LATIN AMERICAN CULTURAL AND MUSICAL CONTEXTS IN MUSIC THERAPY

of related interest

Music Therapy in a Multicultural Context
A Handbook for Music Therapy Students and Professionals
Edited by Melita Belgrave and Seung-A Kim
ISBN 978 1 78592 798 0
eISBN 978 1 78450 807 4

Therapy in Colour
Intersectional, Anti-Racist and Intercultural Approaches by Therapists of Colour
Edited by Dr Isha McKenzie-Mavinga, Kris Black, Karen Carberry and Eugene Ellis
ISBN 978 1 83997 570 7
eISBN 978 1 83997 571 4

The Latinx Guide to Liberation
Healing from Historical, Generational, and Individual Trauma
Vanessa Pezo
ISBN 978 1 80501 021 0
eISBN 978 1 80501 022 7

LATIN AMERICAN CULTURAL AND MUSICAL CONTEXTS IN MUSIC THERAPY

EDITED BY
PATRICIA ZARATE DE PEREZ

Jessica Kingsley Publishers
London and Philadelphia

First published in Great Britain in 2025 by Jessica Kingsley Publishers
An imprint of John Murray Press

I

A CIP catalogue record for this title is available from the
British Library and the Library of Congress

ISBN 978 1 83997 306 2
eISBN 978 1 83997 307 9

Printed and bound in the United States by Integrated Books International

Jessica Kingsley Publishers' policy is to use papers that are natural,
renewable and recyclable products and made from wood grown in
sustainable forests. The logging and manufacturing processes are expected
to conform to the environmental regulations of the country of origin.

Jessica Kingsley Publishers
Carmelite House
50 Victoria Embankment
London EC4Y 0DZ

www.jkp.com

John Murray Press
Part of Hodder & Stoughton Ltd
An Hachette Company

The authorised representative in the EEA is Hachette Ireland,
8 Castlecourt Centre, Castleknock Road, Castleknock, Dublin 15, D15 YF6A, Ireland.

CONTENTS

INTRODUCTION

PATRICIA ZARATE DE PEREZ

In the quest to understand the cultural and musical contexts of music therapy within the Latin American diaspora, we also need to expand our view of the history of music therapy and open the door to the understanding of diverse epistemologies, including Indigenous knowledges. We must also recognize that in Latin America, it is difficult to establish a universal practice, methodology, or policy of music therapy, as Latin America is a complex region with multiple histories entwined in the cultural, social, and economic context of colonialism.

Even attempting to define music therapy in Latin America is problematic. Some music therapy associations use the World Federation of Music Therapy's (WFMT) definition,[1] while others go by the definition from the American Music Therapy Association® (AMTA).[2] Other countries create their own definitions, and even within a single country we may find different definitions and several markedly different concepts of what constitutes music therapy. Some practitioners incorporate both Eurocentric models and Indigenous practices, and prefer not to define music therapy at all. Some Indigenous communities in Latin America reject the field of music therapy altogether, believing that the music therapy profession is another invention of European colonization to change and erase the long-lasting relationship between music and Indigenous healing practices they have developed over centuries.

It is important to note several points regarding the social context of music therapy in Latin America. Music therapists in Latin America may not be recognized as professionals, and they may work without insurance of any kind. They may struggle to make ends meet, and might even lack the financial stability to sustain their music therapy practice. At the same time,

---

1   www.wfmt.info/post/announcing-wfmts-new-definition-of-music-therapy
2   www.musictherapy.org/about/musictherapy

they are remarkably passionate about music and their work. They continu-ally innovate new ways to help the populations they serve, even in remote places with no access to technology, electricity, or water. They experience and experiment with a variety of epistemologies including Eurocentric, African, and Indigenous knowledges, and fight for social justice with their music. Some have access to free music therapy training, and most regularly organize to shape and re-shape the music therapy profession within their countries and communities.

In recent years, music therapy scholarship about multiculturalism in the United States, music therapy in Latin America, studies about music therapy with communities identified as Latinx/e, and individual case studies on Lat-inx/e clients in the US and Europe have emerged as critical academic tools for students and professionals to inform their practice. The Latin American Music Therapy Symposium (Panama), Latin American Music Therapy Net-work (LAMTN) (US), Latin American Music Therapy Committee (Comité Latinoamericano de Musicoterapia, CLAM) (Latin America and the Carib-bean), and a myriad of music therapy associations from all over the region have organized to bring the music therapy Latinx/e diaspora together, to share knowledge and experiences as music therapy providers. In the past decade, Facebook groups, websites, and a series of materials in Spanish and English about Latin America have developed as accessible virtual resources serving different generations of music therapists curious about the Latin American context.

The depth and breadth of Latin American cultural and social contexts is vast—one would need hundreds of books to catalog the stories of music therapists from North, Central, and South America, Caribbean peoples, the Latinx/e community in the United States and Europe, and the larger diaspora spread across the rest of the world. For this book, the focus is on helping people interested in music therapy to understand some of the cul-tural and musical context that influences its diasporic practice.

Chapter 1 narrates the rich and complex history of music therapy within the Latin American diaspora, revealing that the profession has almost always followed chiefly Eurocentric models of creation and development, a fact that has held back the full potential of music therapy in the region, particu-larly by circumventing Indigenous epistemologies and maintaining cultural injustices. The author describes how rapid changes in Latin America have been driven by technological advancements, neoliberalism, and the domi-nance of Eurocentric education, which has brought enormous challenges to defining music therapy across the region, where some groups, particu-larly Indigenous communities, contest the very concept of music therapy. Inquiring into the coloniality of power (which entails racial and ethnic classifications that bring about social hierarchies and marginalization), the chapter calls for a decolonization of music therapy education and practice, advocating for the inclusion of diverse knowledges and approaches, including those from Indigenous traditions. The author challenges the supremacy of Eurocentric models, and animates therapists to embrace a broader range of therapeutic approaches to serve diverse communities better.

Chapter 2 explores the coming together of Puerto Rican culture, identity, and music therapy practice. It highlights the historical, political, and social factors that have shaped Puerto Rican identity, focusing on colonization, marginalization, and the resilience built by Puerto Ricans to overcome them. The aftermath of Hurricane María is shown as a striking example of Puerto Rico's strength in the face of adversity. The author describes the effects of Puerto Rican culture on music therapy, stressing the need for constant development of cultural competence and sensitivity skills in clinical practice. The chapter also looks at the role of music in Puerto Rican healthcare, tracking its historical significance and potential for therapeutic interventions. The author presents the findings from a survey of Puerto Rican music therapists, giving valuable insights into their clinical practices and providing recommendations for all therapists. On the whole, the chapter underscores the importance of integrating Puerto Rican cultural identity into music therapy so as to provide effective and culturally responsive care.

Chapter 3 narrates the birth of the Global Music Therapy Center (GMTC) during the COVID-19 pandemic, which was set to bring together music therapists from all over the world to expand their services online. One critical program of the Center was to certify therapists in Neurologic Music Therapy® (NMT), giving specialized training that was previously limited by location and cost. The author tells the story of Sebastian, a stroke survivor from Chile, who looked for NMT treatment from the GMTC to treat enduring speech difficulties from his trauma. Sessions focused on NMT techniques such as Rhythmic Speech Cueing (RSC) and Therapeutic Singing (TS) to recover his expressive fluency. Despite the challenges in adapting NMT to telehealth, the nine-month treatment resulted in improved fluency for Sebastian. The chapter points out that access to specialized music therapy services, particularly NMT, remains limited in Chile, where issues of privilege are factors. Overall, telehealth has revolutionized music therapy accessibility, with the GMTC aiming to further global connections in the field.

Chapter 4 delves into the profound role of music in promoting health and wellness within Latinx/e communities in the United States. It looks into the cultural significance of music in various aspects of life, such as celebrations and coping with grief, emphasizing its capacity to foster unity and resilience. The author addresses the diversity of Latinx/e communities and the obstacles they encounter when seeking healthcare because of systemic injustices. The chapter underscores the significance of culturally sensitive healthcare approaches, recognizing music as a valuable tool in meeting the distinct healthcare requirements of Latinx/e individuals. The author examines how music mobilizes cultural capital, including linguistic, familial, social, aspirational, and navigational capital, resulting in the active promotion of well-being. Examples are given, such as mariachi music during celebrations and folk songs facilitating emotional expression. The chapter explores strategies to advance equality in healthcare through music, such as expanding access to community music programs and giving more support to bilingual-bicultural professionals. In general, the chapter highlights music's potential to serve as an effective tool in promoting health equality and empowering Latinx/e communities.

Chapter 5 narrates in detail the evolution of intensive care units (ICUs) in Chile and the recent change toward humanized care, highlighting the holistic approach that is needed to address the physical, emotional, and social needs of patients and their families. It delves into the concept of hospital humanization, and the relevance of including families and improving communication in healthcare models. Furthermore, it presents evidence supporting music therapy as a non-pharmacological intervention in ICUs, citing its efficacy in reducing anxiety, pain, and delirium among patients. The author also describes a music therapy intervention conducted in a critical care unit that focused on enhancing the well-being of patients, families, and healthcare staff. The chapter concludes by relating a clinical case that helps to demonstrate the application of music therapy in treating anxiety and improving communication and emotional support for a patient and their family. (This chapter is also provided in Spanish.)

Chapter 6 describes the state of music therapy in Mexico. Recognizing from the outset its musical and healing traditions, Mexico, nevertheless, has not yet formally recognized music therapy as a profession, even though its practice as such is at least 40 years old. The author narrates how practitioners of all levels of training have fostered diverse clinical practices over time, creating a complex landscape for the discipline. The chapter also analyzes survey studies, interviews, and personal experiences, highlighting the challenges, strengths, and distinctive features of music therapy in Mexico. It seeks to stimulate solid discussions among professionals in Mexico and Latin America to expand educational initiatives, regulatory policies, and clinical approaches, and place Mexico within the broader international arena of music therapy practice.

Chapter 7 explores the evolution of music therapy in Argentina, tracing its roots to Indigenous healing traditions and early academic developments. It tells the story of the early practitioners who established the first music therapy association in 1966 and began undergraduate studies, with Dr. Rolando O. Benenzon looking to integrate medical and musical principles. The works of practitioners' associations and the creation of university programs helped boost the expansion of the profession. The chapter highlights that the Argentinian public university system and healthcare infrastructure provide free music therapy education and services. It also argues that despite restricted access to academic knowledge, Argentina has indeed a rich regional practice, enabled by open-access initiatives and local literature. Although education opportunities are limited because of economic constraints, undergraduate degree programs and specialized courses have been created to respond to demand. The expanding significance of music therapy practice can be seen in the strict regulations that have emerged to control it, including National Law 27153 (the Professional Exercise of Music Therapy).[3] The chapter also looks at the growth of research in music therapy, facilitated by inclusion in official research systems, although challenges remain in training and time constraints. The author concludes that Argentina's music therapy community must confront particular challenges while offering valuable contributions globally, stressing the need for non-stop development and knowledge dissemination. (This chapter is also provided in Spanish.)

Chapter 8 summarizes a research study conducted by CLAM on music therapy training in Latin America and the Caribbean, based on data collected throughout 2020 and 2021. The study, directed by CLAM's Training Process Committee (Comisión de Procesos de Formación Profesional), sought to collect information about professional training in music therapy using an e-form that was distributed to educational programs in all countries of Latin America. The dynamic nature of music therapy training in the region is highlighted by the study, where socioeconomic and political realities shape the creation, advancement, or ending of programs, as well as their processes of adapting to those realities. The author points out the long history of music therapy training in Latin America, accounting for the influence of both regional and international training. The author also emphasizes the diversity of formats for music therapy training programs, which increased in response to the COVID-19 pandemic, with virtual, hybrid, and hyper-hybrid approaches becoming increasingly customary. The chapter shows the

3   www.global-regulation.com/translation/argentina/3065250/exercise-profession-al-of-music-therapy.html

importance of both the movement of students within Latin America and abroad for music therapy training as well as the significant influence of international training on the development of music therapy in the region. The author concludes by creating a data map reflecting the curriculum of Master's and Bachelor's degree programs in Music Therapy across Latin America, displaying the complexity and diversity of training processes in the region. Overall, the study works as an introductory exploration of music therapy training in Latin America, bringing to light its potential for development and its role in shaping the discipline globally. (This chapter is also provided in Spanish.)

Chapter 9 discusses the emergence of music therapy in Brazil in the 1960s, and the unique views of the Brazilian therapeutic community on music therapy practice and theory, outlining challenges in combining these views with European methods as well as advocating for them. The author reflects from a Brazilian viewpoint on working as a music therapist, teacher, supervisor, and researcher in different European countries, and speculates on the future of this viewpoint in Europe and other countries.

In sum, music therapy in Latin America has developed within different social and cultural contexts in the Americas and the rest of the world. Many more voices need to be heard, but here is a sample of multidimensional experiences, identities, and epistemologies. If there is anything we should take from the Latin American context it is that the region is vastly diverse, multiethnic, and multilingual, with various epistemological and ontological realms that converge to create musical and cultural contexts that are difficult to define and constantly contested.

CHAPTER 1

DECOLONIZING MUSIC THERAPY—ONE LATIN AMERICAN PERSPECTIVE

PATRICIA ZARATE DE PEREZ

Decolonial vocabulary

binary settler colonial logic: A binary, dualistic perspective of knowledge, peculiar to Eurocentrism, which became globally hegemonic via Europe's colonial domination over the world (Quijano 2020).

borderland: Gloria Anzaldúa (1987) refers to the geographical (and wider) area that is most susceptible to *la mezcla*, neither fully of Mexico nor fully of the United States.

border thinking: Walter Mignolo (2012) developed this concept after Gloria Anzaldúa's *borderland* to expand the idea into the consciousness and epistemic location from which reality is lived and experienced.

coloniality of power: The most general form of domination in the world today associated with the emergence of urban and capital social relations based on the social and historical constructs of modernity and rationality (Quijano 2007; Quijano and Ennis 2000).

colonization: A process of domination established since the 15th century by Europeans in the Americas, Africa, and other locations of the Global South that produced specific social discriminations later codified as "racial," "ethnic," "anthropological," or "national," etc. (Quijano 2007).

decolonial turn: A concept that frames colonization as both a foundational component of modernity and an ongoing process, and decolonization as all the means by which the hegemony of the colonial powers may be resisted and disrupted (Maldonado-Torres 2008).

epistemological disobedience: A form of decolonial thinking or delinking from the web of imperial knowledge (Mignolo 2009).

Global Music Therapy (GbMT): A paradigm shift to understand music therapy in the Global South.

Global South: A catch-all term referring to countries and peoples that have been colonized by a handful of European empires (e.g., Spain, Britain, Germany, Portugal, and France, among others), particularly Latin America, Australia, Africa, and South East Asia.

Gunas: One of the Indigenous communities from Panama. Also known as Kunas.

pedagogies of cruelty: Coined by Argentinian feminist scholar Rita Segato, this concept describes how the violence, cruelty, and terror of capitalism manifest in the education systems of capitalist society. Pedagogies of cruelty seek to erode any sense of solidarity or connection, whether they be social or in communion with nature (Segato 2018).

Pedagogy of the Oppressed: A pivotal book on pedagogy written by Paulo Freire in 1968, where he introduces concepts such as the "banking model of education," which he criticizes as an oppressive system that discourages critical thinking and engagement (Freire 1972).

settler colonialism: A form of colonization that seeks to establish a permanent homeland through displacement of native populations (Cavanagh and Veracini 2016).

settler colonial logic: Refers to the set of ideas, values, structures, and practices that justify, maintain, and reproduce the relations of domination established during colonialism, even long after the colonial empires have formally disappeared. This logic is not limited to territorial occupation or political control, but penetrates deeply into cultural, social, economic, educational, and epistemic aspects (Quijano, 2000; Mignolo, 2005).

wagas: Non-Guna, non-Indigenous from the Americas, white settler, Latinx/e.

Introduction

Music therapy within the Latin American diaspora has a rich and complex history. The creation of the music therapy profession in the region (as with many other scientific and academic disciplines) centered on the development of cross-disciplinary curricula that would be accepted within the broadly Eurocentric educational systems to sustain what Paulo Freire coined the *pedagogy of the oppressed* (1972). This educational mode presents significant challenges: Eurocentric systems have tended to insist on sharp separation between disciplines, whereas most Afro-Latin American and Indigenous perspectives in the region recognize the value in holistic approaches and traditional epistemologies (Mignolo 2019). In this chapter, I will explore the concept of decolonization and coloniality through the ideas of Latin American decolonial thinkers such as Aníbal Quijano, Walter Mignolo, Rita Segato, and others. I will also discuss the context of music therapy training and culture within that theoretical framework, and provide examples from Latin American music therapists' writings along with my own experiences working in the Republic of Panama (Zarate de Perez 2020).

I will also present the concept of Global Music Therapy (GbMT) as a critique on the establishment and continuing implementation of conventional music therapy models from the Global North in the Global South. The dominant music therapy models that focus on Eurocentric ideals have complicated the development of the music therapy field in Latin America. Moreover, this overemphasis on Western concepts of music and its relationship to health has played a part in erasing Indigenous and Afrocentric epistemologies in the Americas for the past 500 years, and continues to do so.

As a model to envision and organize a future of music therapy in the Global South, GbMT aims to utilize the therapeutic approaches of the Global North alongside Afrocentric and Indigenous epistemologies, knowledges, and histories. The ultimate goal is a Global South Music Therapy that treats all these knowledge systems as equally valid, applying each according to the needs and wants of clients from different cultural and ethnic backgrounds.

The Global South

The **Global South** is defined by a relationship to empire. The countries of the Global South are those that were either colonized or simply forgotten by the (mostly European) empires that have dominated the globe for the last 500 years. As such, the nations and peoples of the Global South are generally opposed to all forms of colonialism and imperialism. When I write about the Latin American perspective on **colonization**, I refer to the settler colonialism that began in the Americas (North, Central, and South) in the 15th century with the "discovery" of the Americas by Cristóbal Colón (known to Americans as Christopher Columbus). **Settler colonialism** is characterized by settlers who aim to make colonized lands their permanent home, resulting in continuous and sustained conflict with the Indigenous populations (Englert 2022). While related to colonialism, settler colonialism is markedly distinct, defined by the direct relationship between the colonists and the colonized. As a system defined by these unequal relationships, settler colonialism involves an exogenous collective aiming to locally and permanently replace Indigenous populations. Unlike other types of colonialism, it has no geographical, cultural, or chronological bounds. It is culturally non-specific and can occur at any time, and anyone is a settler if they are part of a collective that seeks to establish a permanent homeland through displacement (Cavanagh and Veracini 2016).

Latin America and the Caribbean region are composed of over 30 countries that hold different groups of peoples that have continuously migrated since the 15th century for different reasons and under different circumstances. Indigenous knowledges have mixed with African and European epistemologies to create new hybrids that have morphed over time in order to survive the pressure of colonization (Kusch *et al.* 2010). Over the past centuries, migrations from India, China, the Middle East, and other regions of the world have also made their mark, and since the 1990s, the rapid development of technology, the establishment of neoliberalism, and the epistemological hegemony of Eurocentric models of education have created additional complexity and conflict in the region. However, beyond all of these factors, the most visible and dramatic source of conflict in Latin America is the level of social and economic inequality.

Panama

Take Panama for example—according to the World Bank, Panama is a "high income country" which at the same time ranks among the most economically unequal countries in the world (World Bank 2024). Its status as a tax haven only serves to deepen this inequality to greater extremes.[1] This combination of immense economic development on the one side and rampant inequality on the other has made the rich richer over the past several decades, while the poor have grown desperately poorer (Vakis and Lindert 2000).[2] Under these circumstances the music therapy profession in Panama faces serious difficulty in reaching everyone who needs it, and this is why it is especially crucial for Indigenous and Afro-diasporic peoples, the population most affected by inequality, racism, and marginalization, to maintain their own traditional musical healing practices.[3]

In Panama, and many other countries in Latin America, the music therapy profession continues to make efforts to adapt to a broken system that undermines the knowledge of Indigenous peoples and maintains cultural and social injustices in the Global South. What's more troublesome is that after millions of dollars spent in trying to lower its poverty rate, Panama remains attached to the dream of development within a modern cultural system that justifies structural violence, where historical discourse around social development conceives of a "third world" in which hunger is a potent social and political force (Escobar 2011).

In general terms, systemic and institutional racism run rampant in the Panamanian healthcare system. The grandmothers of some of my Indigenous music therapy students are under-prescribed and at times even denied pain medication. They experience unusually long wait times at hospitals, and sometimes their doctors refuse to make a diagnosis, even when presented with severe symptoms—in one case, health professionals prescribed water and rest for an elderly patient who was unable to move and complaining of extreme pain and fever (see, for example, Dam Lam and Gasparatos 2023; Fisher 2014).

---

1   During COVID-19, Panama's GDP decreased by more than 17 percent; Panama experienced the highest number of COVID-19 cases per 100,000 inhabitants in Latin America; poverty increased by 2 to 14.9 percent of the population; unemployment reached 18.5 percent; and, if government policies to mitigate the adverse effects of the crisis are not in place in the next year or so [2023], the poverty rate is expected to grow to 20.8 percent of the population (World Bank 2022). We can also note that: the poverty rate in rural areas did increase in Panama, from 29.3 percent in 2022 to 32.3 percent in 2023 (World Bank 2024).

2   A World Bank publication from 2000 states that "poverty among Indigenous peoples of Panama is abysmal…83 per cent of Indigenous peoples live below the poverty line…70 percent of Indigenous peoples can not satisfy their minimum daily caloric requirements even if they allocated all of their consumption to food" (Vakis and Lindert 2000).

3   It is important to note that many Indigenous communities do not consider themselves "poor." The label "poor" may be seen as another way to separate peoples into class, which is another Eurocentric concept that may not be accepted in Indigenous circles.

Many Afro-Panamanian communities suffer from similar disparities in their encounters with the healthcare system. In a publication from the Panamanian Government's Social Security Fund (Caja del Seguro Social) from May 30, 2022, titled "Learn about the medical fragility of being of African descent" ("Conoce la fragilidad médica de ser afrodescendiente") (García 2022) Dr. Francisco Urriola, general physician at the local primary healthcare unit (Unidad Local de Atención Primaria en Salud, ULAPS), explains that there are pathologies inherent to being Black. He comments that the prevalence of certain diseases in different racial populations "has a lot to do with the genes that each race has," claiming a genetic basis for the "higher prevalence and mortality due to hypertension, diabetes, kidney problems, obesity, heart failure, strokes" among Black patients. A far better explanation for the disproportionate occurrence of these illnesses among Black patients is the disproportionate number of Black (not to mention Indigenous) people who live in poverty in Panama, something that the Panamanian public is reluctant to acknowledge. What sort of system tolerates the promotion of scientific racism while at the same time healthcare professionals denounce native healing practices as pseudoscience (Chang *et al.* 2021)?

Border thinking

With the concept of music therapy being contested, even simply defining music therapy in Latin America is a complex issue. Many professionals in Latin America maintain a broad and flexible concept of music therapy, as they work with both Eurocentric models and Indigenous practices, which places music therapists in the **borderland** of epistemic experiences (Anzaldúa, Vivancos Pérez, and Cantú 2021). Music therapists like Dr. Yadira Albornoz from Venezuela describe the spiritual dimension of Indigenous knowledges related to healing practices as something that can only be experienced—they are not possible to comprehend in a "logical" way (Albornoz 2023). In this case, the "logic" in question is the **settler colonial logic** that established racism, capitalism, anthropocentrism, and patriarchy as foundations of our "modern" society.

While settler colonial logic dominates the cultural, musical, and political contexts of music therapy scholarship in Latin America, therapists like Dr. Albornoz experiment with **border thinking** (Mignolo 2012), which operates between the worlds of Indigenous healing practices in Venezuela and Eurocentric music therapy scholarship. Dr. Albornoz works at the border of Western thought and Latin American Indigenous knowledges, and notes that for many Western music therapists, Indigenous practices seem "illogic," but our modern Western ways of thinking and living seem just as illogical for them.

While visiting Ustupu, a Guna Yala island off the coast of Panama, I learned that the Gunas sometimes exile people to Panama City as a punishment, forcing them to contend with the suffering that prevails in modern cities. By the logic of many Indigenous cultures, fundamental dynamics of Western societies and economies (particularly concepts like rent and health insurance, and even money itself) are irrational and insane. Border thinking requires giving this perspective deep consideration.

Walter Mignolo explains that the interrelated phenomena of globalization and migration have highlighted not only the territorial borders of the nation-state but also the existential conditions of migrants. Migrants dwell at the borders, whether residing in the heart of cities like Paris, London, or New York, or at the borders dividing Europe from Africa or the United States from Latin America and the Caribbean. One defining feature of the current global era, which began in 1500, is the contrast between the movement of people and the movement of money and commodities. While people are stopped at borders, money and commodities move freely. People are to be "regulated," while trade is to be "liberated" at all costs (Mignolo 2012).

I would like to expand Mignolo's ideas to the music therapy profession and point out that music therapists in Latin America experience border thinking in their practice when they participate in Eurocentric academic programs while working with Indigenous and Afro-descendant communities at the same time, inside and outside their region. In the borderland of epistemes and cosmologies, these communities continue to suffer from displacement, theft of their land, and cultural appropriation.

Decolonization theory in Latin America

Latin American decolonization theory helps us understand the musical, cultural, and political contexts in which music therapy stands. Latin America and the Caribbean survived colonization through processing Afrocentric, Indigenous, and European knowledges. In this chapter I will focus on the dance between Indigenous and Eurocentric knowledges I have experienced in Panama working with the Guna community.

The **Gunas** are a community of Indigenous peoples who live on the land and the islands of the Caribbean Sea (in Panama and Colombia) and who have also established urban communities in Panama City, Panama. I have worked with Guna students on a series of projects spanning over a decade, which has included opening a children's library, supporting presentations on their musical and healing practices in the Latin American Music Therapy Symposium, and helping document their healing songs. During the annual Symposium I have been questioned several times by the Gunas wondering why it is necessary to create an entire new narrative about the relationship between music and healing when they have known everything I have discussed in my music therapy presentations for hundreds of years.

One of the ways to learn to negotiate these kinds of questions in our music therapy praxis is to understand decolonization theories. Latin American decolonization theories have decades of development and touch an important part of the population including music therapists (Thurner 2019). Since the 1960s, intellectuals like Peruvian sociologist Aníbal Quijano have paid close attention to the historical contexts in which Latin America has developed professional practices within Eurocentric epistemologies. Many professional music therapists question the concepts of capitalism, professionalism, individualism, the wider globalization of neoliberalism (a cultural, social, and economic formula first tried in Chile during the Augusto Pinochet dictatorship), and Eurocentric epistemologies (Fuentes and Valdeavellano 2015).

Quijano (2007, pp.215, 216) points out that Latin America is the "original and inaugural space/time of the first 'indigenization' of the survivors of the colonizing genocide, as the first population in the world subjected to the 'racialization' of their new identity and their dominated place in the new pattern of power." For Quijano (2007), the legacy of European colonialism is embedded in every aspect of today's society and has shaped (even created) the modern world or the concept of modernity: "Europe's hegemony over the new model of global power concentrated all forms of the control of subjectivity, culture, and especially knowledge and the production of knowledge under its hegemony" (Quijano and Ennis 2000, p.540). In other words, under European colonialism, the colonizers gained a monopoly on knowledge, which they organized according to hierarchical binaries.

In the case of the music therapy profession, the legacy of the **binary settler colonial logic** created a system that overvalues "new knowledge," fast productivity, and solitary thinking, inescapably subverting paradigms of connection, mutuality, and collective thinking (Grande 2004, p.3). This binary logic divides the concepts of music and therapy and music therapy from the larger context of healing and life in general. Latin American music therapists continually question the notions of subject, evidence, institutionalization, empirical "effectiveness," and many other aspects of the music therapy profession.

Argentinian music therapist Virginia Tosto poses interesting questions about legitimizing the discipline of music therapy in Latin America from traditional points of view disseminated in the region:

> [Music therapy] is not responsible for theoretically developing a conception about the subject and the health and disease processes that affect them; It does not have, in its own theoretical corpus, instruments that allow it to carry out a diagnosis of the physical, mental or social condition of people. Nor is it responsible for generating theoretical developments in relation to music, considered as an object of study. (Tosto 2016, p.3)

How can we understand, explain, and work with the existing links between subject, music, and therapy in this situation? Working in music therapy is challenging when these terms have different meanings for different people sharing the same space. A **decolonial turn** in music therapy reasoning is crucial to appreciate the contributions of ways of thinking that highlight the relevance of other spaces such as borders. The decolonial turn identifies and critiques racial and colonial dynamics, fostering counter-colonial or decolonial ways of thinking, acting, and being, with the goal of contributing to the decolonization of modern/colonial spaces and ways of thinking (Maldonado-Torres 2022). Although this turn is possible and is already happening all over the world, the change also needs to be reflected in academic circles and institutions.

Music therapists in Latin America have also questioned Eurocentric ideas of white supremacy and patriarchy. Chilean music therapist Emanuel Cerebello-González (2023, p.34) states that "it is through music therapy academic institutions that patriarchal mandates are exercised: masculine corporatism, low empathy, insensitivity, bureaucratism, distancing, technocracy, formality, universality, rootlessness, desensitization, limited bonding, among other characteristics," which decolonial and feminist scholar Rita Segato calls "**pedagogies of cruelty**." Segato (2021) defines these pedagogies as

> acts and practices that teach, habituate and program subjects to transform their lives and their vitality into things. In this sense, these pedagogies teach something that goes much further than killing, teaching the killing of a deritualized death, of a death that leaves only residue in the place of the deceased.

She explains that habitual cruelty is directly linked to narcissistic and consumerist entertainment, and to the isolation of citizens through their desensitization to the suffering of others (Segato 2021). This is one of the main points of my classes: I work to make students aware of how we are constantly taught to experience only some realities while completely ignoring others. In Panama, for instance, where we see blatant systemic violence against Indigenous and Afro-descendant peoples, the World Bank focuses on narratives showing a reduction in the general poverty rate. These stories tend to avoid discussions about specific poverty rates within each community and the ways in which poverty metrics have been fudged in recent decades to highlight Panama's "economic growth" (Cadena *et al.* 2023).

While Panamanians are led to believe that Indigenous communities are less poor than before to anesthetize the more privileged populations, the reality is that Indigenous peoples are getting poorer by Western standards (Madrid Martínez 2020). This does not even take into account that the Gunas use an entirely different set of metrics for poverty, often thinking **wagas** (non-Indigenous peoples) are poorer than them in many respects (e.g., level of access to the rich forests of Panama). Ultimately, our two worlds run parallel; we are not looking through the same eyes.

Other professionals challenge the status quo by questioning biomedical clinical models as well as the interests of multinational pharmaceutical companies working and experimenting in the region (Oselame, Barbosa, and Chagas 2017). These questions were especially relevant during the COVID-19 pandemic, which exposed the global inequity of access to vaccines. According to one paper by Bernabé Malacalza and Debora Fagaburu (2022, p.433), "Some countries, such as Chile and Uruguay, reported complete coverage, while others, such as Jamaica, Nicaragua, and Haiti, reported one-shot vaccination rates below 5 percent," and only 1.4 percent of the region's overall population was able to obtain two shots. Whatever our opinions about vaccines, vaccination rates are a useful metric for understanding the unequal access to health resources in the region. In the case of Panama, I saw how Panamanian elites traveled to Miami to get the vaccine as soon as it was available in the United States, while some of my Guna students from urban communities lost most of the elders of their family to the virus in the first year of the crisis—one small, privileged group of the population having access to all the health resources (including music therapy) while another, much larger group died was unfortunately the case in many countries of the region.

Critical music therapy

The critical views of music therapists in Latin America help us think about what, how, and why we learn what we learn. If we examine the notions of *health* and *disease* in Latin America we realize that in most Indigenous communities *human* and *health* are profoundly connected to their environment. A healthy human cannot be seen as a separate entity from their land. However, the connection between land and human continues to break as Indigenous peoples are displaced and their lands are stolen, with many groups left with unusable land.

Many Indigenous peoples of Latin America refuse to engage in Western academic dialogues until their land is returned. This refusal to participate is a form of **epistemological disobedience**, independent thought, and decolonization (Mignolo 2009). The same happens with the concepts of *human* and *music*, which are thought of as interconnected, without separation. The concepts of music, performance, and audience as separate entities may not exist. Music is part of life and embedded in daily routines to the point that it is not considered music any longer but part of the act that is happening. For example, some Indigenous groups may play music or sing, before, during, and after a hunt. But from their point of view, they are not playing music at any point: they are simply hunting. Western thinking separates the two processes, but this separation is nonsensical in Indigenous thought; one does not happen independent of the other. What would be two acts to a Western mind (making music and hunting or any other practice) is all one act in the Indigenous mind (Halbmayer 2020).

In observing Indigenous healing practices, we might witness a ceremony or a healing act that includes what we would consider many separate elements: music, rest, herbalism, the spoken word, lunar cycles, animal migrations, etc. But for the Indigenous peoples partaking in the ceremony, *all* these elements are integral to the process to the point that without one of them, the process cannot take place, or worse, healing will not happen. This point of view presents a challenge to Eurocentric models of music therapy as some Indigenous populations maintain living epistemological and cosmological traditions as a central facet of their societies.

Eurocentric thought and colonialism have managed to separate the world into constructs that are not separated in reality (Mignolo 2018). In Western thought, including music therapy scholarship, the social sciences and the natural sciences are seen as separate, at times even contrasting points of view. As creative output has become increasingly commodified, art has been detached from other human experiences, creating niches such as "music for entertainment," which is treated as the main function of music today, and for some people, the only one.

The professionalization of music therapy in the Global South has impeded exchange between different knowledges by rejecting Indigenous practices as primitive and ultimately irrelevant, leaving a large swath of the population disconnected from their ancestral healing practices. The idea that scientific studies can validate the effectiveness of one music therapy technique over another is contested by music therapists working at the intersection of Eurocentric and Indigenous epistemologies. The narrowly specialized "rational sciences" developed in Europe are profoundly different from "Native sciences." Native sciences encompass ritual, metaphysics, art, spirituality, community, and creativity, but also "exploration of basic questions such as the nature of language, thought and perception; the nature of proper human relationship to the cosmos; and other questions related to natural reality" (Grande 2004, p.124).

Music therapists in Latin America have access to diverse epistemologies that are not easy to learn in colonized academic settings. While many professionals receive extensive training in Europe or the United States, many experience a disconnect between the social, political, cultural, and musical contexts they encounter at school and the ones they work in when they return home. They face challenges such as serving patients who have never been properly diagnosed, treating illnesses in traumatized populations, serving larger groups than usual, and finding appropriate spaces for music therapy sessions (CAMTI Collective 2022). Their teachers and colleagues in the Global North may be unfamiliar with many or most of these circumstances, as training in these countries often overlooks a great deal of scholarship that is relevant to the Latin American region.

When navigating Central American Indigenous epistemologies one needs to live in the border of epistemes. Recognizing the different dimensions of the healing process, trying to understand and accept Indigenous and Afrocentric epistemologies, their concepts about music and its relationship to individual and communal health, can help us as music therapists to understand how to better help the people we seek to serve in our region of the world.

The coloniality of power

Coined by Aníbal Quijano, the concept of **coloniality of power** has become widely known in academic circles all over the world. It has also been a key component in Latin American scholarship since it was first published in the 1960s:

> The globalization of the world is, in the first place, the culmination of a process that began with the constitution of America and world capitalism as a Euro-centered colonial/modern world power. One of the foundations of that pattern of power was the social classification of the world population upon the base of the idea of race, a mental construct that expresses colonial experience and that pervades the most important dimensions of world power, including its specific rationality: Eurocentrism. (Quijano 2020, p.861)

The historical timeline of Latin America, the Caribbean, and the culture of **coloniality** provoked the social problems of poverty, and objective and subjective violence (Žižek 2008), along with other modern social ills, by way of the genocide of Indigenous peoples, the enslavement of African peoples, the erasure of their epistemologies, and their forced integration into a capitalist world market. In order to create new knowledges within music therapy in Latin America, we must critically engage with the history of the new ways of colonization (including neoliberal globalization) we encounter in our educational curricula and practice:

> All forms of labor, production, and exploitation were in ensemble around the axis of capital and the world market: slavery, serfdom, petty commodity production, reciprocity and salary. In such conditions, each and every one of those forms of labor was not just an extension of its historical antecedents. They were historically and sociologically new, both in themselves and in their relation to each other, because they were articulated to a new pattern of power. And this new pattern of power was capitalist, because capital—as specific social relation—was the axis around which it was articulated. (Quijano 2020, p.302)

As capitalism placed Indigenous peoples of the Global South at the bottom of the hierarchical structures of society, they were marginalized into groups that continue to be entangled in social issues such as poverty, violence, and abuse. The dominant groups continue to oppress peoples of color not only because of external differences, but also because of mental maps and cultural differences that separate peoples into categories.

Quijano concludes that it is this separation of peoples into binary constructs like superior/inferior, black/white, modern/primitive that creates new social historical identities such as "Spanish," "Portuguese," "American," "Negro," and "Indian." Quijano (2020, p.326) remarks that these social constructs based on race "classify the populations in the power structure of the new society, associated with the nature of roles and places in the division of labor and in the control of resources of production."

In order to make space for Global South epistemologies to develop within music therapy practice, we need to understand the process of coloniality in Latin America. Quijano's "coloniality of power" theory describes one of the cornerstones of the global capitalist economy. The coloniality of power is based on the imposition of racial and ethnic classifications that began in the 16th century. Through this classification of peoples, power gains control of individual and communal subjectivities and epistemologies. This process has its origin in the construction of America as both a territory and a sociocultural context. With the constitution of "America" as a geographical and conceptual space, the emerging capitalist power became global, hegemonic, and Eurocentric. To construct a new global society, European powers configured new unidimensional identities: Black, White, Indian, Yellow, and Red peoples who lived in geocultural imaginaries such as America, Africa, the Orient, the Occident, and Europe. These identities were arranged in hierarchies according to various binaries that continue to define our world: rational/irrational, primitive/civilized, traditional/modern.

The binary constructs, Quijano points out, challenge us to think about the separation of knowledges and disciplines and how music interacts with all of them. Does music really affect the cognitive, creative, mathematical, linguistic, and emotional dimensions of the brain separately? Could we imagine music engaging every system simultaneously, in every part of the brain? Indigenous knowledges would find the interconnections of the brain a natural state, as the world is interconnected in every possible sense. However, even in Latin America, where we have access to Indigenous knowledges, we waited for neuroscientists to use brain imaging to "show" how the musical process transforms from electrical to chemical to biological to behavioral in order to recognize the depth of connection between these systems. Such is the depth of the coloniality of power.

Ideologically speaking, the commoditization of music and therapeutic practices and the "selling" of music therapy services are unthinkable in Indigenous paradigms. However, it is also difficult to sell music therapy practices to non-Indigenous populations, as the hyper-commoditization of music has made it difficult to position music therapy as having similar value to other health services. This is one of the reasons why music therapy in Latin America may not pay well and music therapists have a hard time sustaining their work. Institutions that want to "modernize" their medical departments may include music therapy services, especially in places like Argentina, Chile, Brazil, and Colombia, where music therapy has a long history of clinical practice attached to Eurocentric practices of psychiatry and/or psychology. However, these cases are few and scattered across the region, as there is no consensus on how music therapy clinical practice should evolve.

In Panama, I have experienced the clash between Indigenous epistemologies and the concept of modernity. On the one side, Indigenous groups resist Western medical practices and Eurocentric models of relating music and health; on the other, Panama has an intense desire to establish itself as a modern country with medical access of the highest quality. The overwhelming inequality in the country and the difference between servicing one population or the other can only be parsed by understanding the concept of "modernity" in Latin America.

Let's examine Quijano's idea about the construction of America as the future of the European imaginary. After the "discovery of the Americas" in the 16th century, Europe established a concept of its future closely related to the exploration and exploitation of the Americas. When the Age of Enlightenment began in Europe and the Americas, the Americas sought independence from colonial rule: "The production of modern rationality was associated, above all, with the liberational promises of modernity" (Quijano 2020, p.789). In the case of Panama, for example, modernity was symbolized by the Panama Canal, the US project that dominated the country for over a century, and established a solid center of control that would aid the United States with its expansion of power to the rest of the Americas. Panama was "modernized" under colonial rule while liberation (economic, cultural, and political) eluded, and continues to elude, its people. As of this writing (2024), Panama is suffering from some of the worst wealth inequality in the world. The Panama Canal did not necessarily "liberate" Panamanians from the dominion of the US, and the country continues to be attached to US hegemony in social, economic, cultural, and even legal terms.

In the quest to liberate music therapy practices from Western hegemony, Panama has served as both a center for epistemological discourse through the Latin American Music Therapy Symposium, and a laboratory for the development of a new approach to music therapy called Global Music Therapy. The growth of these ideas over the past two decades owes much to the multiethnic, multinational, and multilingual space Panama provides for the development of music therapy.

The Latin American Music Therapy Symposium

Despite rampant inequality, extreme poverty, and profound social injustices, Indigenous peoples, Afro-Panamanians, and their various descendants are profoundly musical, creative, and resilient. Music is used throughout Panama to connect peoples, resist social injustices, and navigate the issues that come with extreme poverty and marginalization. A rich diversity of traditional and modern musical styles in every region of the isthmus, along with centuries of musical development that have led to important transnational musical connections from jazz to reggaeton, have created a fertile ground for the development of music therapy (Zarate de Perez 2023).

Launched in 2013 in Panama City, the Latin American Music Therapy Symposium has attracted thousands of people interested in knowing more about the profession, and has served as a bridge to connect North, Central, and South American music therapists.[4] It has provided a safe space to discuss antagonistic epistemologies and differing views about music therapy, and has opened the door to (sometimes clashing) methodologies that are contested equally by professionals, students, and the general public. The event has drawn music therapists from over 15 different countries, and has organized panels on dozens of music therapy methodologies from different parts of the world. Since COVID-19, the symposium has been a free event open to all, making access to music therapy scholarship available to everyone. It is produced by the Panama Jazz Festival annually thanks to a team of hundreds of workers and volunteers, many of them students enrolled in the new Music Therapy Master's degree program offered by the Danilo Pérez Foundation, the Music Therapy Center of Panama (Centro de Musicoterapia de Panamá, CMP), and directed by myself.

Regardless of the lack of cash sponsorship, the Symposium has strong collaborative ties with organizations such as the City of Knowledge (Ciudad del Saber), which provides valuable access to classrooms and technology, making it available virtually to anyone in the world with internet access. Schedules run from Monday through Friday, from 9am to 5pm, making it one of the longest music therapy events in the region. It is also enriched by the hundreds of activities of the Panama Jazz Festival that run Monday through Saturday, from 9am to 3am, offering diverse cultural and artistic experiences for attendees (Muñoz 2024). It has provided education for many people in Panama, and served as a platform for the development of a music therapy law (Law 332) to regulate the profession that was passed in October 2022.

The Symposium aims to provide a safe space for border thinking and even epistemic disobedience. Conflict can arise among the attendees as the perspectives of militant groups of Indigenous and Afro-diasporic peoples collide with Western worldviews. In Panama, both worlds exist together in a liminal space, yet they do not share the same vocabulary. Epistemologies are contradictory and cosmologies differ significantly. As one side presents music therapy methodologies tied to communities living in privileged positions in modernity, another offers accounts of the systemic violence of the music therapy profession. The concept of "Global Music Therapy" has developed from experiences along this borderline.

---

4   See www.simposiomusicoterapia.com

Global Music Therapy (GbMT)

As a newly defined approach, **GbMT** is based on the interactions between therapeutic and non-therapeutic performance and improvisation, acknowledging the broad and diverse musical styles and languages from different cultures around the world. GbMT lives at the intersection of composition, improvisation, and therapy. Influenced by performer-music therapists such as Colin Andrew Lee and jazz musicians such as Wayne Shorter and Danilo Pérez, GbMT proposes a new way to consider therapy and musicking. It is a model that educates performer-therapists to live in both of these musical worlds simultaneously. Flexibility in moving between artistic and therapeutic manifestations of creative music-making are key roles in advancing GbMT (Zarate de Perez and Wu 2023).

The field of music therapy in Latin America has always been in conversation with decolonization theory, Indigenous epistemologies, and concepts such as the "coloniality of power." The particular case of Panama is an interesting one, since epistemological dilemmas are encountered on a regular basis in events, classes, and the day-to-day therapeutic practice itself. The constant clash between Eurocentric ways of knowing and Indigenous epistemologies is better understood through theories of coloniality first developed in Latin America in the 1960s by scholars such as Aníbal Quijano.

These confrontations between knowledge systems also help develop passionate groups of diverse peoples discussing the field of music therapy and its rationalization within the construct of modernity, promote narratives about the present and future of the music therapy profession, and even, at times, provide a platform for laws to be established. The term "Global Music Therapy" has grown from these dialogues and, as with all decolonial projects, is unfinished and in transition (Murrey 2019).

Discussions of the term "global" are open-ended in different academic circles. The *Oxford English Dictionary* defines it as "a. Relating to or encompassing the whole of anything or any group of things, categories, etc.; comprehensive, universal, total, overall. b. Of, relating to, or involving the whole world, worldwide; (also in later use) of or relating to the world considered in a planetary context."[5] For many decades the word "global" has been attached to the concept of globalization, which, used neutrally, refers to international integration, and has been part of the core of working-class movements in many nation-states, including many countries in Latin America, where unions are called *internacionales*, and the Communist Party and other left-wing organizations sing "La Internacional" in gatherings of every size. However, with the rise of neoliberalism, the

---

5   See www.oed.com/dictionary/global_adj?tab=meaning_and_use#3011976

notion of "globalism" was "appropriated by a narrow sector of power and privilege to refer to their version of globalization," which only serves corporate power and capitalism (Chomsky 2015). In turn, I would like to reclaim "global" to help define and develop the concept of GbMT from a decolonial perspective.

In Latin America, as well as other parts of the world that have suffered from colonization, GbMT is in constant conversation with Indigenous knowledges. Native knowledges are separate from the Western idea of "new knowledge," which arises from the same epistemic binary narratives we constantly rename as we attempt to recycle and adapt Eurocentric models. Indigenous knowledges can help us reflect and provoke thoughts on the meanings of music and health and its relationship to expand our counternarratives of capitalistic forms of knowing and ways of experiencing the world. Thus GbMT curricula and praxes must be much broader and deeper than the common practice and reductive teachings of the Global North.

It is essential for the global music therapist to understand the power of coloniality and Latin American decolonization theory. While many students and professionals learn music therapy curricula that have been based exclusively on a Western rationale, global music therapists are open to different epistemologies and cosmologies. Being open to new knowledges does not always mean we can use them, or even completely understand them—we can never fully comprehend the depths of hardship and suffering in communities that have been violently dispersed through genocide without belonging to one ourselves. Yet it is vital to acknowledge these groups and give them a space in music therapy practice. In the south of Chile you can go to an "Indigenous pharmacy" and find all the herbs and medicine Indigenous peoples use to maintain their well-being. This service is specifically maintained with Indigenous peoples in mind, and they should be afforded the same access to their own healing practices in music therapy. The ultimate ideal would be for Indigenous healers to command the same legitimacy and institutional support as licensed music therapists.

GbMT involves critical thinking and the questioning of how and why the music therapy profession and its curricula develop in the places and directions they do. It is not about the appropriation of aboriginal practices or culture into the music therapy profession by white settlers, but about making a space in our own minds for other forms of knowledge. GbMT resists making assumptions about the historical, socio, and cultural context of peoples. We live in different worlds, and cannot pretend to experience the world in the same way as people who have endured extreme social inequality, poverty, genocide, and war as realities of daily life. As decolonial thinkers do, GbMT questions the history of music therapy and its origins.

Why do we usually begin with Greek philosophers like Plato and not the *machi* of the Mapuche Indians of Chile? What are the obstacles to including aboriginal knowledges in music therapy curricula? Why do we have official and unofficial music therapy programs in Latin America? Why and how do those unofficial programs develop? Perhaps we cannot be satisfied with a monolithic view of music therapy? In the simplest sense, GbMT is about critiquing the profession of music therapy and finding new ways to think about the concept of music and therapy in the context of Latin America without appropriating Indigenous knowledge.

Conclusion

This chapter has explored the intricate history of music therapy within the Latin American diaspora, highlighting that the field has predominantly followed Eurocentric models of creation and development. This adherence has limited the potential of music therapy in Latin America, particularly by overlooking Indigenous epistemologies and perpetuating cultural injustices. We have discussed how rapid epistemological changes in Latin America, driven by the dominance of Eurocentric education, have posed significant challenges to defining music therapy in the region. In some areas, especially among Indigenous communities, the very concept of music therapy is controversial.

We have delved into the concept of the coloniality of power, and the establishment of racial and ethnic classifications that engender social hierarchies and marginalization. This calls for the decolonization of music therapy education and practice, advocating for the inclusion of diverse knowledge systems and approaches, particularly those rooted in Indigenous traditions. GbMT, a new approach to music therapy critique, encourages therapists to adopt a broader range of therapeutic approaches to better serve diverse communities. As a concept born from studies, practice, and observations in Panama, a place of epistemic borderlines, GbMT critically questions the history and development of music therapy as a profession and its present practice, and asks what the future of music therapy could be.

CHAPTER 2

PUERTO RICAN CULTURE AND IDENTITY

Implications for Music Therapy Practice

JENIRIS M. GARAY

"¡Yo soy Boricua—pa'que tú lo sepas!" This line, originally the title and part of the chorus of a song composed in 1995 by Joel "Taíno" Bosch, has become a statement of cultural pride. Any Puerto Rican anywhere in the world could start to chant this line, and all other Puerto Ricans in their vicinity would be able to join in and complete it. It's a code for social connection, a battle cry, and a lullaby, the sound of our love for our heritage.

Countless Puerto Rican songs, musicals, music genres, and other art forms have their genesis in historical, political, and social happenings, and they are a testament to the cultural tapestry of Puerto Rico. This is a particularly significant gap in music therapy curricula throughout the United States, considering that Puerto Ricans, as the second largest subgroup of the large Hispanic minority in the US, have poorer health status compared with their peers (Díaz *et al.* 2020). Puerto Rican identity implies a certain degree of resilience, and while some may wish the synonymy were unnecessary, the truth is that Borikén (the island's Taíno Indian name) is home to some of the world's toughest people. Take, for example, Puerto Rico's brush with Hurricane María in 2017:

> On September 20, 2017, María's eye sliced the island almost straight down the middle, making it impossible for people to escape the nightmare that would follow. She left 100 percent of the island without power or water, bringing down all radars, weather stations, and cell towers. Those of us outside the island rushed to social media to start creating databases of missing families and neighborhoods, connecting people to their loved ones, and trying to find our own along the way. As the seconds passed by sluggishly, I asked for

help from the universe. I was glued to my phone and computer, searching for them tirelessly until, weeks later, family members started emerging in brief, almost robotic replies, restoring the rhythm to my sore heart.

I wrote those words in October 2017, as part of a much longer statement, after nearly three excruciatingly long weeks spent searching for members of my "extended" family (which, for any Puerto Rican, is simply your *family*). Words appeared on those pages expressing a debilitating combination of emotional exhaustion and resentment towards our "part-time American" status. This was the longest and largest major power outage in modern US history (Hernández, Leaming, and Murphy 2017). Four months after María, over 1.3 million Puerto Ricans—US citizens—were still living without power, among them many young, sick, and disabled people. Reported death tolls ranged anywhere from 16 to over 1000, but the official count remained at 64—no one knew why (Robles *et al.* 2017). By February 2018, the death toll towered at nearly 3000 (Hernández, Schmidt, and Achenbach 2018), and the menacing winds of a new hurricane season were but a few months away.

I had always joked with friends and colleagues in Puerto Rico about our second-class citizenship; humor is one of the many coping mechanisms the Puerto Rican community employs to deal with long-standing cultural and political oppression:

I agree with Herbert W. Brown, who writes for the *Miami Herald*, in his April 7, 2004, "Other Views" column:

Puerto Ricans need a way out of limbo... Because of our nation's unresolved colonial relationship with Puerto Rico, the United States should be disqualified from pressuring other countries on civil rights (Duany 2004). (Garcia-Preto 2005, p.254)

As a board-certified music therapist and clinical educator born and raised in Puerto Rico, I have spent over a decade exploring the impact of the Puerto Rican identity on clinical work and relationships as well as training college students from all over the world to work with Puerto Rican clients and families in experiential learning trips. From anecdotal evidence to interviews with professionals from various fields to a review of survey findings, this chapter explores Puerto Rican culture and history and its implications for music therapy practice. Analyzing the impact of colonization and political trauma on the complex identity of Puerto Ricans, the chapter highlights both the homogeneity and diversity of experiences across the island and the Puerto Rican diaspora, examining perspectives from Puerto Rican music therapists, music therapy students, ethnomusicologists, and other community members, as well as my own subjective interpretations as a US-based Puerto Rican music therapist.

This chapter aims at building a starting point to illustrate the uniqueness of Puerto Rican culture and how it may inform clinical work from the standpoint of cultural competence and humanistic service.

The world's oldest existing colony

> Puerto Rico is a beautiful island
> It belongs to the United States
> Our children speak English and Spanish
> And salute our flag every day. (quoted in Denis 2015)

These were the words that students in 1908 would recite every day in school directly after the Pledge of Allegiance gazing at the Stars and Stripes. Nelson A. Denis (2015, pp.21–22) recounts that "within 10 years of U.S. occupation, every subject, in every class, in every public school was being taught in English." This was part of the United States' attempt to replace 400 years of Spanish, Taíno Indian, and African influence on Puerto Rican language and culture.

In 1493, Christopher Columbus seized Puerto Rico as a Spanish territory for Ferdinand and Isabela. In July 1898, toward the end of the Spanish-American war, US forces invaded Puerto Rico and secured the island by August. As strategic and non-democratic as it may have actually been, the narrative has been changed and/or erased from US education, and many mainland Americans today have no idea where Puerto Rico is on the map, do not know that it is a commonwealth of the US, and/or have continued to believe that Puerto Ricans are of immigrant status.

Nevertheless, education is not the only area with room for growth when it comes to understanding and valuing the Puerto Rican people. For example, Puerto Rico has representation in Congress, but Puerto Ricans cannot vote in presidential elections, even though the US president governs Puerto Rico along with the 50 states. As Flores (2000, p.9) states:

> Long after the wave of decolonization swept the so-called Third World in the post-World War II, and at a time when the most fashionable theory of diplomatic affairs goes under the name of the "postcolonial," this island nation is still a colony by all indicators of international relations, economic and political life fully orchestrated by its mighty neighbor to the north, putative of world democracy and sovereignty.

In 2022, Hurricane Fiona hit the Dominican Republic as a category 2, and 7 percent of the population was left without power. Meanwhile, Fiona took out 100 percent of Puerto Rico's power within hours of hitting the island as a category 1. The so-called "reparations" that had been made by the government after Hurricane María's devastation in 2017 were very quickly dismantled by Fiona just five years later, including entire bridges being swept away within the first 24 hours.

There is a larger issue at hand, and people all over the world are beginning to listen. While natural disasters are difficult or impossible to prevent, particularly as climate change worsens, a history of political corruption and lack of pre- and post-disaster support for the Puerto Rican community has become a source of intergenerational trauma. How does someone who has been abandoned financially, medically, socially, politically...begin to trust again? It is imperative that clinicians and service providers consider trauma history, internalized colonialism, and the individual's current sense of identity when treating clients of Puerto Rican descent, both on the island and abroad.

Island residents, diaspora, and identity through the years

> No nací en Puerto Rico.
> Puerto Rico nacío en mi.
> [I was not born in Puerto Rico.
> Puerto Rico was born in me.] (Mariposa (María Teresa Fernández),
> ["Ode to the Diasporican"] "Pa' mi gente") (cited in Pérez Rosario 2014)

In this 1994 poem, Mariposa introduced the term *diasporican* and thus gave language for what seemed an indescribable displacement of a people and a culture throughout centuries of political and social unrest. The relationship between the United States and Puerto Rico is complex and nuanced. The Puerto Rican identity is overshadowed by various confusions depending on context and perspective. When surrounded by Latin American citizens, a Puerto Rican person is typically viewed and treated as the "gringo/a" or "American" one in the crowd. Alternatively, if that same Puerto Rican is placed in a community within mainland United States, they are considered "Latinx/e." These patterns of mis-identifying and re-categorizing Puerto Ricans over time form part of a larger pattern of microaggressions, discriminatory practices, and overall marginalization.

Since becoming a US territory, Puerto Rico has faced endless ostracization and mistreatment that directly impacts the respect and dignity its people are (or are not) receiving from the US. There doesn't even appear to be a clear racial classification for Puerto Ricans on arriving in the United States:

> Since World War II, massive migration from Puerto Rico to the mainland has pitted two racial classification systems against each other: the Puerto Rican one, based largely on physical appearance, and the American one, based largely on ancestry. Thus, when Puerto Ricans move abroad, they confront a different construction of their racial identity. (Duany 2002, p.244)

In fact, most Puerto Ricans tend to consider themselves as an entirely different category when faced with the dichotomous black/white choices in mainland United States.

Duany also recounts the work of New York-based Puerto Rican sociologist Clara Rodríguez:

> Based on the analysis of the Public Use Microdata Sample of the 1980 census as well as her own survey results, Rodriguez reports that many members of the Puerto Rican community in New York resist being classified as either black or white and prefer to identify themselves as "other." (Duany 2002, p. 244)

By contrast, Adrian Florido's 2020 report for NPR, "Puerto Rico, island of racial harmony?," explores more recent self-reports and how some mobilized for change in the 2020 Census, noting that "people in Puerto Rico have only been asked their race on the Census since 2000. Since then, they've overwhelmingly marked themselves as white, much more so than Puerto Ricans in the mainland U.S. do."

Denis (2015, preface) remarks:

> We see so many huge, surrealistic flags during the New York Puerto Rican parade because all Puerto Rican flags were illegal in the island from 1948 until 1957. Even a Nobel Prize nominee, Francisco Matos Paoli, was sentenced to twenty years in La Princesa [a prison in San Juan] for owning one.

It's these types of experiences that shape the conflicted identity of Puerto Ricans, and will inevitably impact the client–therapist dynamic unless honored for its complexity.

It's important to recognize that not all marginalization has been unidirectional from mainland Americans toward Puerto Ricans. Much of the antagonistic and exclusionary behavior toward Puerto Ricans has been a product of fellow Puerto Ricans. One could argue that this is an intergenerational trauma response, yet regardless of the cause(s), it is a key cultural factor to consider in the client–therapist dynamic and treatment process.

Each Puerto Rican client will present an entirely personal and unique circumstance on the spectrum of cultural assimilation and trauma. Puerto Ricans are also a source of comfort for each other, and celebrate cultural traditions together wherever they find each other in the world. For example, while the largest Puerto Rican cultural parade is held in New York City, there are over 50 parades held across the US alone, including cities with high Puerto Rican populations such as Chicago, Philadelphia, and Boston.

Integration of music and health in Puerto Rico

Puerto Rican music and culture exhibits many remnants of its Spanish, African, and Indigenous Taíno and Carib Indian heritage. Some of the resulting genres include, but are not limited to, bomba, plena, trova, salsa, Rock en Español, boleros, and reggaeton. Music can actually be traced back to healthcare and community settings. Noel Allende-Goitía, social and cultural historian of music and research associate of the Colectivo de Estudios Musicales de Puerto Rico (Puerto Rican Music Studies Collective), describes examples of music and its historical role in health and community building in 1930s Puerto Rico. The Asilo de Beneficiencia (Charity Asylum), serving the poor and homeless, the island's first juvenile correctional facility in Mayagüez, and Puerto Rico's first institution for the blind and visually impaired, all formed and housed community bands (N. Allende-Goitía, personal communication, January 16, 2023). It's no coincidence that the Puerto Rican community found music valuable and even necessary in efforts to support vulnerable populations, and it illustrates the natural potential of music therapy in Puerto Rican healthcare.

Implications for music therapy with Puerto Rican clients and families

For decades, Puerto Rican music therapists have been serving in leadership positions and contributing to many organizations including the American Music Therapy Association® (AMTA) and the Latin American Music Therapy Network (LAMTN). In 2021, the Puerto Rican Music Therapy Association (Asociación de Musicoterapia de Puerto Rico, AMTPR) became official. It is a member of the Latin American Music Therapy Committee (Comité Latinoamericano de Musicoterapia, CLAM). The AMTPR consists of members residing in Puerto Rico as well as diasporicans, and it hosted the first Puerto Rican Music Therapy Congress on June 11, 2022.

So how are the field of music therapy and Puerto Rican culture and identity integrated to provide high-quality clinical care to Puerto Rican clients? The theoretical foundation supporting music therapy as a treatment modality involves the effect of music on the human brain as well as the culture and community-building aspects of music. Technological advances in neuroimaging have allowed us to discover that there is no "music center" in the brain, or any one brain area dedicated to processing music. Instead, the vast number of elements involved in music are processed in locations all over the human brain, with some regions analyzing rhythm while others are linked to characteristics such as timbre, pitch, lyrics, dynamics, tempo, melody, and harmony.

Evidence from the fields of psychology and neuroscience support the use of treatment modalities that incorporate music therapy with patients experiencing mental health issues including anxiety, depression, and post-traumatic stress disorder. In examining the psychological and emotional stress that Puerto Ricans have been repeatedly exposed to over centuries of colonization and its aftermath, and considering the deep importance of music in their culture and history, music therapy resonates beautifully with mental health and wellness goals for Puerto Rican clients and families. Its accessibility and reliability allow it to be molded and adapted to each individual clinical situation, and provide opportunities for increased health and a return to physical and emotional homeostasis.

"Perhaps the most important intervention to keep in mind when working with Puerto Ricans is that as therapists we must keep that hope alive while helping them gain access to their rightful resources" (McGoldrick *et al.* 2005, p.254). When faced with crisis, the natural response of Puerto Ricans all over the island and abroad is to gather, pray, sing, and play instruments. Videos of residents playing bomba and plena and creating lyrics about resilience and hope in the middle of flooded disaster zones post-Hurricane Fiona circulated all over the internet. Music is often synonymous not only with Puerto Rican traditions such as weddings, funerals, holidays, and cultural festivals, but also with coping in times of need. This points toward music therapy as a promising method for improving and promoting health and wellness in a culturally sensitive and humanistic way.

My survey

In my quest for clinical considerations specifically when serving the Puerto Rican community, I asked current music therapists who identify as Puerto

Rican to share some of their clinical anecdotes, experience, and advice for future music therapists ("Puerto Rican music therapists' experiences: culture, identity, and clinical practice"). Since the purpose of my survey was to gather initial, qualitative self-reports that are specific to the Puerto Rican population, it was important to also allow clinicians working with Puerto Rican clients to respond, regardless of whether they themselves identified as Puerto Rican or not.

The survey was conducted in January 2023, with a sample size of ten. Participants ranged from young adults to 50+ years of age, with 50 percent being between 25 and 39 years old, 30 percent between 40 and 50, and the remaining 20 percent split evenly between 18 and 24 and 50+ years of age. A total of 69.2 percent identified as female and 30.8 percent as male. The majority of participants, 90 percent, were born in Puerto Rico, and 10 percent in Latin America. When reporting their current place of residence, 70 percent noted Puerto Rico, 20 percent were living on mainland United States, and 10 percent in Peru. Regarding experience in the music therapy profession, 40 percent of participants reported 1–3 years, 10 percent 4–9 years, 30 percent 10–19 years, and the remaining 20 percent reported 20+ years in the field. Participants reported a variety of clinical settings and populations being served, as illustrated in the figure below.

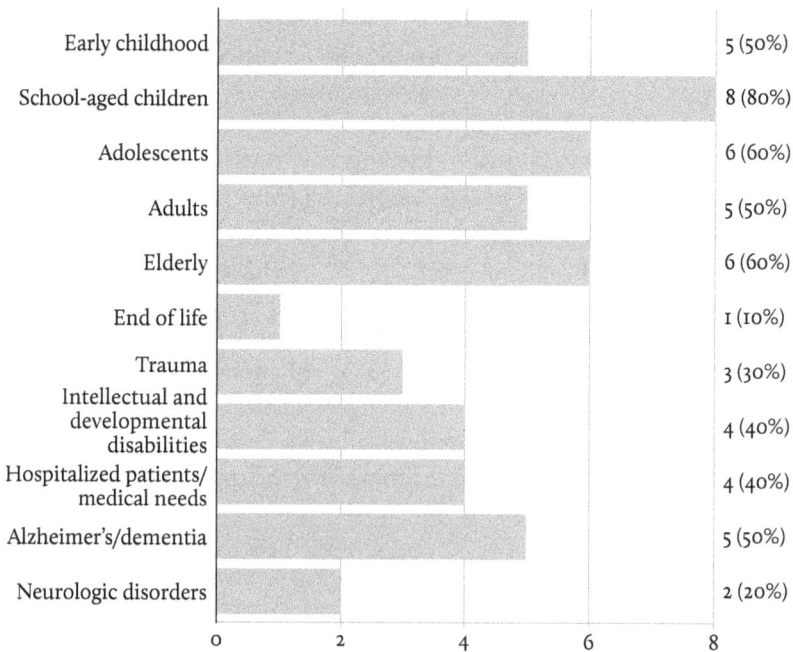

Population	Count (Percent)
Early childhood	5 (50%)
School-aged children	8 (80%)
Adolescents	6 (60%)
Adults	5 (50%)
Elderly	6 (60%)
End of life	1 (10%)
Trauma	3 (30%)
Intellectual and developmental disabilities	4 (40%)
Hospitalized patients/medical needs	4 (40%)
Alzheimer's/dementia	5 (50%)
Neurologic disorders	2 (20%)

POPULATIONS SERVED BY SURVEY PARTICIPANTS

The survey was open for one month and promoted via social media, WhatsApp group chats for AMTPR and LAMTN, and via email sent by the AMTPR leadership team.

The following table is a synopsis of participant themes and responses for each of the four survey prompts.

Survey on clinical interactions where Puerto Rican culture and identity played a role

Survey prompt 1

Think of a clinical interaction you had with a client/family member/colleague that was particular to the Puerto Rican culture and identity. Please share a brief anecdote or memory of it and/or why it was special.

Recurring themes		Quotes and responses
Culture and ethics		• Asking for a blessing (*la bendición*) at the beginning and end of a session • Clients and therapists commonly greeting each other with hugs and kisses on the cheek • Bringing favorite fruit to an elderly patient as a favor for their granddaughter who lives too far away to do so herself • Children automatically dancing along to Puerto Rican songs • Clients immediately opening up to clinicians about their personal struggles once they notice the therapist speaks Spanish and/or is Latinx/e
Song requests		• Older adults—themes of resilience or reaffirming the Puerto Rican identity • Adolescents—drum circles typically making reference to reggaeton, trap, and bomba y plena • Various age groups—Christian music
Interventions	Music appreciation	• Videos and analysis of Puerto Rican singers • Study of Puerto Rican music history, particularly the 1950s to the 1980s
	Music and imagery	• Referencing Puerto Rican landscapes • Utilizing an ocean drum and guitar

cont.

Recurring themes	Quotes and responses
Music-facilitated discussion and rapport building	• "A Spaniard-born man shared his story of how he decided to move to PR [Puerto Rico] 50+ years ago, prompted by the song 'En Mi Viejo San Juan.' It was special... how an outsider can feel deeply embraced and welcomed by the Puerto Rican community." • "I had a patient whose spouse (Cuban) used to live in Puerto Rico for several years. During the patient's session, the spouse was always very involved and interested in initiating conversations with me because I am Puerto Rican. The spouse always expressed his experiences from the years living in PR [Puerto Rico] and asked for 'El Jibarito (Lamento Borincano)' every time I went to visit. It appeared to provide comfort and reminiscence..."
Songwriting as a celebration of culture and bonding	• "A young mother had a stroke during childbirth. I was assigned to treat her in the inpatient rehabilitation center while I also treated the baby in the NICU [neonatal intensive care unit]. We connected immediately and it was evident that the patient wanted her baby to be immersed in the culture from the beginning... We worked on writing a lullaby in Spanish to address the patient's executive function while also providing a platform for them to express how they felt and creating a cultural welcome through music for the baby. We had...a co-treat session with OT and the NICU nurses to bring this song to the baby while the patient held her for the first time. It was one of the most beautiful moments in my 12+ year career as an MT [music therapist]."

Survey prompt 2

In your opinion, what is at least one aspect of the culture and/or identity that any music therapist working with Puerto Rican clients should consider/learn/explore?

Recurring themes		Quotes and responses
Music genres		<ul><li>Salsa</li><li>Reggaeton<ul><li>One participant offered this video resource: "LOUD: The History of Reggaeton," narrated by Ivy Queen[1]</li></ul></li><li>Boleros</li><li>Contemporary music on the radio</li></ul>
Musical elements		<ul><li>Afro-Caribbean rhythms</li><li>Coordination of movement and rhythm</li><li>Syncopation</li></ul>
Music and culture		<ul><li>"Music is embedded in our DNA. We have used music throughout our history to communicate news, express difficult emotions, and enjoy each other's company. Music is also closely related to food. I have never been to a PR [Puerto Rican] household and someone has not invited me to enjoy a *cafecito con galletas* (coffee with cookies) or a sandwich. The PR people are family-centered, and once you cross the doorway you will be greeted with kindness and a warm spirit."</li><li>"If the MT [music therapist] is not Puerto Rican, I would say it is imperative that they get to know the music and culture as well as the subcultural differences within the population."</li></ul>
Clinical boundaries	Politics	<ul><li>"I think we should embrace the language, and culture, but not get into any kind of politics, because that is a sensitive topic that might jeopardize the therapeutic relationship."</li></ul>
	Trust	<ul><li>"Making you part of the family as someone who cares will be very easy, so make sure you establish some type of professional boundary while also giving space for crude and raw emotions to arise in the session."</li></ul>
	Religion	<ul><li>"Faith is a very big component of the culture... Be mindful of the Christian traditions in the Caribbean and how they related to the topic of health."</li></ul>

cont.

---

1   https://futurostudios.org/podcasts/loud-the-history-of-reggaeton

Survey prompt 3

What are at least three songs/interventions/techniques you would recommend that music therapy students practice and include in their clinical repertoire when working with Puerto Rican clients?

Recurring themes	Quotes and responses	
Songs	• "Piel Canela" • "En Mi Viejo San Juan" • "El Jolgorio" • "Preciosa" • "Paz En La Tormenta" • "Levanto Mis Manos"	• "El Coquí" (danza) • "Pescador De Hombres" • "Cuán Grande Es El" • "Calma" • "Verde Luz"
Genres and techniques	• Bomba • Plena • Reggaeton • Salsa • Baladas en español • Seis chorreao	• Using instruments like claves and güiro • Basic Puerto Rican folk patterns on the guitar with a pie-forzado (forced foot) approach
Interventions	• Call and response • Music and movement, as Puerto Rican music is commonly danced to • Syncopated rhythms for memory recall • Reminiscence and resilience work for people struggling with moving off the island • "Plena/bomba drumming layered rhythms: You can add to this having them take turns using a sheet, scarf, or even a skirt so when they shake it you match them on the drum. However, remember to be respectful of the genre's history, especially one of people marginalized by society." • "Use music in tech to create a reggaeton beat, and utilize songwriting methods! Good songs to grab inspiration from: 'Muchos Quieren Tumbarme' by Ivy Queen, 'Loiza' by Tego Calderón, 'Oye Mi Canto' by N.O.R.E., 'Ella Perrea Sola' by Bad Bunny." • "The structure of plena allows clients to work on language while also fostering creativity... Plena was historically used to tell stories. The use of it in a session allows us to learn about situations we might otherwise not have discovered."	

Survey prompt 4

Is there anything else you would like future music therapy students to know about Puerto Rican culture and identity?

Recurring themes	Quotes and responses
Diversity	• "There is a lot of diversity in musical preferences, but something that coincides among many is rhythm paired with movement as well as religious/spiritual music. Music is the thread connecting all areas of the self for many Boricuas. We protest with music, celebrate with music, and remember with music." • "Visit Puerto Rico. Use the time to chat with locals and really dive into the culture. There is no better way to learn than by being immersed." • "We speak, think, and feel in Spanish."
History and identity	• "It is important to be aware of the historical power relationships that exist and how these bleed into a therapeutic relationship with a Puerto Rican client. In a sociopolitical context, Puerto Ricans are subject to a colony (territory) relationship with the US: topics and fears regarding culture, identity, land, and history being eradicated are very present... Over one hundred years, more if you count Spanish colonization, of being used to not receiving adequate protections, not having a voice or a vote to receive more disaster aid... We have learned over time that to get far, you need to know your neighbor. Our communities are our centers for healing, and our key to survival. The therapist must be aware of these hierarchies in relationships and work to increase reciprocity by creating an environment where respect, understanding, and patience is earned, not given. Get to know your Puerto Rican client, and the people that are a part of their circles—how can you contribute to their community of healing/ecosystem of support?"
Authenticity	• "Be culturally responsible, humble. Puerto Rican people are kind and very musical. You can be comfortable asking them what they like." • "Do not assume, always ask—it's okay not to know." • "To be genuine and interested in learning about your client without making assumptions. For example, do not assume that they might like Bad Bunny because they are Puerto Rican. Explore their preferences together and learn from their culture to understand what is the better way to be present for them during sessions."

Conclusion

This survey helped not only to gather preliminary data regarding what music therapists see as significant when serving Puerto Rican clients, but also to shed light on a major limitation of this study: outreach and the subsequent small sample size. This might have been due to a variety of factors, including the fact that the AMTPR had just recently been established and communications were in the process of becoming more streamlined, as well as the fact that Puerto Rican music therapists and music therapy students are spread out all over the world. This makes it difficult to engage participants who may not be connected to the Puerto Rican music therapy community online or living close to other Puerto Rican practitioners. Geographical differences and changes due to the recent COVID-19 pandemic also limit the amount of in-person gatherings that might otherwise facilitate networking, direct outreach, and survey participation. Nonetheless, there is an opportunity to replicate this study on a larger scale, perhaps involving not only more participants, but also a more in-depth look at the clinical work that is being done with Puerto Rican clients and what can be learned from it.

In this study, participants shared a great deal of insight and reflection that provided a taste of how music therapy curricula might be enhanced and elevated to a more culturally sensitive and humanistic level, particularly in the US, to support the growing Puerto Rican population. It was interesting to notice how frequently Puerto Rican music therapists and those working with clients of Puerto Rican descent tend to describe the work within the context of multiple, overlapping layers, remarking on the importance of politics, food, reggaeton, religious music, resiliency, hugs, and kisses. As in many cases within healthcare, and basically any human interaction, it's difficult to consider an individual's experience as isolated in one time, place, or situation. This is due to the myriad of factors that influence that individual's feelings of self-worth, identity, sense of belonging and support, association with music or any other given treatment modality, intergenerational trauma, ability, and so much more. Humans are complex, and Puerto Ricans, whether or not by choice, have developed a collective self-awareness that acknowledges, honors, and even celebrates that complexity.

This is why the first few minutes of a session might involve a kiss on the cheek and a deep dive into a client's medical and social history, all while they invite you to a *cafecito*. It's the reason why a diasporican client might burst into tears the moment they hear their therapist speak Spanish or perform a Puerto Rican classic. It's the reason why "*¡Yo soy Boricua!*" ("I'm Puerto Rican!") will be met with an unapologetic "*¡Pa'que tú lo sepas!*" ("Just so you know!"). There is pride in surviving, overcoming, and reclaiming Puerto Rico's culture. The Puerto Rican essence is woven together in a beautiful blend of history, heritage, and music that is individual and united, layered and integrated, one and all of us.

CHAPTER 3

NEUROLOGIC MUSIC THERAPY IN A TELEHEALTH ENVIRONMENT

Sessions with a Chilean Stroke Survivor

TALIA GIRTON

The COVID-19 pandemic created an atmosphere of confusion and isolation as an unprecedented way of life was forced upon us all with almost no warning. Lockdowns and social distancing meant that our normal daily routines, our work life, and our interactions with others all had to change in order to protect each other from this new disease.

As weeks turned into months, life went on, but business as usual was an impossible task. This left the door open for a fresh breeze of innovation, creativity, and new ways of thinking. It is out of this that the Global Music Therapy Center (GMTC) was born, a coming-together of music therapists and educators from around the world who saw an opportunity to expand the reach of their services as people around the globe moved their lives largely online.

One of the GMTC's first initiatives was to ensure that all its therapists were certified in Neurologic Music Therapy® (NMT). For the first time, the International Training Institute in Neurologic Music Therapy® offered its course online, allowing therapists worldwide access to specialized knowledge that had previously been restricted by location, travel time, work, and other associated costs.

NMT is defined as "the therapeutic application of music to cognitive, affective, sensory, language, and motor dysfunctions due to disease or injury to the human nervous system" (Thaut and Hömberg 2014, p.2). A set of 18 protocols has been developed to assist in sensorimotor, speech/language, and cognitive rehabilitation, and each of these therapeutic music exercises is

49

adaptable to fit client preferences and needs. Like all music therapy modalities, NMT harnesses the power of music to help clients achieve non-musical goals (Thaut 2005).

It was this specialization in NMT that originally inspired Sebastian, a stroke survivor from Chile, to contact the GMTC. He was referred to us by his neurologist who herself was trained in NMT and was impressed by the rigorousness of the scientific basis for treatment: evidence-based medicine, neuroscience-guided rehabilitation, and data-driven therapy (Thaut and Hömberg 2014).

Background
Client profile

Sebastian contacted the GMTC in September 2021 seeking additional support for lingering speech difficulties following a middle cerebral artery (MCA) stroke the year before. After five months of speech therapy, during which he made great gains in speech comprehension, expression, and literacy, a re-evaluation revealed semi-fluent and informative speech, with the presence of latencies and a tendency to self-correct. Adherence to grammatical rules and the production of automatic language was largely preserved, as was word and sentence repetition and denominative language for both objects and actions. Sprinkled throughout these achievements, however, was the presence of phonemic paraphasias as well as a lingering difficulty with semantic and phonemic fluency. Incredibly, Sebastian performed at an accuracy level of 80 percent or above in all other communication tasks.

Prior to our work together, Sebastian had worked with another music therapist as part of his rehabilitation program. These sessions focused on a variety of goals, including improving processing time, visual and auditory coordination, attention span, and memory. In terms of speech and language, his goals were centered around enhancing automatic recall and improving articulation, prosody, and vocal strength.

While his previous music therapist worked to address a wide variety of needs post-stroke, the work Sebastian and I did together was specifically centered around verbal communication through the use of NMT with the simple goal of, in his words, "*hablar bien*"—speaking well. After an initial meeting and subsequent assessment, it was determined that Sebastian wanted to improve his expressive fluency and lingering phonemic paraphasias. He felt comfortable communicating with friends and family, but found some difficulty in the work setting when speaking with people who were not known to him.

Assessment

A modified version of the Mississippi Aphasia Screening Test (MAST, Spanish version) and the Prueba de Articulación de Fonemas (Phoneme Articulation Test) were conducted to identify areas of difficulty. Sebastian scored well on most areas of the MAST with the exception of repetition of long phrases and, as was expected, oral expression. The phoneme articulation test revealed difficulties with the rolled "r" and "d" before a consonant; words that included two consonants back to back with one of these sounds were especially challenging. The diphthongs "ue" and "ie" were also problematic. Assessment was ongoing throughout the treatment period and the treatment plan was regularly updated as additional data was gathered.

Treatment plan

A treatment plan was devised drawing on information from Sebastian's latest speech and language pathology report along with his desired outcomes from therapy. Each intervention was designed to improve his expressive language fluency, and sessions were largely centered around the NMT techniques of Rhythmic Speech Cueing (RSC) and Therapeutic Singing (TS).

Each session lasted for 45 minutes and was designed according to the following structure:

1. Warm-up: Breathing to music
2. Musical realization of target phonemes and words in isolation
3. Song project: Target phonemes and words placed in the wider context of a song:
   a. Call and response, with rhythm only
   b. Client speaks rhythm only
   c. Call and response, with rhythm and melody
   d. Client sings without support from therapist
   e. Therapist demonstrates song with accompaniment (live piano or guitar)
   f. Client and therapist sing along together with accompaniment
   g. Client sings along with accompaniment, without support from therapist

Between each step, any sounds or words that presented difficulty were noted and practiced using RSC. Songs were generally practiced for four to six weeks until 80 percent mastery of target sounds was achieved.

BREATHING TO MUSIC

Sessions with Sebastian always began with a breathing to music exercise. This was to calm the nervous system and reduce any anxiety associated with speaking. Clients with aphasia are aware of the mistakes they make while conversing, which can lead to frustration and anxiety; this can then cause even more mistakes to occur. Starting the session from a place of calm and a sense of groundedness was a good way to avoid this negative loop.

A variety of breathing techniques were used, including:

- Square breathing, to the beat of a drum: breathe in for 4 beats, hold for 4, breathe out for 4, and hold for 4. This was repeated 10–15 times.
- Resonant frequency breathing with piano. Breathing into the belly is encouraged, with the rate of breathing slowed to 3–7 breaths per minute. This was facilitated by music with a slow tempo; inhales were cued with an ascending melodic motif and exhales were cued with a descending melodic motif.
- Three-part breathing with calming ambient music. The client was asked to fill up their lungs a third of the way, then two-thirds, then all the way, before letting out a long exhale.

The practice of Neurologic Music Therapy®

NMT involves implementing a selection of evidence-based protocols that use music to change the way the brain functions (NMTSA 2011). Making use of singing, instrument play, and movement to music, specific musical elements such as tempo, melody, rhythm, pitch, and dynamics are highlighted or altered to create an effective, creative, and enjoyable therapeutic intervention.

NMT techniques fall into one of three categories: sensorimotor rehabilitation, speech and language rehabilitation, and cognitive rehabilitation. Clients with autism, cerebral palsy, Parkinson's disease, Down syndrome, traumatic brain injury, Alzheimer's disease/dementia, cerebrovascular accident (stroke), and a variety of genetic disorders are the target population for NMT protocols.

Speech and language protocols

Eight speech and language protocols were developed to aid clients in improving their communication. These address a wide variety of goals, including improving functional speech responses, facilitating motor planning and muscular coordination, enhancing voice control in terms of pitch, timbre, dynamics, prosody, and breath, and improving articulation.

To improve Sebastian's expressive fluency, we focused on two protocols: Rhythmic Speech Cueing (RSC) and Therapeutic Singing (TS). RSC uses rhythm to control the rate of speech (Thaut 2005). Sebastian tended to produce more phonemic paraphasias when attempting to speak quickly, so we used a metronome as well as more musically interesting backing tracks at varying speeds to train him to slow down and control his rate of speech. When particular words proved tricky, he was encouraged to clap or pat his leg along with the pulse. (This will be discussed in more detail later on.) Therapeutic Singing (TS) is a more general protocol in NMT that refers to a variety of singing techniques to improve speech and language initiation, development, and articulation (Thaut 2005).

As the goals for Sebastian revolved around clearer pronunciation and improved fluency, specific songs were chosen to work on particular sounds he found challenging. Some of these songs were picked from his collection of favorite artists, some were unfamiliar songs, and some were composed with the purpose of practicing a specific phoneme or string of phonemes that proved difficult. Call and response singing was implemented as an enjoyable way to practice minimal pairs and non-words as we moved from treating his aphasia (difficulty with expressive language) to his dysarthria (difficulty with the motor movements of the speech apparatus).

Therapeutic Singing interventions

After an initial warm-up, each session started with practicing target sounds in isolation. This was achieved by call and response singing with the therapist. A simple melody and rhythm was used to deliver the target sound in a musical way for the client to then repeat. For example, the therapist might play a 12-bar blues progression and sing a two-note melody with a variety of words that contained the target sound /ng/, such as *bongo*, *sangre*, and *jungla*. The therapist would sing one word at a time and the client would then sing it back. This intervention was later adapted to practice minimal pairs, for example, *boca* and *poca*. The therapist would sing three words, such as *boca*, *poca*, *boca* and the client would listen and sing them back. The therapist would repeat this several times, switching around the order of the words.

Next, target sounds were placed in the wider context of a song. For example, "Bongos y Congas" was composed specifically for Sebastian to work on the sound combination "ng:"

En las profundidades de la jungla
Hay árboles de mango
Y cien tipos de hongos
Cangrejos de mil y un
Colores, tan rojo como sangre
Rojillo de mi lengua
Compongo esta canción y hay
Bongos y congas, congas y bongos, bongos y congas
Escucho fuertes
Bongos y congas, congas y bongos, bongos y congas
Y ya se acabó.

Another example is "Huevos Revueltos," which was composed to improve Sebastian's "ue" diphthongs:

Estamos de acuerdo
Queremos almuerzo
Tal vez huevos revueltos
Y café luego
Vamos al muelle
Cerca de la fuente
Aquí siempre recuerdo
Cuentos del pueblo.

To further Sebastian's improvement of target sounds, rhythmic lines were added to tongue twisters such as "Fuente de Fuensanta" and "Cuando Cuentes Cuentos."

NOTATION FOR THE COMPOSITION "CUENTOS Y CUENTAS"

Songs were also used to improve Sebastian's control of the rate of his speech. Starting with an old classic in simple 4/4 time, "Piel Canela," he was led in clapping a steady beat as he sang. A metronome was used to aid in this, starting at 60, and then gradually increasing the tempo to 100. Once he was able to clap and sing this song fluently, we moved on to a more challenging salsa rhythm with "Vivir Mi Vida." The same metronome concept was utilized, but this time with a salsa backing track for added enjoyment.

Rhythmic Speech Cueing interventions

RSC techniques were used within the larger context of TS interventions. Each time a song was introduced into a session, Sebastian was asked to clap and speak the words rhythmically before adding the melody. The clapping was either a steady pulse with the spoken word flowing evenly on top, or it was matched to the pattern of speech.

Matching lyrics to musical pulse and speech patterns

Speech pattern	X	X	X	X	X	X	X
Steady pulse	X		X		X		X
Lyrics	Twin	kle	twin	kle	lit	tle	star

Once Sebastian was confident in clapping a steady beat along with his singing, the metronome was introduced. It was soon discovered that he had a hard time slowing down his rate of speech to match a slower metronome beat. The goal of improving the ability to modify the rate of speech was added to his treatment plan, as learning to speak more slowly would lend itself to improved fluency; giving the brain more time to process the desired outputs and form target sounds would reduce his phonemic paraphasias.

RSC was also used when the client had trouble with a particular word. First, the therapist would clap each syllable of the target word while speaking each syllable aloud, and the client would repeat. Next, the client was asked to clap and speak each syllable without a prompt. Finally, the client was asked to say the word naturally, without claps or syllabic division. Each step was repeated three to five times. Then, the word was put back into the larger context of the song.

NMT in an online environment

As one can imagine, a number of challenges came up when planning for NMT sessions in the virtual space. While most can be overcome with creative adjustments, the problem of simultaneous music-making online is something that technology is not yet able to solve. Since many NMT protocols require the use of a steady pulse set by the therapist, with the therapist and client singing or playing instruments in synchrony, much thought must be put into finding workarounds for audio latency.

1. Client Audio Share: Instead of turning on the metronome on my end, I had the client source an online metronome and use the audio share option from their end. This eliminated the latency factor from the equation, and meant I could accurately interpret the client's rhythmic ability.
2. Using Recordings: I would often record the accompaniment to a song and send the track to the client. Then, I would ask them to share their audio, play the track, and sing along. That way, I could hear how they interacted with the music in real time, rather than dealing with a delayed response. I would also record exercises directly from Zoom during our sessions for the client to practice with during the week.
3. Turning Off the Client's Microphone: the latency issue made it impossible to sing together in sync, so I often asked the client to turn off their microphone when we sang together. Since my microphone was on, the client still had the experience of our two voices joined.

Results
Following nine months of treatment, Sebastian reported improved fluency and more ease in communications with his work colleagues. A subsequent modified MAST revealed a score of 87 percent; an improvement, but with some lingering difficulties with oral expression. While stroke patients often make great advances in speech in the first few months of their recovery, 60 percent continue to have lingering difficulties over six months post-stroke (Flint Rehab. 2021).

The role of privilege in Chile in access to services and professional training
Chile finds itself among the most prosperous countries in Latin America, coming second only to Uruguay in GDP per capita out of the 21 countries or territories in the region (World Bank 2021). It is safe to assume that private out-of-pocket services are more accessible to the average Chilean than to people from many of its neighboring countries. Chile is also fortunate to have a formalized music therapy training program—most other countries in the region are underdeveloped in this respect, with only Argentina, Brazil, and Colombia enjoying thriving music therapy communities. As of 2017, there were around 130 trained music therapists in Chile (WFMT 2017).

The University of Chile (Universidad de Chile) offers the only two music therapy programs in the country: the postgraduate Specialization in the Arts Therapies (Music Therapy emphasis) and the Music Therapy diploma. The postgraduate program allows graduates to practice music therapy in Chile while the diploma is aimed at education professionals and offers tools from the realm of music therapy that can be applied in school settings. The Chilean Music Therapy Association (Asociación Chilena de Musicoterapia, ACHIM) is an active professional body that hosts a myriad of events, publishes a variety of articles in conjunction with the University of Chile, and provides resources to members and those interested in the field.

Even so, access to specialized music therapy services in Chile is a privilege enjoyed by few. Out of the 3416 Neurologic Music Therapists around the world, there are currently six in the entire country of Chile, with four located in the capital, Santiago, where Sebastian lives (Academy of Neurologic Music Therapy 2015). Sebastian's high level of education and position as a project manager in a multinational corporation afforded him the means to seek out and pursue NMT treatment.

Conclusion

Through the incredible advances in telehealth and global connection ushered in by the COVID-19 pandemic, as an American music therapist based in London, I was able to successfully plan and execute a remote music therapy treatment plan with a client in Chile. Creative workarounds were implemented to adapt NMT protocols to the online sphere, and impressively, some advantages were found, such as the ability to directly record exercises to be done in between sessions. Music therapy in the virtual space is here to stay, and the Global Music Therapy Center looks forward to continuing connecting clients and music therapists around the world.

CHAPTER 4

MUSIC: HEALING OINTMENT FOR THE HEART (MÚSICA: EL VAPORU DEL CORAZÓN)

Music, Health, and Wellness within Latinx/e Communities in the United States

CYNTHIA PIMENTEL KOSKELA

"Deja tu corazón sentir con la música" ["Let your heart feel with music"].

The use of music to support health and wellness is deeply rooted within Latinx/e communities in the United States. From the use of music in traditional Latinx/e gatherings such as dancing to salsa and bachata during a *quinciañera* or listening to mariachi music to honor loved ones who passed during funerals, music has played a significant role in helping communities collectively process grief, navigate hardships, nurture a sense of unity, and foster a sense of belonging. This chapter will explore the relationship between the healing role of music within Latinx/e communities currently living in the United States, and its ability to mobilize cultural wealth and promote health and wellness. It will also identify areas of growth for applying music in health and wellness practices, including the development of culturally responsive professional music therapy practices within Latinx/e communities. *It is important to note, however, that not all cultural values discussed are applicable for every Latinx/e individual/community, and should not be generalized.*

Latinx/e communities in the United States

For the purposes of this chapter, the term "Latinx/e community" refers to a diverse group of people of Latin American origin or descent living in the United States. The term "Latinx/e" is a gender-inclusive alternative to traditional terms such as "Latino" or "Latina." The Latinx/e community comprises individuals from various countries in Latin America, including, but not limited to, Mexico, Colombia, Brazil, Argentina, and many others (OMH 2023). According to the US Census Bureau, people from the Latinx/e community account for an estimated 63.7 million living in the United States, or approximately 19 percent of the total population (United States Census Bureau, 2023; Moslimani, *et. al.* 2023).

Over the past few decades, the Latinx/e community has played a significant role in driving up US population growth—53 percent of population growth was primarily from this ethnic group (Pew Research Center, 2023). This growth has significant contributions to the United States' cultural and economic landscape. From language to country of origin, diversity within the collective Latinx/e community in the United States is incredibly complex (Estrella 2017). For instance, both immigrants and non-immigrants with origins from diverse countries throughout Latin America comprise a large part of the population, and the number of individuals who identify as Latinx/e who speak English has also increased dramatically—72 percent of Latinx/e aged five and older reported being able to speak English proficiently (Falicov 2014; Pew Research Center, 2023).

Addressing health inequities

Similar to other historically marginalized communities in the United States, Latinx/e face exposure to inequities in healthcare due to factors such as structural racism, or the "normalization and legitimization of an array of systemic—historical, cultural, institutional, and interpersonal—that routinely advantage Whites," which, in turn, directly impact the social determinants of health (Green and Poppe 2021, p.2). The impact of structural inequities includes, but is not limited to, access to healthcare and education and economic disadvantages (Green and Poppe 2021, p.4). For instance, according to UnidosUS, approximately 10.8 million Latinx/e do not have access to healthcare coverage and over 50 percent do not have access to paid sick leave (UnidosUS 2021).

These factors, combined with stressors resulting from immigration status and language differences, contribute to an increase in health disparities among Latinx/e communities in the United States, including higher levels of physical and mental illness and mortality rates (Falicov 2014; Flores *et al.* 2008; Green and Poppe 2021; Vega, Rodriguez, and Gruskin 2009). For instance, research indicates that racialized trauma, or an individual's ongoing discrimination and oppression due to race, has a negative impact on an individual's health and wellness over time (Flores *et al.* 2008; Hadley 2017).

Additionally, individuals in oppressed groups, such as Latinx/e, report experiencing racial/ethnic discrimination including as microaggressions, or the everyday intentional or unintentional act of hostility (verbal or non-verbal) from an individual in the dominant identity to an individual from typically marginalized communities (Hadley 2017). Racism, such as in the form of microaggressions, can take a negative toll on an individual's health and well-being over time (Hadley 2017).

Due to these challenges, access to culturally responsive healthcare treatment is critical in order to best meet the needs of this growing population, as culture plays an important role in how an individual defines and engages in health (Harrison *et al.* 2019). Healthcare professionals and clinicians must be able to utilize culture as a source of strength within treatment and care. This has been associated with engagement and improved health and wellness outcomes (Mulvaney-Day *et al.* 2011; Vega *et al.* 2009).

Music and health in the Latinx/e community

There is a current need to implement culturally responsive practices in healthcare to effectively address the unique health needs of Latinx/e-identifying individuals and communities. People from Latinx/e communities in the US hold a variety of strengths within traditional wellness practices, including the active utilization of music for health and wellness. Music is a strong form of cultural expression, and plays a significant role in supporting well-being and addressing the unique health needs of individuals within the Latinx/e community.

This section highlights how music is used to mobilize cultural capital—drawing on elements of Yosso's (2005) asset-based cultural wealth model—to support the health and well-being of the Latinx/e community in the United States.(Cuadrado-Garcia, 2023; Mcleod, 2024; Yosso, 2005). *It is important to note that not all experiences relate to the entire Latinx/e community, and should not be taken as a prescription for treatment and diagnosis.*

Mobilizing cultural capital with music

These are five identified areas of cultural capital that can be mobilized through the use of music for health and wellness within the Latinx/e community:

1. Linguistic: Emotional expression
2. **Familial:** *Familismo*
3. Social: Collectivism

4. Aspirational: Spirituality or religion
5. Navigational: Identity development

Linguistic capital: music for emotional expression

CIELITO LINDO
Ay, ay, ay, ay
Canta y no llores
Porque cantando se alegran, cielito lindo, los corazones.
[Ay, ay, ay, ay
Sing and don't cry
Because singing makes the hearts happy, my dear sweetheart.]

From *mariachi* to *boleros*, music is used within Latinx/e communities to express deep feelings, for example, celebrating moments of joy during community gatherings such as *quinciañeras* (coming of age ceremonies), nurturing hope, or processing challenging emotions such as grief in the death of loved ones during funerals. For instance, the song "Amor Eterno" by Juan Gabriel was played by local Uvalde mariachi musicians in June 2022 for the community to mourn the lives of children murdered after the tragic school shooting (Martinez 2023). The ability for music as a source of emotional expression through non-verbal means is an ideal form of mental health support within the Latinx/e community, because there can be a stigma within the community in receiving talk therapy within mental health treatment, as it may "create embarrassment and shame for the family, resulting in fewer people seeking treatment" (Mental Health America 2023; National Alliance on Mental Illness, 2023); Thoughts and emotions that may be challenging to express verbally are often more effectively communicated and processed—both consciously and unconsciously—through artistic expression (Fajardo, 2009).

Music has the unique ability to support Latinx/e immigrant communities living in the United States to process and navigate the challenges of the immigrant experience. For instance, within Norteño or corrido music, a musical style originating from Mexico that incorporates storytelling, there are many groups, such as Los Tigres del Norte, that write songs expressing the experience of immigrants living in the US.

Los Tigres del Norte has identified that their music serves "as a consolation" for newly arrived individuals who are navigating multiple challenges in living within a new country, and who are "an example of fighters who want to make a better life for themselves" (Flores 2020, p.1). This, in turn, has created an opportunity for Latinx/e immigrants and first-generation immigrants to utilize this music as a linguistic cultural health capital (Dubbin,

Chang, and Shim 2013), as music is a linguistic or communication style that provides a channel for emotional expression and a tool for acculturation, in turn generating resiliency (Yosso 2005).

Familial and social capital: music to elevate *familismo* and collectivism

From the use of Latin music genres such as cumbia and salsa to gather communities in dance during gatherings and family celebrations to the use of fandango jarocho, a mix of African, Indigenous, and Spanish-influenced music native to Veracruz, Mexico, to build community and strengthen immigrant cultural values in the United States, Latin music can be a primary conduit for connection and a source of hope (Gonzales 2019). These forms of community music engagement are central, as there is a natural influence from family and participatory engagement within Latin music. Genres such as son jarocho highlight the Latinx/e cultural values of collectivism (placing a community's needs above individuals), and *familismo* (the importance of family participation and inclusiveness) (Ayón, Marsiglia, and Bermudez-Parsai 2010).

An understanding of family dynamics is extremely important in this collectivistic culture, as psychosocial functioning is expressed in *familismo* by placing family members' needs over one's own and placing an importance on connectedness within family units (Fernando 2008). *Familismo* and collectivism are sources of strength that play a critical role in supporting individual health and well-being, acting as protective factors in mitigating the risk of mental illness. (Estrella 2017; Valdivieso-Mora *et al.* 2016). These cultural values can be found expressed within Latin music and utilized in therapeutic treatments.

Community music engagement is an expression of both collectivism and *familismo* and a tool in building community and supporting health and wellness within historically marginalized groups (Ayón *et al.* 2010; Murray and Lamont 2012). For instance, during the COVID-19 pandemic, people of color were disproportionately impacted, and experienced increased rates of mental health illnesses (Saltzman *et al.* 2021). The use of music to connect communities became increasingly important, such as with the Cumbiatón collective (a group dedicated to finding new creative ways to connect to undocumented immigrant and queer communities through its virtual dance parties) (Trinh 2022). Within this movement individuals were able to generate safe spaces to combat isolation, build community, and support physical and mental health. In addition, by holding collective music experiences focused on empowerment and community connection, this challenges the dominant social representation of the community through a deficit-based lens, and can promote well-being by providing individuals with a source of strength, joy, and confidence (Murray and Lamont 2012).

Aspirational capital: music in spirituality

The traditional use of folk medicine and spirituality are accessible supports for health and wellness within Latinx/e communities, given the inaccessibility of traditional models of care (Hernandez Romero 2019; Mental Health America 2023). Coping through the use of music within spirituality or religion can be used to maintain hope and dreams for many Latinx-/e-identifying individuals, making it a mobilizer for aspirational wealth and a protective factor in mental health (Caplan 2019; Mental Health America, 2023). Therefore, the use of spiritual music to mobilize coping skills through self-reflection within spiritual or religious healing practices is greatly recommended for religious or spiritual Latinx/e individuals confronting psychosocial challenges. However, it is important to be aware that not all members within the Latinx/e community utilize religion as a protective factor, and religion can inversely contribute to stigma in receiving mental health services (Caplan 2019). Therefore, the use of spiritual music within a religious context and used as an anti-stigma intervention is recommended for Latinx/e individuals who utilize religion or spirituality in their health and wellness practices.

Navigational capital: music in identity development

Research shows that exposure to systemic inequities, including racial discrimination, can negatively impact an individual's sense of cultural identity and health and wellness outcomes (Torres, Driscoll, and Voell 2012). The use of music as a source of cultural identity and pride within the Latinx/e community can support racial-ethnic identity development, and serve as a protective factor in health for many individuals from historically marginalized communities, especially for those navigating intersectionality, such as for people identifying as LGBTQA+ and Latinx/e (Case 2021; Myrie, Breen, and Ashbourne 2022; Villa 2019). Engaging in music-based experiences may provide empowerment for individuals and communities navigating systems of inequity through challenging stereotypes and providing a platform for self-expression and visibility, thus assisting in building navigational capital.

Advancing health equity through music

Despite increasing numbers of Latinx/e-identifying communities in the United States, structural racism in healthcare policy greatly impacts access to quality healthcare services (Yearbey, *et. al*, 2022). This may also include access to music therapy, an established health profession in the United States which utilizes music to accomplish non musical goals and is conducted by a board certified music therapist (American Music Therapy Association, 2023; Yearby, Clark, and Figueroa 2022). Inequities impacting care and treatment include access to affordable insurance, the training and education of providers who share a similar cultural background, and other factors that directly impact implementation of culturally responsive healthcare services for this population (Velasco 2016; Yearby *et al.* 2022). Music in the Latinx/e community should be utilized as an asset-based healthcare tool, as it is a participatory practice that can be used as a catalyst for community dialogue and social change (Gonzalez 2020).

Here are some suggested areas of focus in elevating the role of music for Latinx/e health and wellness:

- *Increasing access to the use of community music to support Latinx/e health.* Healthcare providers, including music therapists, advocates, and communities serving Latinx/e communities, are recommended to engage in collaborative advocacy to increase access to healthcare services centering community music and health. Utilizing community music experiences to support Latinx/e health is an ideal form of engagement, as it incorporates the cultural value of collectivism. Additionally, this evolution in culturally responsive treatment is a strengths-based approach that utilizes the cultural wealth of communities as an integral asset in the therapeutic process and in supporting health and wellness.

- *Recruitment, employment, and the support of bilingual-bicultural professionals.* Research indicates that the presence of clinicians of similar race or ethnicity in healthcare able to communicate in their patient's preferred language is greatly beneficial, including, but not limited to, enhanced quality of care due to factors such as an increase in trust and communication (Mental Health America 2023). Limited ethnic diversity in healthcare providers is a current concern, including in the field of music therapy, as 88% of practicing music therapists identify as white and 3.6% as Hispanic or Latinx/e (AMTA 2021).

- *Engaging in ongoing education centering diversity equity, inclusion, and belonging.* Authenticity from the clinician and other healthcare providers in exploring their biases and worldview and accepting that a participant is the expert on their culture is necessary in the development of successful and meaningful therapeutic relationships and best practices (Falicov 2014; Mulvaney-Day *et al.* 2011).

Conclusion

There is significant potential for growth in the use and application of music to support the health and wellness of the Latinx/e community in the United States. Targeting these identified areas of mobilizing cultural wealth through music is essential in supporting wellness and in expanding accessible and culturally responsive healthcare services. The role of music in supporting Latinx/e health and wellness can be elevated by schools, health-care providers, and other community-based organizations, as achieving equitable healthcare requires active cross sector engagement within the community and multisector partnerships (Baumann et al, 2023).

Collaboration within healthcare, education, and other sectors is highly recommended to generate new innovations in the use of music to advance health equity. These collaborations are in a unique position to elevate the use of music in fostering a sense of empowerment, belonging, and *esperanza* (hope) within Latinx/e communities. By utilizing this effective approach to healing and well-being, music has the unique capability to be utilized as "*el vaporu del corazón*" (healing ointment for the heart).

CHAPTER 5

CONTRIBUTIONS OF MUSIC THERAPY IN INTENSIVE CARE UNITS IN CHILE

RICARDO MAYA

Dedicated to the memory of R.O. and to his entire family, for all the love given during the process.

Introduction

Intensive care units (ICUs) began to emerge in the 1950s in order to provide specialized priority treatment for patients in more serious medical situations. The application of music therapy as a non-pharmacological intervention in ICUs to achieve clinical objectives in critically ill patients has been studied and supported in different publications.

In recent years there has been a paradigm shift toward humanized care in ICUs. In these models of care, care not only for the patient but also for their family and clinical staff is considered a central element that contributes to healing. From this point of view, it is worth asking if music therapy should include work not only with patients but also with their families and care teams.

The main objectives of this chapter are to help the reader learn about the needs and situation of critical patients and their families, to understand what the humanization of intensive care consists of, and to consider how music therapy can contribute in this environment. In addition, a brief bibliographic review of music therapy in ICUs is included, as well as an account of the experience of patients, families, and the clinical team in the Critical Patients Unit (Unidad de Pacientes Críticos, UPC) of the University of Chile Clinical Hospital (Hospital Clínico Universidad de Chile, HCUCH) between 2019 and 2020.

The critically ill patient

Spending time in an ICU has a strong impact on every dimension of a patient's life. It can often feel strange and hostile for patients: being admitted means being removed from their home and the family environment, and may involve invasive or painful treatments in a context of extreme stress. Even if the physical ailments are successfully addressed, a trip to the ICU can be a traumatic experience that will impact the patient's life in the long term. Patients admitted to the ICU are typically in a serious condition, and may need to be connected to various monitoring and life support technologies. Clinical staff must often perform treatments that cause pain, discomfort, and various side effects. These procedures, along with the illness itself, may impose severe limitations on a patient's mobility and autonomy.

At a cognitive level, some patients may experience delirium: an acute alteration of cognition that presents with fluctuating states of disorientation, delusional ideas, agitation, and alteration of attention, perception, and memory. This condition is associated with a longer stay in the unit and higher mortality. Delirium cannot be attributed to a single cause, since it depends on the interaction of various factors, such as the medication administered, the patient's previous psychological state, the traumatic experience of the disease, and the stress induced by the stay and treatments carried out in the ICU.

At an emotional level, anxiety, stress, despair, and confusion are common among ICU patients (Gómez-Carretero *et al.* 2007). People admitted to the ICU are likely to experience fear and concern regarding their own death (which they may perceive as imminent), the uncertainty of their current and future situation, and the well-being of their family. In addition, they may experience feelings of guilt, lack of independence and control, and anguish. All this leads to a loss of self-esteem (Blanca Gutiérrez *et al.* 2008). Ayllón Garrido, Álvarez González, and González García (2007) studied the most stressful factors for critically ill patients, concluding that these were thirst (62.6 percent), difficulty/inability sleeping (42.9 percent), tubes in the nose or mouth (35.2 percent), and not knowing the time (34.1 percent). Patients who suffered from delirium perceived disorientation or hallucinations as stressors.

On a social level, patients are separated from their home environment, family, and friends. Visiting hours are more or less restricted depending on hospital policy. This isolation from their normal environment can favor the development of depressive states and disorientation.

Blanca Gutiérrez *et al.* (2008) distinguish five types of needs expressed by critically ill patients:

- Communication: they need to spend as much time as possible inter-acting with their family and with other people, to combat loneliness and boredom.
- Personalization: they request humanized and individualized treat-ment, which considers their preferences and privacy.
- Security: they need to trust the team that serves them and the tech-nology that surrounds them.
- Information: they need to receive as much information as possible, in a structured and empathetic way.
- Spiritual: they need their beliefs and values, religious or not, as a source of comfort to cope with this process.

The family of the critically ill patient

The admission of a person to the ICU puts the family in a crisis situation, where the usual roles and dynamics of the group are altered. As pointed out by Blanca Gutiérrez *et al.* (2008), families experience great uncertainty regarding the status of their loved one—stress, anxiety, sadness, helpless-ness, restlessness, pain, and uncertainty. They can also experience feelings of hope and security in their relations with the health team.

Pardavila Belio and Vivar (2012) identify four groups of needs for the families of critically ill patients:

- Cognitive: the knowledge of family members about the patient's condition and the functioning of the ICU. The family need updates on their family member's health status, level/quality of rest, vital signs, prognosis, and comfort, but they also need to know about the technology, the professionals caring for their loved one, and hospital rules. This information should ideally always be provided by the same staff, in a clear, structured, and empathetic manner.
- Emotional: the closeness with the admitted family member and the emotional support from the team. The family needs to spend as much time with their loved one as possible, and be supported by the health team.
- Social: the need for families to interact with other people in their immediate environment, such as extended family or friends.
- Practices: the elements of the physical environment that contribute to or hinder the comfort of the family, such as waiting rooms, access to a telephone, bathrooms, lighting, color of the walls...

The concept of hospital humanization and models of humanized care

Critically ill patients demand humanized treatment, and in recent years, many ICUs have implemented protocols and practices to address this in their facilities. But what does it mean to "humanize" intensive care?

As Rojas (2019, p.121) points out:

> humanizing intensive care is focusing on the person we care for, understanding that they are unique, preserving their dignity and values, caring based on the best available evidence, making rational use of resources, including to family members and making them part of the process, remembering that health is a fundamental right of every human being and finally it is also giving back to the health team the vocation and meaning for what they do.

Here is an overview of some of the most important elements medical institutions should consider when working to humanize intensive care.

The view of the patient and their health

According to the World Health Organization, "health is a state of complete physical, mental, and social well-being, and not only the absence of illnesses or diseases."[1] This refers to one of the central elements of humanized care: the health of patients depends on more than the diagnosis and treatment of their physical illnesses. There are also psychological and social aspects that must be included in analysis of the care system. In humanized care models, the vision of the patient broadens beyond the clinical setting and includes strategies to promote their overall well-being.

Family group inclusion

Another defining concept of humanization in hospital environments is the view of the family as a central element in the patient's recovery. For example, the patient- and family-centered care model, proposed by the American Institute of Medicine, considers families essential agents in quality healthcare, defining them as an active part of the healing process (Rojas *et al.* 2019, p.121). Family involvement in decision-making and in simple procedures (such as patient hygiene) can produce benefits for the family members, for the patient, and also for the care team, facilitating close communication and empathy between everyone involved.

---

1   www.who.int/about/governance/constitution

Traditionally, ICUs have implemented fairly limited visiting hours, under the premise that this will benefit the care team's work and the patient's recovery. However, experience in other units (pediatric and neo-natal ICUs) has shown greater benefits than risks associated with extending the visiting schedule and encouraging family participation. These include reduction of complications, improvement of communication with the team, and an increase in patient and family satisfaction.

Team–family–patient communication
Training in skills and routines that promote fluid communication within the ICU, involving the team, patients, and family members, promotes a climate of trust and respect, and facilitates joint decision-making.

Environment
Humanized facilities should consider light, temperature, acoustics, materials, and decoration, improving the functionality of the facilities and promoting more comfortable experiences in them.

Care for the clinical team
ICU staff are constantly exposed to stress, and as a result may experience "burnout syndrome," low self-esteem, and emotional fatigue. Humanized models for intensive care indicate that the professional, physical, psychological, and emotional needs of caregivers must also be taken into account.

Prevention of post-intensive care syndrome
Between 30 and 50 percent of critically ill patients are affected by this, which is related to traumatic experience while in the ICU, and causes physical (persistent pain, weakness, malnutrition, ulcers, sleep disturbances), neuropsychological (memory, attention, and information-processing alterations), and emotional (anxiety, depression) symptoms. It can affect both patients and families.

To understand, in depth, the different aspects of hospital humanization, it is worth reviewing the work of Heras La Calle, Martín, and Nin (2017), who, through their project "HU-CI," have designed a conceptual framework with eight work areas around the humanization of ICUs. Taking these elements into account, I would like to propose a definition of humanization of care that reflects these dimensions.

Humanizing ICUs means establishing an empathetic care system that understands and cares for each patient in all their dimensions (physical, mental, social, and spiritual), respecting their social ties and worldview, maintaining open and fluid communication about their health status, and including their family in the process. This system must also include care and attention to the needs of both the clinical team and the patient's family.

Evidence of the use of music therapy in ICUs

Over the last two decades, various papers have been published regarding music therapy or musical intervention in critical hospital areas, specifically in ICUs. These interventions have placed music therapy in a non-pharmacological therapy role aimed at preventing and treating, mostly, anxiety, pain, and delirium. Another objective that the clinical teams consider for music therapy interventions in intensive care is to reduce the amount of medications that patients must consume, thereby reducing the risk of aggravating their clinical situation.

Hunter *et al.* (2010) used active and responsive music therapy techniques in critically ill patients with mechanical ventilation. They evaluated the parameters of anxiety (self-reported and by recording vital signs), days required to withdraw from mechanical ventilation, patient satisfaction, and nurse satisfaction. The results showed a positive response to incorporating music therapy as a complementary treatment during the process of weaning off mechanical ventilation. In addition, a decrease in anxiety was recorded, both self-reported and in terms of heart and respiratory rate. Both patients and nursing staff showed greater satisfaction during this process.

Heiderscheit, Chlan, and Donley (2011) used self-administered musical listening techniques through headphones and music previously selected by the music therapist based on the tastes of each patient to measure parameters of anxiety, stress, time of dependence on mechanical ventilation, and stay in the ICU. The results obtained show a positive impact on patients who actively participated in managing their symptoms of anxiety and distress. Additionally, music provided a distraction from the stressful environment.

Chlan *et al.* (2013) used self-administered musical listening techniques through headphones and music previously selected by the music therapist based on the tastes of each patient with the objectives of sedoanalgesia and anxiety management. The patients were on mechanical ventilation. The results showed a significant decrease in anxiety levels, as well as in the intensity and frequency of pharmacological sedation.

Gullick and Kwan (2015) measured the effect of music therapy for 373 mechanically ventilated patients. The intervention consisted of listening to music selected according to the patient's tastes. The results showed that targeted music therapy and noise-canceling headphones could be useful and cost-effective, and contribute to an improvement in anxiety parameters and sedation exposure.

Johnson, Fleury, and McClain (2018) conducted a study with the objective of evaluating the effects of music therapy in preventing delirium in critically ill patients. The method used was the administration of music with headphones, with a slow tempo, simple rhythms, and low pitch, for one hour twice a day. Significant differences were found in heart rate and systolic blood pressure. No participant suffered from delirium. The authors concluded that music therapy addressed the pathophysiological mechanisms that contribute to delirium, making it an effective tool for prevention.

Fallek *et al.* (2019) evaluated the effect of music therapy on pain, anxiety, heart rate, and respiratory rate in 150 patients. Different active and receptive techniques were used, and a significant decrease in pain and anxiety was found after each session.

Golino *et al.* (2019) measured the effect of active music therapy in critically ill patients. Thirty-minute sessions were carried out, with a record of vital signs before and after the intervention, as well as a self-reported measurement of anxiety and pain. The results showed a significant decrease in heart and respiratory rates, self-reported pain, and anxiety. No changes in oxygen saturation were observed. These results support active music therapy as a useful, non-pharmacological intervention modality without side effects.

Álvarez-Trutié *et al.* (2020) conducted a study on a sample of 40 patients to assess the effectiveness of implementing a music therapy program as an alternative to control agitation and sedation in patients with mechanical ventilation. They concluded that music therapy improved mean arterial pressure, heart rate, and respiratory rate, reducing the dose of sedatives and reducing agitation and disorientation in the study group. In addition, the anxiety levels of both professionals and patients were lowered.

Almerud and Petersson (2003) conducted a study to determine if music therapy was effective in promoting relaxation in critically ill patients on mechanical ventilators. Analysis of the quantitative data showed a significant drop in systolic and diastolic blood pressure during the music therapy session, and a corresponding increase after treatment discontinuation. All changes were found to be statistically significant. The conclusion was that intensive care nursing staff could beneficially apply music therapy as a non-pharmacological intervention.

McCaffrey (2006) and McCaffrey and Good (2000) conducted two studies to measure the impact of a musical intervention on delirium in patients undergoing knee or hip surgery. Music was administered with headphones to postoperative patients, when they woke up from anesthesia, and in the subsequent period. The authors found that patients who received music therapy had significantly fewer periods of confusion or delirium during hospitalization compared to those who did not receive additional therapy.

From this brief review of articles about the application of music therapy in critically ill patients, it can be concluded that the most studied areas were: anxiety, pain, stress, sedoanalgesia, the process of withdrawing from mechanical ventilation, and the degree of satisfaction or comfort in the ICU. In all these areas, music therapy has demonstrated its effectiveness, reducing the need for pharmacological treatment in patients. Pharmacological treatments for the disorders described have important side effects (nausea, vomiting, weakness, muscle atrophy, infections, hypotension, delirium, etc.), which can largely be avoided by applying these music therapy techniques.

Music therapy in the University of Chile Clinical Hospital's Critical Patients Unit

Between 2019 and 2020, I participated in a music therapy intervention that took place in the UPC of HCUCH, in the context of my university practice as a music therapist, which I carried out in the music therapy division of the Integrative Medicine Unit (Unidad de Medicina Integrativa, UMI), under the supervision of music therapist Patricia Lallana Urrutia.

The work was designed with three purposes in mind:

- To carry out focal music therapy interventions with all the actors involved in the UPC, namely: health personnel, patients, and families.
- To generate two investigations to provide evidence of the mixed nature (quantitative–qualitative) of the impact and perception of interventions for health personnel and families/patients. (The research related to the impact on families/patients has not yet been published, due to its delay after the COVID-19 pandemic.) The research team was made up of: Verónica Rojas (university nurse), Patricia Lallana Urrutia (music therapist), Gabriel Zamora (music therapist in training), Ricardo Maya (music therapist in training), Cecilia Plaza (doctor), Loreto Alcade (university nurse), Rolando Aranda (occupational therapist), **María Angélica Berasain (university nurse),** Solange Quiroz (university nurse), **Viviana Calfuñanco (university nurse)** and Carlos Romero Patiño (doctor).
- To initiate music therapy processes with some of the patients and their families, following the referral criteria, the instructions of the UPC team, and the session records belonging to the study.

I will now describe the context in which the intervention was developed, the publication that was produced on the use of music therapy with clinical staff and finally, a clinical case to illustrate professional practice with patients and families.

The University of Chile Clinical Hospital (HCUCH) was founded in 1952 in the city of Santiago de Chile as a public entity, although it currently follows a private management model. The Critical Patients Unit (Unidad de Pacientes Críticos, UPC) is located on the second floor of the hospital and has been in operation since the late 1960s. It works under a multidisciplinary model and has a humanistic vision of intensive medicine—the family of admitted patients is recognized as a fundamental actor in the recovery process, and instances such as the informative and psychoeducational meetings with family members and the team, the permissiveness of group visits, and the use of conventional and complementary therapies that involve the family unit take on special relevance for treatment.

Music therapy care at the UPC was part of collaborative activity between the UPC and the Integrative Medicine Unit (Unidad de Medicina Integrativa, UMI), founded in 2018 and currently closed. A multidisciplinary health team made up of doctors, nurses, kinesiologists, nutritionists, and music therapists worked at the UMI. Providing an intervention-based model of care to restore the health and well-being of patients and their families was central to their mission. This vision of health was characterized by incorporating not only the physical but also the social, mental, and spiritual aspects of healing, recognizing the relevance of the therapeutic link in care, and allowing the patient to actively participate in the task of maximizing their well-being.

This intervention followed a line of work based on the humanization of intensive care, and focused on promoting well-being not only in critically ill patients, but also in their families and the unit's clinical team. Intervening from this perspective, with all the actors involved, is what, in my opinion, makes this work remarkable and novel. Although there is evidence about the use of music therapy with critically ill patients, it has not been reported in the case of the clinical team and the patient's family.

Intervention focused on the critically ill patient and their family

The first of these interventions was carried out with critically ill patients and their families, who were referred by the UPC clinical team under one or more of the following criteria: pain management, delirium prevention, and anxiety management.

In addition to the clinical objectives, the team set out to evaluate the impact and degree of satisfaction of the family members who participated in the sessions. A voluntary questionnaire was designed for family members, self-administered pre- and post-session, which included aspects related to the perception of the patient's condition by their family as well as an assessment of the satisfaction and usefulness of the session for family members.

In total, 51 unique sessions lasting approximately 30 minutes were carried out with 51 patients and their families. An average of two family members participated in each session, mainly children and partners, and active, receptive, and mixed techniques were used. Participating families reported a greater sense of relief, company, and the ability to express their emotions, as well as a lower degree of stress and physical discomfort. The results of this intervention allowed the team to conclude that music therapy sessions positively affected the physical, social, and emotional state self-reported by family members.

Intervention focused on the clinical team

The results of this intervention were published in the study, *Impact of Music Therapy on the Members of the Clinical Team of a Critical Patients Unit: A View from the Caregiver Care* (Rojas *et al.* 2020). Its objective was to evaluate the impact of a group music therapy session on the level of stress self-reported by the UPC clinical team. A pre-post session self-administered questionnaire was designed that included two numerical scales to grade the level of anxiety and stress, as well as a question to indicate the usefulness of the music therapy session on a personal level.

Six group music therapy sessions were held lasting approximately 30 minutes, in which a total of 71 participants from the UPC clinical team participated (31 percent nurses, 53 percent nursing technicians, 13 percent assistants, and 3 percent administrative staff). Receptive (3 sessions), active (2 sessions), and mixed (1 session) techniques were used.

The results showed that self-reported anxiety and stress levels decreased after the music therapy sessions, and that they helped UPC staff relax, distract themselves from their worries, and have fun. Rojas *et al.* (2020) conclude that music therapy sessions positively impact the reduction of self-perceived stress and anxiety by employees, and also provide a space for self-care during the workday.

Clinical case: R.O. and family

The music therapy process presented here was carried out with a patient admitted to the UPC of the HCUCH and his family between the months of September 2019 and November 2020. It should be noted that this process was interrupted in March 2020 due to COVID-19, which is why the end of the treatment process had to be postponed until November of that same year, taking place in the family home.

Diagnostic approach and general objectives

The patient (R.O.) was a 63-year-old Chilean man, born in Santiago de Chile. He was referred by the UPC clinical team under the criteria of anxiety management, delirium prevention, pain management, and emotional support.

He presented in the ICU in a very serious condition and with a prognosis of long hospitalization due to lymphoma. The disease was in an advanced stage, resulting in paralysis that affected all his limbs except his left arm, which he could move slightly. It also preserves mobility in the neck and head and facial expressiveness. Due to his injury, R.O.'s ability to make vocal sounds had been severely affected. It was also very likely that he would not recover mobility in his extremities, although he would receive speech therapy treatment to recover swallowing and speaking abilities. At the time of the initial evaluation, the patient did not have pain as a result of taking medication.

The patient did not show any signs of disorientation or cognitive impairment; he remained lucid and aware of what was happening around him, able to interact with his family and the team through facial gestures. He was knowledgeable about the conditions related to his illness and the recovery process he faces. He said he felt encouraged by the opportunity to share a music therapy space with his family. However, he explained that he felt anxious and had a hard time resting.

Regarding sonic identity, R.O. referred to his taste for classical music and pop from the 1970s. His main uses of and associations with music involved relaxation, stress reduction, enjoyment in family company or being alone, and also during work. He also enjoyed nature sounds: the wind, the sea, the rain, and the chirping of birds.

In the social sphere, R.O. had solid and close family and social relationships. At the time of the initial assessment, his wife, two of his daughters, and his sister were present, all of whom maintained physical/verbal/visual contact with him at all times, exchanging displays of mutual affection. Furthermore, R.O. expressed how important the love of his family, and specifically of his wife, were to him.

R.O. was the youngest of eight brothers and sisters. His two older sisters were the closest to his nuclear family, with whom he shared the most time. His mother and his father were dead, the latter dying recently. He had been married to his current partner since adolescence. Four daughters and sons were born from this relationship, aged between 18 and 40. R.O.'s eldest son had two teenage boys, who lived with him in the United States. His other children and grandchildren lived in Santiago.

Generational patterns can be identified regarding the family's sonic identity. R.O.'s generation, his sisters, and his wife identified with dance music, especially the pop music of the 1970s and 1980s—the great hits of Música Libre were shared by this generation. R.O.'s children had diverse tastes, ranging from cumbia to rock, pop and reggaeton.

The family members present in the first sessions (one of his sisters, his wife, and three of his children) conveyed their high level of stress and physical and emotional discomfort regarding R.O.'s situation, although they reported feeling strongly linked to both him and the health team, as well as feeling emotionally supported.

On a pre-post assessment questionnaire at the first meeting, the family rated their experience as very positive, and wanted to have regular sessions. They reported a decrease in their own stress and physical discomfort at the end of the session. They also observed a change in R.O., who, from the first session, showed an improvement in his mood.

Once the team carried out the first diagnostic assessment session, the general objectives of the intervention were established:

1. Promote instances of accompaniment, expressiveness, and emotional containment for R.O. and his family during the hospitalization process.
2. Decrease anxiety in R.O. and his family.
3. Pain management for R.O.

Framing

The therapeutic process took place over 20 weekly sessions lasting approximately 40 minutes each. R.O. and the music therapist were present in all sessions. R.O.'s wife participated in most of the sessions. His sisters, his daughters and son, and two co-therapists from the UMI music therapy team participated in many of the sessions. Some of R.O.'s friends and his family, health personnel, and other patients were present at some sessions.

The table on the following page shows the relationship of each family member to the patient and the number of sessions attended, illustrating the degree of family participation in the process.

The sessions with R.O. took place in a context in which the team visited other patients in the UPC before and after the music therapy session. This entailed a high risk of transmission of pathogens, which are especially dangerous in the case of critically ill patients. To minimize these risks, physical contact of team members with R.O. was prohibited, and the team observed the World Health Organization (WHO) guidelines for hand washing five times during the care of a critically ill patient:

1. Before contact with the patient
2. Before performing an aseptic task
3. After risk of exposure to body particles
4. After contact with the patient
5. After contact with the patient's environment

Family participation in the therapeutic process for R.O.

Family member	Number of sessions attended
R.O.	20
Wife	12
Sister	6
Sister	4
Eldest daughter	6
Youngest daughter	3
Son	3
Grandchildren	1
Aunt	1
Son-in-law	1

The team also used personal protective equipment—latex gloves and disposable aprons—and all instruments used in the session were disinfected before and after use, using alcohol-soaked compresses. Instruments with fabric or wool components (drumsticks, rattles, hooves) were not introduced because they were difficult to disinfect; plastic, metal, and wooden instruments were preferred.

Regarding the spaces in which the sessions were carried out, the first took place in the UPC; however, when R.O. showed sufficient improvement, he was transferred to another area within the same UPC called Medical Intermediate (Intermedio Médico, IM). For framing purposes, these two instances were very different: in the ICU, patients were in separate rooms, where they could enjoy greater privacy and less exposure to noise. In the IM, patients were in larger rooms with between one and five other patients (in addition to the healthcare personnel), occasionally separated by curtains. In both environments, however, life support machines were present, emitting a series of high-volume sounds. There were also frequent interruptions in the sessions (especially at the beginning of the process, in the ICU), due to the arrival of a family member or health official who had to carry out a check or medical procedure.

Given the nature of the environment and the situation—a hospital and a critical patient—these interruptions became part of the daily process, and were considered when planning interventions. A family member would likely visit R.O. during the course of a session, or an urgent or unplanned medical procedure might arise. The team's approach in these situations was not to interrupt the session, unless it was strictly necessary or what R.O. clearly wanted. This meant finding ways of integrating these interruptions into the flow of a session. Due to the SARS CoV-2 virus and the declaration of a global pandemic, the end of the treatment process was interrupted. By the time it could be resumed, R.O. was already back at home, so the last session took place in the family home.

The instruments used in this intervention included guitar, ukulele, quena, small percussion instruments such as shakers/maracas, steel tongue drum, melodica, kalimba, rain stick, triangle, metallophone, music mobile, claves, Tibetan bowls, cultrún, tambourine, elliptical tambourine, and a drum. In addition, a cell phone with a small speaker was used to play music and create environments through different applications.[2] R.O. expressed his preference for the guitar from the beginning of the process, and it was always or almost always present, with the music therapist playing it. Given R.O.'s mobility and condition, he was only able to play along in some sessions towards the end of the process with small shakers tied to his left hand with a surgical glove and an elliptical tambourine tied around his wrist. A cell phone with video and audio recording applications was used to record the sessions.

Techniques used

The team employed active (in which the patient and family were encouraged to play an instrument), receptive (techniques based on listening), and mixed (involving elements of both) music therapy techniques. These included:

- Musical improvisation: the team performed short musical improvisation sessions in conjunction with R.O. and his family. These improvisations were free or with some instructions.
- "Freestyle" soundpainting: R.O. acted as the conductor of an orchestra—made up of the music therapist's team and R.O.'s family. R.O. chose the instruments for the participants and conducted the orchestra through moving his hand and head.

---

2   Not only is music played on devices, but applications are also used to play sounds to create sound environments, for example sounds from the sea, the forest, animals or rain.

- Historical-musical-cultural tour: via the figure of a tree with spaces to write on its branches, R.O., his wife, and the music therapist investigated the couple's biography, placing different works of art (musical, pictorial, cinematographic...) on the tree as milestones of their shared history. The work was titled "The tree of love."
- Songwriting: the music therapist and R.O. created a song together.
- Phonomimic: the music therapist played and sang a song selected by R.O., who moved his lips, following the lyrics without making a sound, in a kind of playback.
- Relaxation techniques: breathing and body awareness exercises were performed while creating a musical environment.
- Guided visual imagery: an imaginary journey was proposed to R.O., guided by the music therapist and accompanied by breathing techniques.
- Selection and listening to songs that were meaningful to R.O. and his family.
- Lyrical discussion: the lyrics of the songs were explored in depth, associating them with some significant aspect for R.O. or his family.
- Sound bath: the family and team played for R.O., recreating an environment they chose, with instruments they had previously chosen.

Stages of the therapeutic process

Stage	Objectives	R.O. and family difficulties	Techniques used	Main milestones
Stage 1	Establish the therapeutic bond Evaluate anxiety in the family group Know sound identities Promote emotional expressiveness and containment in the family group	Very serious condition (R.O.) Anxiety (R.O. and family) Difficulty sleeping and discomfort (R.O.) No vocalizing capacity (R.O.) Low mood (R.O. and family)	Sound bath Listening to a song that is meaningful for R.O.	R.O. falls asleep during the session R.O. remembers his father after listening to a selected song

cont.

Stage	Objectives	R.O. and family difficulties	Techniques used	Main milestones
Stage II	Manage anxiety in patient Promote emotional expressiveness and containment in the family group Improve communication with the patient (lip reading and gestures)	Very serious condition (R.O.) Anxiety (R.O.) Difficulty sleeping and discomfort (R.O.) No vocalizing capacity (R.O.)	Sound bath Relaxation Guided imagery Phonemics	Familiar images and meanings appear during relaxations (memory of R.O.'s mother) R.O. performs the song "Cariñito" dedicated to his wife
Stage III	Facilitate the patient's adaptation to the IM unit Stimulate bonding with other patients in the ward Pain management Celebrate progress in the recovery process	Appearance of pain due to medication withdrawal Chemotherapy side effects Discomfort due to change of environment (increased noise, shared room)	Listen and perform R.O.'s favorite songs Relaxation Guided imagery	Improvement in R.O.'s physical condition, although his condition remains serious Removal of some life support technology Participation of other patients in the room in the session (group singing and listening)
Stage IV	Explore the history of the bond between R.O. and his wife Manage chemotherapy side effects Facilitate family intimacy spaces Stimulate self-knowledge	Chemotherapy side effects Nasogastric tube discomfort	Select and listen to meaningful songs Lyrical discussion Relaxation Guided imagery Improvisation Soundpainting	Improvement in R.O.'s physical condition, within the severity R.O. can perform sessions semi-sitting up (sitting on the bed or a chair) R.O. plays an instrument for the first time

Stage V	Carry out a joint review of the process Prepare a song that captures what has been experienced Establish future plans and projections	Chemotherapy side effects Anxiety about imminent departure	Joint singing Selecting and listening to meaningful songs Improvisation	Notable improvement in R.O.'s health Emergence of vocalizing capacity

Regarding the evaluation of this therapeutic process, based on the qualitative and quantitative records collected throughout, the music therapy team was able to conclude that the objectives set at the beginning were achieved. The bonds built with the patient and his family taught me that during a crisis, although traumatic events may unfold, there is always possibility: the music of life continues to play. In my case, I was privileged to walk with R.O. and his family on a sensitive path full of possibilities for affection, respect, and fun, thanks to their great warmth and generosity.

Based on my experience, and taking into account the evidence that was generated from the HCUCH, I believe that it is not only possible, but necessary, to implement music therapy programs in ICUs that follow models of humanization of intensive care. To do this, music therapists must have a systemic vision of the unit, develop an approach that combines the clinical with the preventive, and make diagnostic approaches and design sessions equally for patients, families, and the clinical team in order to promote the well-being of all within the system.

APORTES DE LA MUSICOTERAPIA A LAS UNIDADES DE CUIDADOS INTENSIVOS EN CHILE

RICARDO MAYA

Dedicado a la memoria de R.O. y a toda su familia, por todo el cariño entregado durante el proceso.

Introducción

Las Unidades de Cuidados Intensivos (UCI) comienzan a surgir en la década de los 50 con el fin de tratar específicamente a los pacientes en situación de mayor gravedad dentro las instituciones hospitalarias. La aplicación de musicoterapia como intervención no farmacológica en las UCI para alcanzar objetivos clínicos en pacientes críticos, aun siendo relativamente reciente, ha sido estudiada y avalada en diferentes publicaciones.

En los últimos años se ha producido un cambio de paradigma hacia la atención humanizada en las UCI. En estos modelos de atención, el cuidado no solo al paciente, sino a su familia y al personal clínico es considerado como un elemento central que contribuye a promover la salud y mejorar el trabajo en la unidad. Es bajo esta mirada bajo la cual cabe preguntarse si la musicoterapia debe incluir el trabajo no sólo con pacientes sino con sus familias y el equipo que los atiende.

Uno de los objetivos del siguiente texto es que el lector pueda conocer a las necesidades y la situación de los pacientes críticos y sus familias, y entender en qué consiste la humanización de los cuidados intensivos, y cómo puede la musicoterapia contribuir en este sentido. Además, se hará una breve revisión bibliográfica sobre el uso de musicoterapia en las

UCI, y se expondrá la experiencia que tuvo lugar con pacientes, familias y equipo clínico en la Unidad de Pacientes Críticos (en adelante UPC) del Hospital Clínico Universidad de Chile (HCUCH) entre los años 2019 y 2020.

El paciente crítico

El paso por una unidad de cuidados intensivos tiene un fuerte impacto en la vida de los pacientes en todas sus dimensiones. El ambiente de la UCI resulta, en muchas ocasiones, extraño y hostil para los pacientes: estar ingresado significa ser alejado del entorno familiar, del hogar, y posiblemente suponga tratamientos invasivos o dolorosos, en un contexto de extrema gravedad. Esto puede derivar en una vivencia traumática que dejará importantes secuelas en la vida del paciente. En un nivel físico, los pacientes que ingresan a la UCI se encuentran en un estado grave, pudiendo hallarse conectados a diversas tecnologías de monitorización y soporte vital. Para revertir esta situación, es probable que el personal clínico deba realizar tratamientos que generan dolor, molestias y diversos efectos secundarios. Además, su movilidad y autonomía han podido verse severamente afectadas por su estado de salud y por los procedimientos realizados.

A nivel cognitivo los pacientes pueden experimentar delirium: una alteración aguda de la cognición que cursa con estados fluctuantes de desorientación, ideas delirantes, agitación y alteración de la atención, la percepción y la memoria. Este padecimiento se asocia con una mayor permanencia en la unidad y con mayor mortalidad. La aparición de delirium no responde a una sola causa, ya que depende de la interacción de diversos factores como la medicación administrada, el estado psicológico previo del paciente, la vivencia traumática de la enfermedad y el estrés inducido por la permanencia y los tratamientos llevados a cabo en la UCI.

A nivel emocional la ansiedad, el estrés, la desesperación y la confusión son algunas de las alteraciones mayoritariamente manifestadas por los pacientes de las UCI (Gómez-Carretero *et al.* 2007). Es probable que las personas ingresadas en la UCI experimenten miedos y preocupaciones con respecto a su propia muerte (la cual perciben como inminente), a la incertidumbre de su situación actual y futura y al bienestar de su familia. Además, vivencian sensaciones de envejecimiento, culpabilidad, falta de independencia, falta de control y angustia. Todo ello desemboca en una pérdida de autoestima (Blanca Gutiérrez *et al.* 2008). Ayllón Garrido, Álvarez González, y González García (2007) estudian los factores más estresantes para los pacientes críticos, concluyendo que fueron sed (62,6%), dificultad/imposibilidad para dormir (42,9%), tubos en nariz o boca (35,2%) y no saber la hora (34,1%). Los pacientes que padecieron delirio percibieron como estresores la desorientación o alucinaciones.

A nivel social, los pacientes se encuentran alejados de su entorno, familia y amigos. Los horarios de visita son más o menos restringidos según la política del hospital. Este aislamiento de su entorno puede favorecer la aparición de estados depresivos y de desorientación.

En cuanto a las necesidades expresadas por parte de los pacientes críticos, Blanca Gutiérrez *et al.* (2008) distinguen cinco tipos de necesidades:

- De comunicación: necesitan pasar el máximo tiempo posible con su familia y relacionarse con otras personas para combatir la soledad y el aburrimiento.
- De personalización: solicitan un trato humanizado e individualizado, que considere sus preferencias y su intimidad.
- De seguridad: necesitan confiar en el equipo que les atiende y en la tecnología que les rodea.
- De información: necesitan recibir toda la información posible, de manera estructurada y empática.
- Espirituales: necesitan de sus creencias y valores, religiosos o no, como una fuente de confort para sobrellevar este proceso.

La familia del paciente crítico

El ingreso de una persona en la UCI pone a la familia en una situación de crisis vital, donde se alteran los roles y dinámicas habituales del grupo. Tal y como señalan Blanca Gutiérrez *et al.* (2008), las familias experimentan una gran incertidumbre con respecto al estado de su ser querido, sienten estrés, ansiedad, tristeza, impotencia, desasosiego, dolor e incertidumbre. También experimentan sensaciones de esperanza y seguridad en el equipo de salud.

Pardavila Belio y Vivar (2012) distinguen cuatro grupos de necesidades en las familias de pacientes críticos:

- Cognitivas: referentes al conocimiento de los familiares acerca del estado del paciente y el funcionamiento de la UCI. Necesitan explicaciones sobre el estado de salud, nivel/calidad del descanso, los signos vitales, el pronóstico y el confort de su familiar, pero también necesitan conocer el equipo tecnológico, el equipo profesional y las reglas del hospital. Además esta información idealmente debe ser facilitada siempre por el mismo personal, de manera clara, estructurada y empática.

- Emocionales: referentes a la cercanía con su familiar ingresado y con el apoyo emocional por parte del equipo. La familia necesita acompañar el mayor tiempo posible a su ser querido, y ser acompañada y contenida por el equipo de salud.
- Sociales: referentes a la necesidad de las familias de relacionarse con otras personas de su entorno cercano, como la familia extensa o los amigos.
- Prácticas: los elementos del entorno físico que contribuyen o dificultan la comodidad de la familia, como las salas de espera, acceso a un teléfono, baños, iluminación, color de las paredes...

Aproximación al concepto de humanización hospitalaria y los modelos de atención humanizada

Como se ha comentado en el anterior apartado, entre las necesidades expresadas por los pacientes críticos, estos demandan un trato humanizado, y en los últimos años, muchas UCI están implementando protocolos y prácticas en este sentido en sus instalaciones. Pero, ¿qué quiere decir humanizar los cuidados intensivos?

Tal como señala Rojas (2019, pg.121):

> humanizar los cuidados intensivos es centrarnos en la persona a la que atendemos, entendiendo que es única, preservando su dignidad y valores, cuidando en base a la mejor evidencia disponible, haciendo uso racional de recursos, incluyendo a los familiares y haciéndolos parte del proceso, recordando que la salud es un derecho fundamental de todo ser humano y finalmente también es devolver al equipo de salud la vocación y el sentido por lo que hacen.

A continuación, se propone un compendio de elementos que describen algunos de los aspectos más relevantes para la humanización en cuidados intensivos.

La mirada sobre el paciente y su salud

Para explicar lo que significa la humanización de los cuidados hospitalarios conviene comenzar revisando la conocida definición de la Organización Mundial de la Salud: "La salud es un estado de completo bienestar físico, mental y social, y no solamente la ausencia de afecciones o enfermedades."[1]

Esta conceptualización hace referencia a uno de los elementos centrales del cuidado humanizado: la salud de los pacientes no solo depende

---

1   www.who.int/about/governance/constitution

del diagnóstico y tratamiento de sus enfermedades físicas, también se ven implicados aspectos psicológicos y sociales que deberán ser incluidos dentro del sistema de cuidados. En los modelos de atención humanizada la visión que se tiene del paciente trasciende el ámbito clínico, e incluye estrategias para promover su bienestar global dentro de la unidad.

Inclusión del grupo familiar

Otro de los conceptos definitorios de la humanización en entornos hospitalarios es la consideración del grupo familiar como elemento central para la recuperación del paciente. Bajo esta mirada, el modelo de Atención Centrada en el Paciente y la Familia (Patient- and Family-Centered Care), propuesto por el Instituto Estadounidense de Medicina, considera a las familias agentes esenciales para lograr una atención sanitaria de calidad, situándolas como parte activa del proceso (Rojas 2019, pg.121).

La implicación familiar en la toma de decisiones y también en procedimientos sencillos como la higiene del paciente puede traducirse en efectos positivos para ellos mismos, para el paciente y también para el equipo, facilitando la comunicación cercana y la empatía entre todos los actores presentes.

Tradicionalmente, las UCI han implementado horarios de visita bastante acotados, bajo la premisa de que esto será beneficioso para el trabajo del equipo y la recuperación del paciente. Sin embargo, la experiencia en otras unidades (UCI pediátricas y neonatales) ha evidenciado mayores beneficios que riesgos asociados a la ampliación del horario y participación familiar (reducción de complicaciones, mejora de la comunicación con el equipo, aumento de la satisfacción del paciente y la familia).

Comunicación Equipo-Familia-Paciente

El entrenamiento en habilidades y rutinas para la fluidez de la información al interior de la UCI, implicando al equipo, pacientes y familiares, favorece un clima de confianza y respeto, y facilita la toma conjunta de decisiones.

Entorno

Unas instalaciones humanizadas deberían permitir el desarrollo del proceso asistencial en óptimas condiciones de luz, temperatura, acústica, materiales y decoración, mejorando la funcionalidad de las instalaciones y promoviendo experiencias más confortables en ellas.

Cuidado al equipo clínico

Los profesionales presentes en la UCI se ven expuestos a numerosas situaciones de estrés. El "síndrome de burnout", la percepción de ofrecer cuidados no adecuados, la baja autoestima o la fatiga emocional son algunos de los cuadros que se pueden presentar entre el personal de la UCI como consecuencia de ello. Los modelos humanizados para los cuidados intensivos señalan que también deben tenerse en cuenta las necesidades laborales, físicas, psicológicas y emocionales de los cuidadores.

Prevención del síndrome post-cuidados intensivos

Entre un treinta y un cincuenta por ciento de los pacientes críticos se ven afectados por este síndrome, que guarda relación con una vivencia traumática del paso por la UCI y cursa con síntomas físicos (dolor persistente, debilidad, malnutrición, úlceras, alteraciones del sueño), neuropsicológicos (alteraciones mnémicas, atencionales y de procesamiento de la información) y emocionales (ansiedad, depresión). El síndrome puede afectar tanto a pacientes como a familias.

A este respecto, para conocer en profundidad las diferentes aristas de la humanización hospitalaria conviene revisar el trabajo de Heras La Calle, Martín y Nin (2017), quienes a través de su proyecto "HU-CI" han diseñado un marco conceptual con ocho áreas de trabajo en torno a la humanización de las UCI. Teniendo en cuenta estos elementos me gustaría proponer una definición de humanización de los cuidados que refleje estas dimensiones antes comentadas.

Humanizar las UCI significa establecer un sistema de cuidados empático, que entienda y atienda a cada paciente en todas sus dimensiones (física, psíquica, social y espiritual), respetando sus vínculos y su cosmovisión, facilitando mediante una comunicación fluida su acceso a la información sobre su estado de salud e incluyendo a su grupo familiar en el proceso. Dicho sistema debe incluir el cuidado y la atención de las necesidades tanto del equipo clínico como de la familia del paciente.

Evidencia del uso de musicoterapia en la UCI

A lo largo de las últimas dos décadas se han realizado diversas publicaciones referentes a la intervención musicoterapéutica o musical en las áreas hospitalarias críticas, en concreto en las unidades de cuidados intensivos. Estas intervenciones han situado a la musicoterapia en un rol de terapia no farmacológica dirigida a prevenir y tratar, mayoritariamente la ansiedad, el dolor, y el delirium. Otro de los objetivos que los equipos clínicos contemplan para las intervenciones musicoterapéuticas en la unidad es reducir la cantidad de medicamentos que deberán consumir los pacientes, impactando sobre el riesgo de agravar su situación clínica. A continuación se describen algunas de las publicaciones realizadas en la última década respecto al uso de la musicoterapia en la UCI.

Hunter *et al.* (2010) usaron técnicas de musicoterapia activa y receptiva en pacientes críticos con ventilación mecánica. Evaluaron los parámetros de ansiedad (autorreferida y mediante registro de signos vitales), días requeridos para la retirada de la ventilación mecánica, satisfacción del paciente y satisfacción de la enfermera. Los resultados mostraron una respuesta positiva a la incorporación de la musicoterapia como tratamiento complementario durante el proceso de retirada de la ventilación mecánica. Además se registró una disminución de la ansiedad tanto autorreferida como en términos de frecuencia cardíaca y respiratoria. Tanto los pacientes como el personal de enfermería, mostraron mayor satisfacción durante ese proceso.

Heiderscheit, Chlan y Donley (2011), utilizaron técnicas de audición musical autoadministrada mediante audífonos y previamente seleccionada por el musicoterapeuta en base a los gustos de cada paciente para medir parámetros de ansiedad, estrés, tiempo de dependencia de la ventilación mecánica y estancia en la UCI. Los resultados obtenidos muestran un impacto positivo en pacientes que participan activamente de la gestión de sus síntomas (ansiedad y angustia). Además, la música proporciona una distracción del entorno estresante.

Chlan *et al.* (2013), usaron técnicas de audición musical autoadministrada mediante audífonos y previamente seleccionada por el musicoterapeuta en base a los gustos de cada paciente con objetivos de sedoanalgesia y manejo de la ansiedad. Los pacientes se encontraban con ventilación mecánica. Los resultados muestran una disminución significativa en los niveles de ansiedad, así como en la intensidad y frecuencia de la sedación farmacológica.

Gullick y Kwan (2015) midieron el efecto de la musicoterapia en 373 pacientes con ventilación mecánica. La intervención consistió en una escucha de música seleccionada siguiendo los gustos del paciente. Los resultados muestran que la musicoterapia dirigida y los auriculares con cancelación de ruido pueden ser útiles, rentables y contribuir a una mejora en parámetros de ansiedad y exposición a la sedación.

Johnson, Fleury y McClain (2018) realizaron un estudio con el objetivo de evaluar los efectos de la musicoterapia en la prevención del delirium de los pacientes críticos. El método utilizado fue la administración de música con auriculares, tempo lento, ritmos simples y tono bajo, durante una hora dos veces al día. Se encontraron diferencias significativas en la frecuencia cardiaca y la presión arterial sistólica. Ningún participante padeció delirium. Los autores concluyen que la musicoterapia aborda los mecanismos fisiopatológicos que contribuyen al delirio, por lo que es una herramienta efectiva para la prevención.

Fallek *et al.* (2019), evaluaron el efecto de la musicoterapia sobre el dolor, la ansiedad, la frecuencia cardiaca y la frecuencia respiratoria en 150 pacientes. Se utilizaron diferentes técnicas activas y receptivas, y se encontró una disminución significativa del dolor y la ansiedad después de cada sesión.

Golino *et al.* (2019), midieron el efecto de la musicoterapia activa en pacientes críticos. Se realizaron sesiones de treinta minutos, con un registro de signos vitales antes y después de la intervención, así como un autorregistro de ansiedad y dolor. Los resultados muestran una disminución significativa en la frecuencia cardiaca y la respiratoria, en el dolor autoinformado y en la ansiedad. No se observaron cambios en la saturación de oxígeno. Dichos resultados respaldan la musicoterapia activa como una modalidad de intervención útil, no farmacológica y sin efectos secundarios.

Álvarez-Trutié *et al.* (2020) realizó un estudio sobre una muestra de 40 pacientes para valorar la eficacia de implantar un programa de musicoterapia como alternativa para el control de la agitación y la sedación en pacientes con ventilación mecánica. Los autores concluyeron que la musicoterapia mejoró la presión arterial media, frecuencia cardiaca y respiratoria, disminuyendo la dosis de sedantes y disminuyendo la agitación y desorientación del grupo a estudio. Además, los niveles de ansiedad tanto de profesionales como de pacientes fueron menores.

Almerud y Petersson (2003) realizaron un estudio para determinar si la musicoterapia era efectiva para promover la relajación en los pacientes críticos con ventilador mecánico. El análisis de los datos cuantitativos mostró una caída significativa en la presión arterial sistólica y diastólica durante la sesión de musicoterapia y un aumento correspondiente después de la interrupción del tratamiento. Se encontró que todos los cambios eran estadísticamente significativos. La conclusión fue que el personal de enfermería de cuidados intensivos puede aplicar beneficiosamente la musicoterapia como una intervención no farmacológica.

McCaffrey (2006) y McCaffrey y Good (2000) realizaron dos estudios para medir el impacto de una intervención musical en el delirium de pacientes sometidos a cirugía de rodilla o cadera. Se administró música con auriculares a pacientes post operatorios, cuando despertaban de la anestesia y en el periodo posterior. Los autores encontraron que los pacientes que recibieron musicoterapia presentaron significativamente menos períodos de confusión o delirium durante la hospitalización, en comparación con los que no recibieron terapia adicional.

De esta breve revisión de artículos acerca de la aplicación de musicoterapia en pacientes críticos se puede concluir que los ámbitos más estudiados son: la ansiedad, el dolor, el estrés, la sedoanalgesia, el proceso de retirada de la ventilación mecánica y el grado de satisfacción/confort en la unidad. En todas estas áreas la musicoterapia ha demostrado su efectividad, reduciendo la necesidad de tratamiento farmacológico en los pacientes. Los tratamientos farmacológicos de las alteraciones descritas tienen importantes efectos secundarios (náuseas, vómitos, debilidad, atrofia muscular, infecciones, hipotensión, delirium...), que pueden ser evitados en gran medida aplicando las técnicas de musicoterapia mencionadas.

Dispositivo de musicoterapia en la Unidad de Pacientes Críticos del Hospital Clínico Universidad de Chile

Entre los años 2019 y 2020 participé de la intervención musicoterapéutica que tuvo lugar en la UPC del HCUCH, en el contexto de mi práctica universitaria como musicoterapeuta, la cual realicé inserto en el dispositivo de musicoterapia de la Unidad de Medicina Integrativa (UMI), y bajo la supervisión de la musicoterapeuta Patricia Lallana Urrutia.

El trabajo que se realizó fue proyectado con un triple propósito:

- Realizar intervenciones musicoterapéuticas de carácter focal con todos los actores implicados en la UPC, a saber: personal de salud, pacientes y familias.
- Generar dos investigaciones que proporcionen evidencia de carácter mixto (cuantitativa–cualitativa) acerca del impacto y la percepción de las intervenciones con el personal de salud y con las familias/pacientes. La investigación relativa al impacto con familias/pacientes no ha sido publicada aún, debido a su retraso tras la pandemia COVID-19. El equipo de investigación estuvo integrado por: Verónica Rojas (enfermera universitaria), Patricia Lallana Urrutia (musicoterapeuta), Gabriel Zamora (musicoterapeuta en formación), Ricardo Maya (musicoterapeuta en formación), Cecilia Plaza (médico), Loreto Alcade (enfermera universitaria), Rolando Aranda (terapeuta ocupacional), María Angélica Berasain (enfermera universitaria), Solange Quiroz (enfermera universitaria), Viviana Calfuñanco (enfermera universitaria) y Carlos Romero Patiño (doctor).
- Iniciar procesos musicoterapéuticos con algunos de los pacientes y sus familias, siguiendo los criterios de derivación, las indicaciones del equipo de la UPC y los registros de la sesión pertenecientes al estudio.

A continuación pasaré a describir el contexto en el que se desarrolló la intervención, la publicación que se realizó sobre el uso de musicoterapia con personal clínico y, por último, un caso clínico que pueda ilustrar el hacer profesional con pacientes y familias.

El HCUCH se ubica en la ciudad de Santiago de Chile, fue fundado en el año 1952 y aunque nació como una entidad pública, actualmente sigue un modelo de gestión privada. La UPC está ubicada en la segunda planta del hospital y funciona desde finales de la década de los años sesenta. Esta unidad trabaja bajo un enfoque multidisciplinar y posee una visión humanista de la medicina intensiva. Bajo esta mirada, la familia de los pacientes ingresados es reconocida como un actor fundamental en el proceso de recuperación, e instancias como los encuentros informativos y psicoeducativos con familiares por parte del equipo, la permisividad de visitas en grupo, las instancias de acompañamiento a las familias y el uso de terapias convencionales y complementarias que involucren a la unidad familiar cobran especial relevancia dentro del tratamiento.

La atención musicoterapéutica en la UPC formó parte de la actividad colaborativa entre la UPC y la UMI, fundada en el año 2018 y actualmente clausurada. En la UMI trabajó un equipo de salud multidisciplinario formado por médicos, enfermeras, kinesiólogos, nutricionistas y musicoterapeutas. El elemento central de la misión de la UMI era ofrecer un modelo de atención basado en intervenciones para restaurar la salud y el bienestar de los pacientes y sus familias. Su visión de la salud se caracterizaba por incorporar tanto los aspectos físicos, como las dimensiones sociales, mentales y espirituales, reconociendo la relevancia del vínculo terapéutico en la atención y permitiendo al paciente participar activamente en la tarea de maximizar su bienestar.

Esta intervención siguió una línea de trabajo basada en la humanización de los cuidados intensivos y puso su foco no solo en promover el bienestar en pacientes críticos sino también en sus familias y en el equipo clínico de la unidad. El intervenir desde esta perspectiva, con todos los actores implicados, es lo que, a mi parecer, hace de este trabajo algo reseñable y novedoso, ya que, pese a que existe evidencia acerca del uso de musicoterapia con pacientes críticos, ésta no se ha reportado en el caso del equipo clínico y la familia del paciente.

Intervención centrada en el paciente crítico y su familia

La primera de estas intervenciones se realizó con pacientes críticos y sus familias, quienes fueron derivados por el equipo clínico de la UPC bajo uno o varios de los siguientes criterios: manejo del dolor, prevención del delirium y manejo de ansiedad.

Además de los objetivos clínicos, el equipo se propuso evaluar el impacto y el grado de satisfacción de los familiares que participaron de las sesiones. Para ello se diseñó un cuestionario voluntario para familiares, autoadministrado pre y post sesión, que recogía tanto aspectos relacionados a la percepción del estado del paciente por parte de su familia, como una valoración acerca de la satisfacción y utilidad de la sesión para los familiares.

En total se realizaron 51 sesiones únicas de una duración aproximada de 30 minutos a 51 pacientes y sus familias. En cada sesión participaron de media dos familiares, principalmente hijos/as y parejas, y fueron utilizadas técnicas activas, receptivas y mixtas. Las familias participantes reportaron una mayor sensación de alivio, compañía y posibilidad de expresar sus emociones, así como un menor grado de estrés y malestar físico. Los resultados de esta intervención permitieron al equipo concluir que las sesiones de musicoterapia afectaron de manera positiva en el estado físico, social y emocional autorreportado por los familiares.

Intervención centrada en el equipo clínico

Los resultados de esta intervención fueron publicados en el estudio *Impacto de la musicoterapia en los integrantes del equipo clínico de una unidad de pacientes críticos: Una mirada desde el cuidador cuidado* (Rojas *et al.* 2020). Este estudio tuvo el objetivo de evaluar el impacto de una sesión de musicoterapia grupal sobre el nivel de estrés autorreportado por el equipo clínico de la UPC. Para ello se diseñó un cuestionario autoadministrado pre-post sesión que incluía dos escalas numéricas para graduar el nivel de ansiedad y estrés, y un ítem para señalar la utilidad de la sesión MT a nivel personal.

Se realizaron seis sesiones grupales de musicoterapia con una duración aproximada de 30 minutos en las que participaron un total de 71 participantes del equipo clínico de la UPC (31% enfermeros/as, 53% técnicos de enfermería, 13% auxiliares y 3% administrativos). En las sesiones se utilizaron técnicas receptivas (3 sesiones), activas (2 sesiones) y mixtas (1 sesión).

Los resultados de esta investigación muestran que los niveles de ansiedad y estrés autorreportados disminuyeron tras la aplicación de musicoterapia, y que las sesiones sirvieron al personal de la UPC para relajarse, distraerse de sus preocupaciones y divertirse. Con estos resultados, Rojas *et al.* (2020) concluyen que las sesiones de musicoterapia impactan positivamente en la disminución del estrés y la ansiedad autopercibidos por los funcionarios y proveen un espacio de autocuidado durante la jornada laboral.

Caso clínico: R.O. y familia

El proceso musicoterapéutico que se presentará a continuación fue llevado a cabo con un paciente ingresado en la Unidad del Paciente Critico (UPC) del Hospital Clínico Universidad de Chile (HCUCH) y su familia entre los meses de septiembre de 2019 y noviembre de 2020. Cabe destacar que este proceso se vio interrumpido en marzo del 2020 por la llegada de COVID-19, por lo cual el cierre del mismo tuvo que posponerse hasta noviembre de ese mismo año, llevándose a cabo ya en el domicilio familiar.

Aproximación diagnóstica y objetivos generales

El paciente (R.O.) es un varón chileno de 63 años, natural de Santiago de Chile. Fue derivado por el equipo clínico de la UPC bajo los criterios de manejo de la ansiedad, prevención del delirium, manejo del dolor y acompañamiento emocional.

Se encuentra en la UCI en estado muy grave y con un pronóstico de larga hospitalización a causa de un linfoma. La enfermedad se encuentra en un estado avanzado, resultando en una parálisis que afecta a todas sus extremidades menos a su brazo izquierdo, el cual puede mover levemente. Conserva también la movilidad en cuello y cabeza y la expresividad facial. Debido a la lesión, su capacidad para emitir sonidos vocales se ha visto severamente afectada. Es, además, muy probable que no recupere la movilidad en sus extremidades, aunque sí recibirá tratamiento fonoaudiológico para recuperar las capacidades de deglución y habla. En el momento de la evaluación inicial el paciente no presenta dolor debido a la medicación.

En el ámbito psicológico, el paciente no presenta signo alguno de desorientación o deterioro cognitivo, permanece lúcido y consciente de lo que ocurre a su alrededor, siendo capaz de interactuar con su familia y el equipo a través de gesticulación facial. Es conocedor de las condiciones relativas a su enfermedad y el proceso de recuperación que afronta. Dice sentirse animado por la oportunidad de compartir un espacio de musicoterapia con su familia. Sin embargo, explicita que se siente ansioso y le cuesta descansar.

En cuanto a su identidad sonora, R.O. refiere sus gustos musicales en torno a la música clásica y el pop de los años setenta. Los momentos y usos principales de la música en su vida se acercan a la relajación, la reducción del estrés, el disfrute en compañía familiar o en soledad, y también durante el trabajo. Le agradan sonidos de la naturaleza como el viento, el mar, la lluvia y el trino de los pájaros.

En el ámbito social, R.O. es una persona con relaciones familiares y sociales sólidas y cercanas. Al momento de la valoración inicial están presentes su esposa, dos de sus hijas y su hermana, quienes en todo momento mantienen contacto físico/verbal/visual con él, intercambiando muestras de afecto mutuo. Además, R.O. manifiesta lo importante que para él es el amor de su familia y en concreto de su mujer.

R.O. es el menor de ocho hermanos y hermanas. Sus dos hermanas mayores son las más cercanas a su familia nuclear, con quienes más tiempo comparte. Su madre y su padre fallecieron, éste último hace poco. Está casado con su pareja actual desde la adolescencia. De esta relación nacieron cuatro hijas e hijos con edades comprendidas entre los cuarenta y los dieciocho años. El mayor de los hijos de R.O. tiene dos hijos varones adolescentes, que viven con él en Estados Unidos. El resto de sus hijas/o y nietos viven en Santiago.

En cuanto a la identidad sonora familiar, se identifican patrones generacionales. La generación de R.O., sus hermanas y su esposa se identifican con música bailable, dentro del estilo pop de los años 70 y 80—los grandes éxitos de *Música Libre* son compartidos por esta generación. La generación de los hijos/as tiene gustos diversos: desde la cumbia al rock pasando por el pop o el reggaetón.

Los familiares presentes en las primeras sesiones (una de sus hermanas, su esposa y tres de sus hijos), transmitieron su alto nivel de estrés y malestar físico y emocional con respecto a la situación de R.O. Refirieron, sin embargo, sentirse fuertemente vinculados/as tanto a él como al equipo de salud, así como sentirse emocionalmente acompañados/as.

Aplicado un cuestionario pre-post de valoración en el primer encuentro, la familia valora la experiencia como muy positiva, y solicita regularizar las sesiones. Refieren una disminución en su propio estrés y su malestar físico al finalizar la sesión. Además observaron un cambio en R.O., quien, a partir de la primera sesión manifestó una mejoría en su estado anímico.

Una vez el equipo realiza la primera sesión de valoración diagnóstica, se establecen los objetivos generales de la intervención:

1. Promoción de instancias de acompañamiento, expresividad y contención emocional de R.O. y su familia durante el proceso de hospitalización.
2. Disminución de la ansiedad en R.O. y su familia.
3. Manejo del dolor en R.O.

Encuadre

El proceso terapéutico tuvo lugar a lo largo de veinte sesiones con una frecuencia semanal y una duración aproximada de cuarenta minutos. En cuanto a la participación en las sesiones, R.O. y el musicoterapeuta estuvieron presentes en la totalidad de las sesiones. Su mujer participó en la mayor parte de las sesiones. Sus hermanas, sus hijas e hijo y dos coterapeutas del equipo de Musicoterapia de la UMI participaron en buena parte de las sesiones. Algunos amigos/as de R.O. y su familia, el personal de salud y otros pacientes estuvieron presentes en algunas sesiones.

El grado de participación familiar en el proceso fue el siguiente:

Familiar	N.º de sesiones a las que asiste
R.O.	20
Esposa	12
Hermana	6
Hermana	4
Hija mayor	6
Hija menor	3
Hijo	3
Nietos	1
Tía	1
Yerno	1

La tabla muestra el grado de parentesco de cada familiar y el número de sesiones a las que asiste. Las sesiones con R.O. se desarrollan en un contexto en el cual el equipo visita antes y después a otros pacientes en la UPC. Esto conlleva una elevada probabilidad de transmisión de patógenos especialmente peligrosos en el caso de los pacientes críticos. Para minimizar estos riesgos se prohíbe el contacto físico de los miembros del equipo con R.O. y se siguen los criterios de la OMS para el lavado de manos en cinco momentos durante la atención a un paciente crítico.

1. Antes del contacto con el paciente
2. Antes de la realización de una tarea aséptica
3. Después del riesgo de exposición a partículas corporales
4. Después del contacto con el paciente
5. Después del contacto con el entorno del paciente

Además, en la atención de R.O. se utilizaron por parte del equipo elementos de protección personal: guantes de látex y delantales desechables. Por otra parte, se desinfectaron todos los instrumentos utilizados en la sesión antes y después de su uso, mediante compresas bañadas en alcohol. No se introdujeron instrumentos con componentes de tela o lana (baquetas, sonajas, pezuñas) por resultar de difícil desinfección. Se prefirió usar instrumentos de plástico, metal y madera.

En cuanto a los espacios en los que se llevó a cabo las sesiones, las primeras tuvieron lugar en la Unidad de Cuidados Intensivos, sin embargo, cuando R.O. manifestó la suficiente mejoría, fue trasladado a otra área dentro de la misma UPC llamada Intermedio Médico (IM). A efectos de encuadre estas dos instancias resultan muy diferentes: en la UCI los pacientes se encuentran en salas separadas, donde se puede interactuar con el paciente dentro de un contexto de mayor intimidad y de menor exposición a ruidos. Por el contrario, en el IM los pacientes se ubican en salas más grandes donde hay entre uno y cinco pacientes más, separados por cortinas en algunos momentos (además del personal sanitario). En ambos entornos, no obstante, acompañarán el proceso diferentes máquinas de soporte vital, que emiten una serie de sonidos a un elevado volumen, presentes en todo momento. Además, se producirán frecuentes interrupciones en las sesiones (sobre todo al inicio del proceso, en la UCI), motivadas por la llegada de algún familiar o funcionario de salud que debe realizar alguna comprobación o procedimiento.

Dada la naturaleza del entorno y la situación, un hospital y un paciente crítico, estas interrupciones pasan a formar parte de lo cotidiano en el proceso, y se contemplan dentro del encuadre. Es probable que un familiar visite a R.O. durante el transcurso de una sesión, o que surja algún procedimiento médico impostergable o no planificado. El posicionamiento del equipo ante estas eventualidades es no interrumpir la sesión a no ser que sea estrictamente necesario o de clara preferencia por parte de R.O. Se trata de incluir el procedimiento que realiza el funcionario de salud o la visita familiar dentro de la sesión. En este punto es necesario señalar que, debido a la llegada del virus SARS CoV-2 y la declaración de estado de pandemia a nivel mundial, el cierre del proceso se vio interrumpido, y cuando se pudo retomar este cierre, R.O. ya se encontraba en su domicilio. La última sesión del proceso se llevó a cabo en el hogar familiar.

El setting instrumental utilizado en esta intervención está compuesto por: guitarra, ukelele, quena, pequeños instrumentos de percusión tipo shakers/maracas, tambor de lengüeta de acero, melódica, kalimba, palo de lluvia, triángulo, metalófono, móvil de música, claves, cuencos tibetanos, cultrún, pandero, pandereta elíptica y tambor. Además, se utiliza un celular con un pequeño altavoz para reproducir música y crear ambientes a través de diferentes aplicaciones.[2] R.O. manifiesta su preferencia por la guitarra desde el inicio del proceso, y será un instrumento siempre o casi siempre presente, siendo el musicoterapeuta el encargado de tocarlo. Dada

---

2   No solo se reproduce música en dispositivos, sino que también se utilizan aplicaciones para reproducir sonidos y crear ambientes sonoros, por ejemplo, sonidos del mar, del bosque, de animales o de lluvia

la movilidad y el estado de R.O., sólo pudo tocar en algunas sesiones hacia el final del proceso unos pequeños *shakers* anudados a su mano izquierda con un guante quirúrgico y una pandereta elíptica anudada alrededor de su muñeca. La parte del setting utilizada para el registro audiovisual de las sesiones consistió en un celular con aplicaciones de grabación de video y audio.

Técnicas utilizadas

Durante el proceso se utilizaron técnicas de musicoterapia activas (aquellas en las que se propone al paciente y a la familia que toquen algún instrumento), receptivas (técnicas basadas en la escucha), y técnicas mixtas (que implican elementos de ambas categorías). Las técnicas utilizadas fueron:

- Improvisación musical: el equipo realiza sesiones breves de improvisación musical en conjunto con R.O. y su familia. Estas improvisaciones son de carácter libre o con alguna consigna.
- Soundpainting "estilo libre": R.O. actúa como director de una orquesta, conformada por el equipo de MT y su familia. Elige los instrumentos para los participantes y dirige la orquesta a través de los movimientos de su mano y su cabeza.
- Recorrido histórico-musical-cultural: a través de la figura de un árbol con espacios para escribir en sus ramas, R.O., su mujer y el MT indagan juntos en la biografía del matrimonio, situando diferentes obras de arte (musicales, pictóricas, cinematográficas...) en el árbol como hitos de su historia compartida. La obra fue titulada "el árbol del amor."
- Composición de canciones: musicoterapeuta y paciente crean juntos una canción.
- Fonomímica: mediante esta técnica, el MT toca y canta una canción seleccionada por R.O., quien mueve sus labios, siguiendo la letra sin emitir sonido, en una suerte de playback.
- Técnicas de relajación: se realizan ejercicios de respiración y toma de conciencia corporal mientras se crea un ambiente musical.
- Imaginería visual guiada: se propone un viaje imaginario al paciente, guiado por el musicoterapeuta y acompañado de técnicas de respiración.
- Selección y escucha de canciones significativas para el paciente y la familia.
- Discusión lírica: se profundiza en la letra de las canciones, asociando ésta a algún aspecto significativo para el paciente o la familia.
- Baño sonoro: se propone que familia y equipo toquen para R.O., recreando un ambiente de su preferencia con instrumentos previamente elegidos por él.

Etapas del proceso

Etapa	Objetivos	Dificultades del paciente y la familia	Técnicas utilizadas	Hitos principales
Etapa I	Establecimiento del vínculo terapéutico Evaluación de ansiedad en el grupo familiar Conocer identidades sonoras Favorecer expresividad emocional y contención en el grupo familiar	Estado muy grave (R.O.) Ansiedad (R.O. y familia) Dificultad para dormir e incomodidad (R.O.) No capacidad vocalizadora (R.O.) Bajo estado de ánimo (R.O. y familia)	Baño sonoro Escucha de canción significativa para R.O.	R.O. se duerme durante la sesión R.O. recuerda a su padre después de escuchar una canción seleccionada
Etapa II	Manejo de la ansiedad en paciente Favorecer expresividad emocional y contención en grupo familiar Mejora de comunicación con el paciente (lectura de labios y gestos)	Estado muy grave (R.O.) Ansiedad (R.O.) Dificultad para dormir e incomodidad (R.O.) No capacidad vocalizadora (R.O.)	Baño sonoro Relajación Imaginería guiada Fonomímica	Aparecen imágenes y significados familiares durante las relajaciones (recuerdo de la madre del R.O.) R.O. interpreta la canción "Cariñito" dedicada a su esposa
Etapa III	Facilitar la adaptación del paciente a la unidad de Intermedio Médico Estimulación del vínculo con otros pacientes de la sala Manejo del dolor Celebración de avances en el proceso de recuperación	Aparición del dolor por retirada de medicación Efectos secundarios de quimioterapia Incomodidad por cambio de ambiente (aumento de ruido, sala compartida)	Escucha e interpretación de las canciones preferidas Relajación Imaginería guiada	Mejoría en estado físico del R.O., dentro de la gravedad Retirada de parte de la tecnología de soporte vital Participación de otros pacientes de la sala en la sesión (canto y escucha en grupo)

cont.

Etapa	Objetivos	Dificultades del paciente y la familia	Técnicas utilizadas	Hitos principales
Etapa IV	Realizar un recorrido histórico del vínculo entre R.O. y esposa Manejo de efectos secundarios de la quimioterapia Facilitación de espacios de intimidad familiar Estimulación del autoconocimiento	Efectos secundarios de quimioterapia Incomodidad por sonda nasogástrica	Selección y escucha de canciones significativas Discusión lírica Relajación Imaginería guiada Improvisación Soundpainting	Mejoría del estado físico del R.O., menor gravedad R.O. puede realizar sesiones semi-incorporado (sentado en la cama o una silla) R.O. toca un instrumento por primera vez
Etapa V	Revisión conjunta del proceso realizado Elaboración de una canción que recoja lo vivido Establecer planes y proyecciones a futuro	Efectos secundarios de quimioterapia Ansiedad por inminente salida	Canto conjunto Selección y escucha de canciones significativas Improvisación	Notable mejoría en la salud del R.O. Aparición de capacidad vocalizadora

En cuanto a la evaluación de este proceso terapéutico, en base a los registros cualitativos y cuantitativos recogidos a lo largo del mismo, el equipo de musicoterapia pudo concluir que se alcanzaron los objetivos planteados al inicio. A este musicoterapeuta, el vínculo construido con el paciente y su familia le ha enseñado que en el discurrir de una crisis, aunque eventos traumáticos puedan llegar a suceder, la música de la vida tiene la posibilidad de seguir sonando. En mi caso, pude recorrer con R.O. y su familia una parte de ese sensible camino lleno de posibilidades de cariño, respeto y diversión del que me hicieron parte.

Bajo mi experiencia, y teniendo en cuenta la evidencia que se generó desde el Hospital Clínico Universidad de Chile, creo que es no solo posible, sino necesario, implementar programas de musicoterapia en las UCI que sigan la línea de la humanización de los cuidados intensivos. Para ello los musicoterapeutas deben poseer una visión sistémica de la unidad, tener un enfoque que combine lo clínico con lo preventivo y hacer aproximaciones diagnósticas y diseñar sesiones por igual para pacientes, familias y equipo clínico en pos de promover el bienestar de todos los elementos del sistema.

CHAPTER 6

MUSIC THERAPY PRACTICE IN MEXICO

A Look Back to Move Forward

EUGENIA HERNANDEZ-RUIZ

Introduction

According to the World Federation of Music Therapy (WFMT) (2011), music therapy is

> the professional use of music and its elements as an intervention in medical, educational, and everyday environments with individuals, groups, families, or communities who seek to optimize their quality of life and improve their physical, social, communicative, emotional, intellectual, and spiritual health and wellbeing. Research, practice, education, and clinical training in music therapy is based on professional standards according to cultural, social, and political contexts.

Although music for healing has its roots in ancestral traditions, some of which can be found in Mexican Indigenous cultures, the emergence of music therapy as a healthcare profession, with codes of ethics, higher education programs, and standards of clinical practice and training, can only be traced back to the 20th century. In Mexico, music therapy as a profession is not regulated by any law, there are no higher education programs in music therapy, and only recently (2018) was a national association (Asociación de Musicoterapeutas en México, AMME) created to support the development of this profession.

Despite this, Mexico does have a small number of individuals who have practiced music for health in different forms throughout the last 40 years (Hernandez-Ruiz and Sullivan 2023), with some dissemination (e.g., social media presentations) and training programs (e.g., short courses, diplomas, master's[1]). Dissemination and education are essential components of a three-pronged approach to developing the profession. Indeed, we need public awareness to sustain a profession, which is facilitated by dissemination efforts. We also need quality higher education programs to build the workforce. However, without clinical practice, which is at the core of what we do as music therapists, no other effort will transcend. Clinical practice, by its private and confidential nature, is often less visible—making music therapy practice in Mexico visible is much needed to develop the discipline.

Without attempting to be a historical study, in this chapter I present some of my own and others' experiences of developing music therapy clinical practices in Mexico. I will highlight the achievements of some of these pioneers, as recounted by themselves. As part of the narrative, I will also present the challenges that some of us have encountered when trying to establish our practice, and will consider the situational and systemic challenges that impede the development of music therapy in Mexico, such as higher education systems, stigma, economic and social unrest. The final section provides a vision for music therapy in Mexico, based on our collective perspectives, expertise, enthusiasm, and hope for the profession.

My background

I will begin by outlining my own perspective, as everything that I write is colored by my own experiences. I am a Mexican music therapist trained in the United States. I studied Music Theory and Composition at the Center for Research and Music Studies (Centro de Investigación y Estudios Musicales, A.C.), a private institution that at the time had agreements to provide certification and degrees with the Associated Board of the Royal Schools of Music of London and Trinity College London. My Bachelor's degree in Music Theory was thus awarded by Trinity College London.

During a trip to Europe (France) in 1998, I discovered music therapy. At that point, I had been involved for several years with an association that worked against domestic violence. Music therapy seemed like the perfect combination of my interests. So, in 1999, I searched out training options in Mexico, where I learned about the then recently formed Institute of Humanistic Music Therapy (Instituto Mexicano de Musicoterapia Humanista, IMH). However, the IMH did not offer a degree, and it did not require

---

1 Diplomado refers to a short weekly or monthly training (6 – 12 months) often not regulated by educational authorities. Similarly, in Mexico, a máster (different from maestría or master's degree) refers to an unregulated training, of different durations, with varied prerequisites and graduation requirements, often provided by private institutions, and not a graduate degree.

applicants to be musicians. I then looked to the US for degree programs, and was fortunate to earn a Fulbright scholarship in 2001 to complete a Master's degree at the University of Kansas. I returned to Mexico in 2004 and started a music therapy agency, MusiCura, S.C. Some of my ensuing adventures are interweaved throughout this chapter.

Beginnings

Some of the earliest references to music therapy programs in Mexico go back to the 1980s, with Consuelo Deschamps and José Guillermo Villegas, who founded Therapy and Education I.A.P. (Terapia y Educación I.A.P.), to provide services to disabled people with music therapy strategies and psychomusic (AMME n.d.). Mariela Petraglia, another pioneer, provided training during the 1980s and represented Mexico when the Latin American Music Therapy Committee (Comité Latinoamericano de Musicoterapia, CLAM) was founded in 1993 (Conservatório Brasileiro de Música 2011). Esther Murow was a US-trained music therapist, who developed a music therapy private practice during the 1980s and 1990s. Unfortunately, there is limited documentation for most of this history, which is mainly recounted by those who had direct knowledge of these people and their efforts.

In the 1980s, Víctor Muñoz Pólit also began providing workshops to address participants' "neurosis" utilizing music as one of its strategies (Muñoz Pólit, personal communication, August 9, 2022). These workshops included up to 80 participants and 10 facilitators simultaneously, and were group stand-alone weekend experiences that happened once a year. According to Muñoz Pólit, they were the "first music therapy workshops in Mexico" (personal communication, August 9, 2022). Muñoz Pólit's training stands out as he is not formally trained as a music therapist; he is a physician with a Master's in Humanistic and Gestalt Psychotherapy, with piano training from his childhood. In his youth he also performed in several music ensembles as a vocalist. From 1995 to 1997 he received training in Mexico in the Guided Imagery and Music (GIM) Bonny Method from Ginger Clarkson, MT-BC, from the US. From his early music experiences combined with his psychotherapeutic training, he then developed his own model of music psychotherapy, or humanistic music therapy, through the IMH, which was founded in 1998.

The first trainings were directed at psychotherapists who wanted to use music within their practices. Direct services and different training opportunities based on this model have since been offered, including a Master's degree that is recognized by the Mexican Ministry of Public Education (Secretaría de Educación Pública). However, maintaining registration for this program was costly, cumbersome, and time-consuming, and the Master's degree was only offered for a few years (Juan Carlos Camarena, personal communication, July 4, 2022). The trainings were then converted into a master.

According to Muñoz Pólit, services and training at the IMH included all types of live and recorded music experiences, although there is evidence that the facilitators were often not trained musicians—a recent survey of self-identified music therapists (Hernandez-Ruiz and Sullivan 2023) found that some graduates of the program do not play a musical instrument. This is one of the most salient characteristics of the development of the discipline in Mexico. Although professionals in other countries may find it difficult to envision a music therapist who is not a musician, a self-identified music therapist in Mexico can be a facilitator who uses recorded music in a therapeutic process, or a musician with no or very limited therapeutic training. Whether this perception has promoted or hindered public recognition of music therapy is a matter for debate.

In fact, other professionals in Mexico have questioned whether the humanistic model can be considered "music therapy." The debate is ongoing, as some musicians have indeed been trained under this model, highlighting the model's flexibility and growth, and the emerging quality of music therapy in Mexico. It is possible that, as the discipline grows, some of these models will be modified to be more aligned to a more common definition of music therapy. In the meantime, it is important to consider the achievements, challenges, and processes that some of these pioneers underwent to contribute to the public awareness of the discipline in Mexico.

Developing a private practice

As I returned to Mexico to start clinical practice as a board-certified music therapist, I attempted different ways of developing my private practice. One of the first projects I engaged in was a series of 20-hour professional development workshops for general education teachers housed in the Secretariat of Public Education (Secretaría de Educación Pública). I provided the workshops as part of my commitment to the National Fund for Culture and the Arts (Fondo Nacional para la Cultura y las Artes) that had partially funded my Master's degree in the US. The workshops were never intended to train music therapists, but rather to introduce educators to music therapy as an established profession, to show music strategies that could be helpful in the classroom, and to create awareness of the use of music to address the different social, emotional, and academic needs of children with disabilities. Ten of these workshops were provided to approximately 300 educators in Mexico City, from September 2004 to March 2005.

As I presented the workshops, several educators saw the value and potential of music therapy for the children with whom they worked. They also requested recorded materials to use in the classroom as they did not feel comfortable implementing the strategies with their limited music skills. From these experiences, two concrete developments occurred: (1) referrals for private practice and (2) the creation of didactic materials (a CD and manual) to use music strategies in the home and in school settings (*Cantando Crecemos*™2).

I received several referrals for music therapy sessions that jump-started my private practice. Some of these sessions happened in clients' homes and, starting in 2005, some in a rented office. Two important challenges to start private practice included the cost of rented space, which, in Mexico City, can be prohibitively expensive, and the fact that all services were paid for by parents or caregivers. Since music therapy was (and is) not a formally recognized profession, insurance companies would not cover these services. Further, medical insurance in Mexico typically only covers major expenses (e.g., hospitalizations) and not ongoing treatment; it is also very expensive, and very few families have access to it. Unfortunately, these two challenges (the high cost of rental space and patients paying for treatment out-of-pocket) continue to exist to this day for music therapists.

Several music therapists who have practiced within the last decade shared similar challenges in setting up their private practice. Juan Pedro Zambonini is an Argentinian music therapist who received his Bachelor's degree in Music Therapy from the University of Buenos Aires (Universidad de Buenos Aires, UBA), Argentina. He lived in Mexico during his secondary education, and then came back to Mexico to practice music therapy from 2014 to 2016. He developed a private practice in Cancún, Quintana Roo. He faced similar challenges to the rest of us: limited understanding of the profession and families paying for treatment. Interestingly, he also mentioned two unique experiences. First, and contrary to Argentina's culture and his own experience, he found that Mexican people were not so open to therapy as Argentinians. He shared that in Argentina "everybody has their therapist." In Mexico, a person who seeks therapy faces the stigma of "insanity," and mental health and disability are still considered through a lens of shame. Such beliefs sometimes prevent families from asking for and receiving services. Compounded with the lack of insurance and institutional funding, music therapy services can therefore be difficult to access. Juan Pedro left Mexico to pursue a Master's and then a doctoral degree in the US after only two years' practice.

---

2 Digital recordings and booklets that share music strategies with parents and non-music professionals to support children's development.

A second unique experience that Juan Pedro reported was the ability to connect with another Argentinian music therapist living in Mexico for a few years, María Fernanda Barbaresco. The possibility of networking with a professional with similar training allowed him to build his client base and supervise his own clinical practice in a way that previous practitioners may not have been able to do. In my own experience, the lack of music therapists with similar training in Mexico City induced me to establish an interdisciplinary network with psychologists, special educators, and other therapists for professional development. This experience seems to be common for other music therapists, who report that they supervise their own clinical practice with educators, psychologists, or other humanistic music therapists (Hernandez-Ruiz and Sullivan 2023). On the other hand, this interdisciplinary perspective became a catalyst for my clinical development and, eventually, my research approach.

Juan Carlos Camarena is a music therapist trained under the humanistic model developed by Muñoz Pólit. He started his practice in 2016 and shared with me that one of the biggest challenges to starting a music therapy practice in Mexico was the fact that the profession was not yet immersed within institutions, leaving all the responsibility of creating a job to the professional. Success in a private practice is dependent on the individual's ability and resources to create a clientele, find an appropriate space, and continue to market their services. Similarly, Elske de Jong, a Danish music therapist who arrived in Mexico City in 2014, resorted to private practice after attempting to create institutional positions, but the difficulty in finding clients who could pay for treatment themselves as well as affordable and appropriate spaces limited the development of her practice. She eventually returned to Denmark at the beginning of 2020.

Lack of institutional recognition and/or funding

Since music therapy, as a discipline and as a profession, was not in public awareness in 2004, I was presented with the challenge of differentiating my services from a music teacher, an entertainer, an educator who "includes music" in her classes, and a special educator who uses music to address children's needs in school. In the process of establishing my practice, I was offered several positions that seemed attractive, but that I ultimately rejected. In 2005, I was offered a position as a "song and games" teacher in a public special education school. This position is often available to any musician or educator with minimal music training who uses music to create activities for children in special education. Although the work seemed interesting, the school director was clear that I would never be able to use "music therapy" and "music therapist" as labels, and that I could not practice within a therapeutic model in the school system. Although the income was greatly needed, I decided to forego this opportunity. Another concurrent opportunity happened in a private preschool in the form of early childhood music classes for "enrichment." For a brief period, I provided services, with the understanding that music therapy would eventually begin. However, when it became apparent that the latter would not happen, I concluded my contract. Although these decisions were difficult and impactful to my income, I was adamant that my services should be understood and acknowledged as music therapy.

This lack of understanding of music therapy as a unique and foundational discipline, and not as an accessory or substitute for music education or music enrichment, is echoed by other professionals. As mentioned, Esther Murow developed a private practice in the 1980s and 1990s. When I met her in 2004, she seemed dejected at the lack of institutional support she had experienced. She mentioned that "music therapy will never be recognized here [Mexico] as a true profession." Unfortunately, she passed away when music therapy was still not recognized. I am hopeful that her work, and the work of many others, have paved the way to ensure a different experience for younger generations of music therapists.

Lourdes Best studied for a graduate diploma, or specialty, in music therapy at the University of Nantes, France. Although not a musician by training, her theatre degree supported the use of her voice as her main instrument. Lourdes designed and implemented a music therapy program at the Mental Health Hospital of Tijuana (Hospital de Salud Mental de Tijuana), in Baja California in 2012. This psychiatric hospital had recently been built, and the director was "a person who was very open to including different types of therapies for the patients" (Lourdes Best, personal communication, July 15, 2022). Lourdes provided group sessions for psychiatric patients for four years. She shared that one of the main challenges was to ensure that other professionals acknowledged her services as foundational to the patients' care, and not only as an entertaining activity. As an example, she mentioned that as soon as her sessions started, she would close the door and not allow nurses to take the patients out of the session. Sometimes, this refusal meant strained work relationships, but she considered this request indispensable advocacy for the profession.

Unfortunately, the hospital in Tijuana was restructured during 2015–16 and some services were closed, including the music therapy program. Similar to Elske, Lourdes resorted to private practice for a few years. She is currently dedicating most of her energy and time to her theatrical career and is not practicing as a music therapy clinician, although she remains involved in the field through supervising students in some of the diploma courses that are currently available.

As mentioned earlier, Elske de Jong is a Danish music therapist who lived in Mexico from 2014 to 2020. Her first attempts to develop a music therapy practice in Mexico included writing and presenting a music therapy program for children to different hospitals and schools. Although she found significant interest from several institutions and was even allowed to provide "courses" to pregnant women in a state women's hospital (Hospital de Gineco Obstetricia (HGO) No. 4, Instituto Mexicano del Seguro Social) for a short period, she was not able to consolidate a program due to lack of funding. She then developed a music therapy course as a continuing education option for musicians in the national university, the National Autonomous University of Mexico (Universidad Nacional Autónoma de México, UNAM). Her intent was never to train music therapists but to provide an introductory course for musicians. She mentioned that this was her main job and source of income until she returned to Denmark at the beginning of 2020.

I had a similar experience to Elske while developing a hospital program in 2004–05. Having completed my internship in a medical setting, my first attempt to develop a music therapy program targeted pediatric hospitals and happened in collaboration with a foundation. After nine months of interviews and discussions, we were accepted into the Pediatric Hospital of the National Medical Center (Centro Médico Nacional Siglo XXI), the largest federally funded pediatric hospital in the country. As with Lourdes's experience, a forward-thinking group of medical doctors and administrators made this possible. However, the foundation (that would provide the funding for the services) had to close its doors as the program was about to start. Due to my immediate need of income, I switched gears to different clinical fields.

Opening doors

When the pediatric hospital opportunity closed, I looked for options to supplement my income. At this point, I had a few private clients, and was attempting to replicate my thesis project (Hernandez-Ruiz 2005) in a non-profit institution that worked against gender violence, Fortaleza, Center for Comprehensive Care for Women and the Family (Centro de Atención Integral a la Mujer y la Familia, A.C.). This was led by another forward-thinking professional, psychiatrist Wendy Figueroa, who opened the doors to music therapy. Coincidentally, at that time a federal funding program to combat gender violence had started. I developed and proposed a music therapy program, and the institution applied for funding. We received initial funding, which was renewed for the following five years (2005–09). Several different music therapy programs emerged as a result of this: individual and group sessions with the women in the shelter, group sessions with their children, mother–child sessions for children aged from birth to five, group-building sessions with the staff, and sessions for men who were working to dismantle their patriarchal and violent behaviors and beliefs (at the outpatient center). With the families' permission, we also produced a professional CD with a compilation of songwriting projects developed by the women and children during sessions.

Also in 2005 I became aware that the Mexican Clinic of Autism and Developmental Disorders (Clínica Mexicana de Autismo y Alteraciones del Desarrollo, A.C., CLIMA) was looking for a music therapist. I was intrigued as this professional label was barely known at the time. I attended an interview for a volunteer position, which turned into a job interview, and started a working relationship that continues to this day. As in other settings, forward-thinking leaders, Mtra. MariCarmen Marroquín Segura, whom I first met, and later Dr. Carlos Marcín, saw the value of music therapy and allowed me to develop a full music therapy program. I started with a three-hour week contract that eventually developed into a full-time job with benefits. To my knowledge, this position was the first music therapy job to receive social security benefits (pension and healthcare) under that job description in the country. The music therapy program grew to include individual and group sessions, parent workshops, training opportunities for professionals, dissemination, and research. After I left in 2014 to pursue my PhD in the US, we maintained a very cordial relationship, which has allowed us to collaborate on clinical research projects (Hernandez-Ruiz 2023) and parent virtual workshops. Other programs are in the making.

Other professionals have also made inroads in developing practices that include music therapy or music for well-being. Previously mentioned humanistic music therapist Juan Carlos Camarena has talked about the co-creation of community workshops with Cultural Brigades (Brigadas Culturales) funded by the Department for Cultural Dissemination (Departamento de Difusión Cultural) from UNAM. The purpose of these community workshops was to provide emotional support to people in shelters immediately after the 2017 earthquake in Mexico City. Musicians from the university orchestra provided 90-minute music sessions in the shelters, which allowed participants to create a sense of community and safety. Juan Carlos and other humanistic music therapists worked as facilitators during those sessions to encourage active listening and emotional processing. Juan Carlos acknowledged that these events may not be considered "music therapy" as they were one-time, limited occurrences.

After these workshops, UNAM asked for other community workshops in an established setting. Similar to Muñoz Pólit's first experiences, these were open to the public and did not follow a therapeutic process of assessment, treatment planning, implementation, or termination (Knight, LaGasse, and Clair 2018). Rather, the 90-minute sessions happened once-weekly, for three months, in a public space (Casa del Lago). The humanistic music therapists or facilitators planned group music activities to work on "the shock [of the earthquake] and PTSD" (Juan Carlos Camarena, personal communication, July 4, 2022). Participants could attend as many sessions as they wanted, and some attended regularly. Similar brief workshops were developed in schools, to help children process their grief and shock during this period, in this case funded by Mexico City's government. Although questionable in their therapeutic rigor, these community music experiences built relationships with institutions and created public awareness of the use of music for well-being.

Patricia Altieri is a music therapist and psychologist who first trained in GIM, with Ginger Clarkson in 1998, and then graduated from her Bachelor's in Music Therapy in Heidelberg, Germany, in 2004. She returned to Mexico in 2006 and developed a private practice that included music therapy strategies (Patricia Altieri, personal communication, June 28, 2022). Patricia shared that at some point she co-treated with another German music therapist, also living in Puebla, Mexico. Because Patricia was also a psychologist, she secured a job as a high school counselor in 2007, where she included music therapy workshops with the students. Similar to my experience in the special education school, her role was considered educational, which limited her therapeutic practices. However, and again, paralleling other professionals' experiences, her ability to include music therapy strategies depended on visionary administrative leaders. She mentioned that a "very open-minded director allowed [her] to do a lot of music therapy with the students" (personal communication, June 28, 2022). She also engaged in brief training with teachers, which introduced them to the profession and advocated for music therapy services.

As her first degree was in Psychology, she continued her Master's degree in Educational Psychology. In 2014, she took a position as higher education professor in an early education program. In this capacity, she trained early educators in the use of music with young children for socioemotional and motor development. During her doctoral studies (2018–22), her clinical practice was limited, but her doctoral research addressed the use of music in the educational setting. Patricia considers that this research allowed her to advocate for music therapy with psychology and education professionals who may not have had previous knowledge of the discipline.

Recent developments

More recently, other professionals have continued to open doors for music therapy.

Daniel Torres is a Mexican professional musician who got his bachelor's in music therapy at the UBA, Argentina. Since his return to Mexico in 2018, his music therapy efforts have been mostly dedicated to training and dissemination. Given that he is also a professional musician, Daniel's time for music therapy is limited (Torres, personal communication, July 20, 2022). In 2020, he took over the continuing education course developed by Elske de Jong in UNAM. From Daniel's perspective, his most important accomplishment has been to grow this course and offer it to several cohorts of students. It is important to note that despite being housed in UNAM, the training does not yet have a degree or certificate recognition, and, in Daniel's words, "does not train music therapists" (Torres, personal communication, July 20, 2022). One of the challenges, of this and other training in Mexico, is the limited supervised practical training, which in some courses can be non-existent or as low as 20 hours total (Hernandez-Ruiz and Sullivan 2023). Finding institutions that will allow students to engage in clinical training and trained professionals who can supervise are some of the challenges and most urgent needs in the country (Hernandez-Ruiz and Sullivan 2023).

Regarding clinical practice, Daniel currently spends a few hours a week in the Voice Clinic (Clínica de la Voz), a private organization, where he works with patients with vocal damage. Previously, he provided music therapy sessions to patients "with neurological damage" and mental health needs through private practice (Torres, personal communication, January 20, 2023). He also provides music therapy sessions to his students in UNAM "who want to experience music therapy themselves" (Torres, personal communication, July 20, 2022). More recently, he has initiated conversations with the National Cancer Institute (Instituto Nacional de Cancerología) to create a music therapy program for cancer patients, foundations to provide services with refugees in Tijuana, and other institutions.

Other professionals have also had recent success in developing music therapy clinical practices, even if only in volunteer positions. Florencia Morales Volosín is an Argentinian music therapist and graduate of the UBA, Argentina, who came to Mexico because of her husband's job relocation in December 2019. Due to the immigration process and the COVID-19 pandemic, she has faced obstacles in creating a clinical practice. Interestingly, she received training in music therapy for neonatal intensive care units (NICU-MT) just before moving to Mexico. Her first intention was to practice her newly acquired skills, so she requested permission to volunteer in several NICUs in public hospitals. Eventually, the president of the College of Neonatologists (Colegio de Neonatólogos) supported her application, and she secured permission to provide volunteer services in a NICU during the first few months of 2022. As other professionals before her, part of her efforts have included educating medical residents, nurses, and doctors in the research evidence and clinical efficacy of music therapy. Florencia is currently providing volunteer services in the NICU on a part-time basis; she constantly receives requests for more. Her constant advocacy and optimal qualifications seem to be opening doors for future developments.

Other actors, such as Alicia Picazo, Mexican psychologist and music therapist trained under the humanistic model, Teresa de Jesús Mazadiego Infante, retired researcher and professor living in Veracruz, Mexico, Teresa Fernández de Juan, Cuban professor and researcher in the Colegio de la Frontera Norte, and more recent voices within and outside of Mexico, such as Samuel Gracida, Mexican music therapist trained and currently living in Germany, have also contributed in several ways to the development of the discipline in the country. Unfortunately, some of them were not available for interview, or some of their efforts do not constitute clinical practice, which is the focus of this chapter.

As mentioned, this is in no way a historical study; formal research is still needed to uncover all the ways in which music therapy has emerged in Mexico. A first national survey study of self-identifying music therapy professionals and students was implemented in April–May 2022 (Hernandez-Ruiz and Sullivan 2023). Results of the survey corroborate the interviews depicted here, most notably the enthusiasm and commitment of different actors to support the professionalization of music therapy in Mexico.

Social challenges

Social challenges that may slow the professionalization of music therapy in Mexico include the higher education structure and systems, social unrest, and economic limitations. At its core, music therapy is a profession that requires training in multiple disciplines (therapy, healthcare, science, music; see AMTA 2021). Mexico's higher education differs from other countries (e.g., the US) in that prospective students declare a major *before* they enter the university, apply only to that specific major (and not general admission to the university), have limited options to change it, and typically study within their own school for the full four years. Cross-discipline courses are limited, if they exist at all, and no common core courses are expected (see, for example, UNAM 2022). Creating an undergraduate degree in music therapy would thus require a unique collaboration of many schools, administrators, and faculty. With limited understanding of music therapy in Mexican academia, this collaboration is still not apparent.

Broader issues relate to social unrest and violence and economic limitations that have been apparent in the last two decades in this country.

Unfortunately, Mexico has suffered a significant increase in criminality and violence (e.g., 25.7 percent increase in homicides between 2012 and 2018; INEGI 2019). Paired with economic duress—such as an inflation rate of 7.82 percent in 2022, the highest since 2001 (CONASAMI 2023) and 52.8 percent of families below the poverty line (CONEVAL 2022)—federal and state funding is currently directed to priorities that require immediate resolution. Although higher education is one of the most powerful tools for social and economic progress, it may take decades for its effects to be felt (Baum and Payea 2013). As Patricia Altieri mentioned (personal communication, July 9, 2022), music therapy advocates would do well to understand these social challenges and to align their proposals with these priorities. Music therapy has much to offer to support families and individuals. However, music therapists need to be well trained and show evidence of their ability to address the most pressing social needs.

Lessons learned

Although limited, my own experiences and the interviews here reported give an initial picture of the development of music therapy in Mexico. Some lessons for the future of the discipline can be drawn from these experiences:

- Forward-thinking administrators are essential to develop clinical practices. Many key actors mentioned that their success in creating both private practices and institutional programs went hand in hand with the support of visionary administrative leaders. In several cases, "knocking doors" until a forward-thinking leader took notice was essential to create these programs.
- Research-based information when presenting music therapy services opens doors. In most cases, interviewees' experiences as well as my own showed that when research evidence was presented, healthcare professionals and administrators were soon convinced of the validity and value of music therapy services. Being knowledgeable and up to date with the research literature is a necessity for clinicians who want to open new venues for their services.
- Qualifications (and particularly music therapy degrees) are an asset and urgently needed. Appropriate qualifications are essential to get one's foot in the door and the attention of an administrator. For example, both Florencia Volosín and myself developed a program by presenting our credentials for a volunteer experience. In my case, those qualifications quickly led to a full-time paid position. In Florencia's case, the process is ongoing. Developing educational

standards and guidelines embedded in Mexico's educational system, the development of university programs, as well as professional regulation, are essential next steps to give newer generations of music therapists a better future.

- Persistence, accountability, flexibility, and collaborative work are critical for success. In all cases, professionals who were able to establish and maintain a clinical practice showed persistence in "knocking doors," building professional relationships and clientele, accountability for their services, and flexibility in creating new ideas for programs. Due to the novelty of music therapy in the country, and the lack of university degrees, educating professionals and creating public awareness takes much time and energy. It is an effort that nobody has done or can do alone. Fortunately, the creation of AMME and other groups has ignited interest, particularly through the use of social media. More of these collaborative efforts are needed.

- Acknowledgment of and building on previous work can support the future. Mexico is experiencing a major surge in new music therapy services, training, and professionals (Hernandez-Ruiz and Sullivan 2023). As in any other country where music therapy has been established (Ridder and Tsiris 2015), working cooperatively to build on the assets created by pioneers and current key actors is critical for the future of the profession.

A look to the future

When interviewees were asked how they envision the future of music therapy clinical practice in Mexico, common themes emerged. Most of the comments highlighted the optimism and enthusiasm towards the future of music therapy, awareness of the need for university programs, excitement about various possible opportunities in both public institutions and private practice, and the need to work collaboratively among different groups and approaches. Further, several of us are aware that the economic, political, and social climate of the country may slow down the professionalization of music therapy, although we feel optimistic that the newly established AMME, and the emerging relationships with CLAM, the WFMT, and other countries, will provide the foundation for internal development. Professionals from other countries who want to support these efforts are invited to become knowledgeable of Mexico's social, political, and educational systems, as well as to respect the organic processes that Mexican key actors and organizations are undergoing, to avoid colonizing practices. Much work and collaboration are needed, but Mexican music therapists are up to the task.

CHAPTER 7

THE EVOLUTION OF MUSIC THERAPY IN ARGENTINA

Benenzon and Beyond

GRACIELA BROQUA

Introduction

While widespread histories locate the origin of modern music therapy in Europe and the US, in work with victims of the First and Second World Wars (Bright 1991; Ferreira 2015), Argentinians hold a different view. As was common in the rest of the Americas, the Indigenous peoples of Argentina maintained shamanic traditions. Shamans dealt not only with physical ailments, but also with emotional and personal difficulties (Ferreira 2015). They used sound, silence, rhythm, singing, dancing, music, and musical instruments to soothe people's suffering. Argentinian therapists need look no further than the history of their own land and the people who lived there to find the roots of their discipline.

Perhaps that is why the academic development of the profession began early, relative to the rest of the world. In 1966 in Buenos Aires, a cross-disciplinary group of professionals (music teachers, healthcare professionals, specialists in body work and body expression) founded the first association of music therapy, the Asociación Argentina de Musicoterapia (ASAM), which still operates today (Cárdenas *et al*. 2008; Tosto 2016).

At that time (in the 1960s) there were few academic music therapy programs anywhere in the world, and their reach was limited with no effective way to carry out distance education (Broqua 2023a, c). Neighboring countries such as Uruguay, Chile, Paraguay, and Bolivia had not yet developed programs (Broqua 2023c), and, according to Rejane Méndez Barcellos and Carvalho Santos (2021), the first music therapy program in Brazil was not founded until 1969 in Paraná. Records of a music therapy program developed later in Rio de Janeiro, in 1972 (Ferreira 2015; Rejane Méndez Barcellos and Carvalho Santos 2021) had been found, but the team working in Argentina had to develop their program without a direct model, lacking Music Therapy degrees themselves.

Argentinian higher education laws require that any profession linked to the fields of health or education may not practice without a diploma from an undergraduate degree program. According to Argentinian law, postgraduate degrees certify academic studies, but do not confer the right to practice a discipline. In other words, the founders of ASAM knew that there would have to be an undergraduate degree program for Music Therapy in order to have practicing music therapists in Argentina. So, in 1966, they founded the first course of study in Music Therapy at the College of Medicine of the University of Salvador (Facultad de Medicina, Universidad del Salvador, USAL), a private institution in Buenos Aires. The program launched in 1967, opening the door to the establishment of music therapy as a profession in Argentina (Cárdenas *et al.* 2008; UBA 2013).

Later, in 1973, the University of the Argentine Social Museum (Universidad del Museo Social Argentino, UMSA) (also private) supported a second music therapy program for a number of years, until the death of the program's founder, Dean Dr. Julio Bernaldo de Quirós (Elencwajg 2020; UBA 2013). Despite its unfortunately short duration, this program garnered international endorsements from prominent musicians, educators, music therapists, and psychologists such as Juliette Alvin, Edgar Willems, and Julián de Ajuriaguerra (UBA 2013).

One of the Argentinians who propelled the early development of the profession was Dr. Rolando Benenzon, who had studied medicine and was examining the effects of music on patients with several different pathologies (Benenzon 1976; Benenzon and Yepes 1972). Dr. Benenzon was responsible for spreading concepts such as the ISO principle, or sound identity of a subject or a group (Benenzon 1976), to various corners of Argentina through his work in different cities.

Music teachers were also among the early pioneers of music therapy in Argentina, and they demonstrated how various musical activities (playing rhythms, practicing instruments, moving to a beat) improved the motor skills of their students, even those with disabilities. Ideas developed by pedagogues such as Carl Orff, Zoltán Kodály, and Émile Jacques-Dalcroze were adapted to achieve therapeutic goals (Benenzon and Yepes 1972; Elencwajg 2020; Sabbatella 2004).

Dr. Benenzon continued developing new ideas and spread them not only throughout the rest of Argentina, but also the world (Rejane Méndez Barcellos and Carvalho Santos 2021). He was not alone—Argentina was becoming home to an ever-increasing number of music therapists with undergraduate degrees granting them authorization to practice the profession. After ASAM, the Association of Music Therapists of the Argentine Republic (Asociación de Musicoterapeutas de la República Argentina, AMURA) emerged, and although it was later dissolved, it laid the foundation for broader and greater participation between music therapists working in Argentina.

Little by little, education and health institutions and professionals began to appreciate the results of music therapy interventions, and interest in the discipline grew. In 1993, with the help of Vida Brenner de Aisenwaser (Chuchuy 2023; Elencwajg 2020), a music therapy degree was added in the College of Psychology of the University of Buenos Aires (Facultad de Psicología, Universidad de Buenos Aires, UBA), a national and public institution. The first class began in 1994, opening the way for a new wave of students in Argentina to pursue undergraduate studies in music therapy at a public institution, tuition-free (Chuchuy 2023).

Music therapy for free

In addition to free undergraduate tuition, public universities in Argentina offer other free services for the whole population in the national territory. This arises from the idea that higher education is a public and a social good, and that access to this benefit is a right that any inhabitant of Argentina should enjoy (Cannarozzo 2020b). As of this writing (2024), UBA (an important and internationally recognized institution) remains the first and only public university in the Americas to offer a tuition-free Spanish-language undergraduate degree program in Music Therapy, having begun in 1994 (Broqua 2023a). Such programs remain uncommon overseas, making the offering in Argentina pertinent for the international music therapy community as well.

Initially, in 1994, applicants for the program at UBA were required to be music teachers. If they had no teaching degree, but they did have equivalent musical knowledge, they could take an entrance exam (UBA 2013). These requirements indicate that the university expected high levels of both musicality and academic aptitude from applicants for the Music Therapy program. At the present moment, this requirement stands: applicants for the undergraduate program at UBA do not need a teaching diploma, but they must pass an entrance exam evaluating their background knowledge in music.

The program is taught in-person in Avellaneda, in the province of Buenos Aires (although some subjects were taught remotely during the COVID-19 pandemic). When the undergraduate program launched in 1994, the approved study plan consisted of 2652 hours of in-person instruction, granting students a Music Therapist (Musicoterapeuta) diploma on completion (UBA 2013). This diploma was offered until December 31, 2014 (Ministerio de Educación Nacional 2014). Later, in 2004 the study plan was updated to consist of 3046 hours of in-person instruction taken over a period of at least five years, awarding students a Bachelor's in Music Therapy (Licenciado en Musicoterapia) (Chuchuy 2023). For several years, the two programs coexisted, with students having the option of choosing either the diploma or the degree path.

Argentina does not use ECTS (European Credit Transfer and Accumulation System) academic credits. Instead, each program records the number of hours of classes. This includes only the time that students spend with teachers, professional practice, and (in the case of the UBA program) a standard number of hours allotted for preparing the thesis. Hours of study, reading, exercises, homework, research, participation in university extension projects, or voluntary assistance and internships are not included.

On completing their coursework for the program and passing exams, students were (and still are) required to write a thesis before receiving their diploma or degree (UBA 2013). In 1994, this made the Music Therapy program more rigorous than the undergraduate degree in Psychology, whose students did not have to write a thesis to earn their degree (although they now must). This gives an indication of how rapidly the standard of academic rigor was rising in music therapy compared to other professions (Chuchuy 2023).

A free undergraduate degree at a public university vastly expanded the possible base of applicants. UBA also offers free tuition to foreign students, and continues to receive applicants from across the globe today, considerably augmenting the number of trained music therapists in Argentina.

But public education was not the only factor that spurred on the development of the profession. There is also a public health system in Argentina, with public hospitals offering free health services. As those hospitals began to add music therapists to their teams, and patients were able to receive free music therapy treatments, more people began to see the potential value of music therapy, and the profession became more established (Berenstecher *et al.* 2022; Cannarozzo 2020a; Cannarozzo *et al.* 2021; Díaz 2023; Gaiada 2020; Lanzoni and Gómez 2020; Reibel 2022; Rodríguez 2017; Vesco and Marasco 2021).

Some hospitals offer residencies (*residencias*) for certain professions. These are postgraduate courses of study and research for professionals who already have their undergraduate degree. Applicants must pass an entrance exam to be considered, and during their residency a music therapist will work from Monday to Friday, at hospitals, offering interventions for patients, in addition to studying, writing, and publishing. Each therapist receives a small economic benefit to supplement their income and help sustain the demanding workload. Although there are still few residencies available for music therapists, the number has grown in recent years (Carrizo 2021; Uzal 2016). These represent a significant leap towards better training and quality of care in Argentinian public hospitals, and help continue to legitimize music therapy at the same level of specialization and rigor as other therapeutic techniques.

Disability treatment represents another important factor in the development of music therapy in Argentina. In 1981, National Law 22.431 was passed to protect the rights of people with disabilities. Since then, the Argentinian government has paid special attention to the needs of this population and the treatments they require (Poder Ejecutivo Nacional 1981a, b). The law has been periodically updated over the years, and in 2016 a new law, and a subsequent decree in 2018, created a major opportunity for music therapists working in the fields of disability or functional diversity (Congreso de la Nación Argentina 2016).

The 2016 law establishes that each person with a disability or functional diversity has the right to obtain a Unique Disability Certificate that grants access to numerous rights within Argentina (Congreso de la Nación Argentina 2016). One of these is to receive any treatments that their doctor considers necessary, free of charge, throughout their life. This includes music therapy, greatly expanding the population of patients and clients who can access the service, and creating a great deal of potential work for music therapists in Argentina.

Open source

In terms of access to academic knowledge, the situation in Argentina is very different from the rest of the world. Despite what Barbara Wheeler expressed in the Foreword for *Music Therapy Methods in Neurorehabilitation: A Clinician's Manual* (Wheeler 2006), music therapists working in rehabilitation in Argentina in the 1990s found it difficult to get hold of resources, journal articles, or books from foreign countries. Translating and developing their own literature was essential. But translations were not readily accessible. Only a handful of music therapy books published abroad were translated into Spanish and found their way onto the Argentinian market. These included *Music in Geriatric Care: A Second Look* (Bright 1991) and *Music Therapy and its Relationship to Current Treatment Theories* (Ruud 1990), both translated by Gregorio Tisera López, and a text from Edith Lecourt translated by Violeta Hemsy de Gainza (Lecourt 2006). Progress has been made, but there is still work to be done (Broqua 2023d; Sokolov and Curcio 2021).

If translations were difficult to come by, the prolific publishing around the rich regional practices helped balance the situation. There are plentiful texts from diverse Argentinian authors, events, and institutions that record the work, ideas, and challenges of the local community of practitioners (Broqua 2022; Federico 2016; Federico and Tosto 2018; Ferrari 2013; Gallardo 1998; Gauna *et al.* 2008; Papalía 1998; Pfeiffer and Zamani 2017; Rodríguez Espada 2020; Satinosky 2006; Schapira *et al.* 2007; Zain 2014). The authors of these texts went to great effort to get hold of copies, even if they could only get a few, so that they could disseminate their findings within the Argentinian therapeutic community.

It is widely held in Argentina that knowledge belongs to the whole of humanity, and as a result there are numerous continuing education and networking opportunities open for music therapists, students, and professionals from other disciplines. Many events, conferences, workshops, and even congresses can be attended for free online. Academic publication practice also follows this principle, for example, the International Congress of the College of Psychology of the UBA publishes its proceedings every year online for free, including papers on music therapy, with international indexation to make searching for texts easier.

Regarding music therapy specifically, the journal *ECOS* (launched in 2016) is the main producer of open access academic knowledge. To date, it can be found in more than ten academic indexes, databases, and catalogues. *ECOS* uses a double-blind peer review process and makes its full contents available online, charging no fees to its readers or authors (Godetti *et al.* 2020). *ECOS* is edited by the Cátedra Libre at the National University of La Plata (Universidad Nacional de La Plata), a public university in the province of Buenos Aires. As there is no undergraduate music therapy degree at the university, the Cátedra Libre consists of volunteer music therapists and students who organize music therapy talks, conferences, and academic events, and publications, interviews, and projects disseminate useful research and information about the profession to the university's student community (Cannarozzo and Diaz Abrahan 2023).

Up to this point we have mentioned two universities (one public and one private, because the University of the Argentine Social Museum's program no longer exists) where people can train to practice music therapy in Argentina, hospitals where music therapists can work and continue their education after receiving their diploma, and the Cátedra Libre, which disseminates concepts and practices of Music Therapy. But this is only the foundation for the ongoing training, policy work, and research that music therapists are engaged in in Argentina.

Training and updates

Training abroad in music therapy is unrealistic for most practitioners in Argentina due to the country's economic situation compared to the rest of the world. That is why, for Argentinians, the establishment of quality training spaces within Argentina itself is so crucial. Moreover, as mentioned before, only individuals with an authorized undergraduate degree are eligible to practice music therapy in Argentina, meaning that therapists with foreign diplomas are often not considered qualified.

Before university music therapy programs were common, Dr. Benenzon and others taught courses in various countries to spread knowledge of the profession (Rejane Méndez Barcellos and Carvalho Santos 2021). Now, in 2024, Argentina alone has seven degree programs where students can obtain a Bachelor's in Music Therapy (CLAM 2021). One is offered by a public university, while the other six are run by private universities. Four are in Buenos Aires city, the public program is in the province of Buenos Aires, another is located in the city of Rosario (in the province of Santa Fe), and the seventh is run by a university in the province of Mendoza (Broqua 2023a, c; Elencwajg 2020). It is possible for a student to complete any of the private programs in four years, while the public university requires a minimum of five years of study. Each program requires students to engage in a period of supervised professional practice before being awarded the diploma.

Because music therapists in Argentina must pass undergraduate degree programs, music therapy in Argentina is practiced with a level of rigor similar to physiotherapy, psychology, or speech therapy, whose practitioners work through similar programs at their universities over the same period of years. The rigor of their university education allows music therapists to participate in interdisciplinary exchanges with their colleagues, aiding the evolution of music therapy as a profession, and helping to legitimize it within healthcare institutions (Broqua 2020).

Bachelor's degrees in Music Therapy provide a wide spectrum of general knowledge that equips their graduates to begin practicing the profession in any context; however, the extensive development of the discipline in Argentina demands that therapists specialize and continually educate themselves. As such, various associations and individual therapists have developed courses to focus on specific applications of music therapy, intended for practitioners who have already obtained their diploma (Broqua 2023b).

The considerable size of Argentina poses an obstacle in disseminating this training to music therapists throughout the country, and distance or hybrid learning formats have become popular among practitioners. Online training also allows music therapists from all over the world to access this specialized knowledge, a significant detail considering that there are few countries in the world with robust continuing education options for music therapists who have completed their degrees (Broqua 2023a, b, c).

In recent years, some universities have begun offering postgraduate music therapy training specifically for practitioners who already have an undergraduate degree in Music Therapy. To differentiate these from postgraduate programs that seek to disseminate music therapy research across disciplines, or those that focus on training professionals from different disciplines to practice music therapy, we will call them "postgraduate update courses" (Broqua 2023a, b, c).

Among the university postgraduate update courses in Music Therapy are the Diploma in Community Music Therapy from Favaloro University (Universidad Favaloro) (Isla and Demkura 2023) and the Accessibility in Music Therapy with Assistive Technology course from UBA (Broqua 2023b, c). Both offer the possibility of remote study for therapists who do not live in Argentina.

To date, there are no postgraduate specialization programs, Master's degrees or doctorates in Music Therapy in Argentina. In the Argentinian university system, these three types of postgraduate programs typically last between one and three years (or more, depending on the nature of the study), and students receive their diplomas after completing a thesis or final academic work. These are pending accounts that will involve high-level specializations to which, in Argentina, professionals from other disciplines could not apply, but only music therapists with diplomas from universities. It is important to remember that postgraduate degrees in Argentina are considered only to be academic. Therefore, specialization courses, Master's degrees and doctorates grant diplomas, but do not authorize the practice of any given profession in Argentina.

All these factors so far have contributed to the broad development that Argentinian music therapy has seen in recent decades; however, one of the most crucial moments in the development of the profession was not in training methods but in policy: the sanction of the Law of Professional Practice (Congreso de la Nación Argentina 2015).

The law

As I mentioned at the first InternationalConference of the CRE Program on Neuro-Socio-Psychological Rehabilitation at Rayat-Bahra University in Punjab, as we acquire more rights, we must take on more responsibilities we must fulfill (Broqua 2021).

In 1995, Article 43 of the Argentinian Higher Education Law established that there were professions that were considered "risky" because they involved public interest and the health or rights of the people they served (Congreso de la Nación Argentina 1995; Marquina 2004). Music therapy meets the criteria for being considered such a profession, meaning that music therapists in Argentina bear greater responsibilities than those of many other professions.

In 2015, National Law 27153 was approved to regulate the professional practice of music therapy in Argentina. Its text dictates the qualifications a person must have to practice the profession in any part of Argentina (Congreso de la Nación Argentina 2015). These regulatory demands are even greater than those that were already being met throughout the nation before the legislation was passed. This implies that, to ensure a properly developed profession, just as other disciplines must respect a great many regulations that ensure the rigor and safety of their practice (Marquina 2004), all music therapists must comply with all standards: the previous ones, the implicit ones, and the new ones.

The law passed in 2015 stipulates that any person who wants to practice music therapy in Argentina must have an undergraduate degree in the field (Broqua 2023a, c). This degree must meet the standards required in the country: it must be issued by a university authorized in the territory, it must be regulated, and students must take a minimum of 2600 hours of classes and clinical training (not including homework) over a period of at least four years (Marquina 2004). This meant that the music therapy diplomas awarded by shorter courses of study no longer authorized the practice of the profession, and that those who held degrees from those programs had to undergo additional education to bring their professional qualifications into compliance with the law. On the upside, this meant elevating the academic standards of the discipline, but it also placed greater demands on therapists.

This law also introduced a requirement for those who studied music therapy abroad to validate their degree in Argentina to work as a music therapist. This validation would confirm that the content and skills someone learned in their program at a foreign university were equivalent to the programs authorized within Argentina. This is the crucial point, and creates a problem, taking into account the disparity between music therapy training in Argentina and other countries, where music therapists often receive their training in postgraduate programs.

The issue is that a Master's degree in Music Therapy with 60 ECTS is not equal to an Argentinian degree. One European credit represents between 25 and 30 hours of study and work (Palacios Picos 2004), so a 60-ECTS postgraduate program would be around 1800 hours of both classes and study time, a figure much lower than the Argentinian requirement of 2600 hours of classes alone. This creates potential difficulties for someone with a Master's degree in Music Therapy wishing to practice in Argentina, while those who have studied abroad in undergraduate degree programs of similar rigor to those in Argentina have a more direct path to having their music therapy diplomas approved by the Argentinian government. However, the federal requirements are not always the only barrier.

Under National Law 27153, each province in the country must decide whether to develop their own provincial law regarding the practice of music therapy, or to adhere to the text of the national law (Congreso de la Nación Argentina 2015). Some provinces, such as Buenos Aires and Entre Ríos (Gobierno de la Provincia de Buenos Aires 2006; Poder Legislativo Provincial de Entre Ríos 2012), have enacted their own provincial laws, mandating that music therapists who want to work in those territories must meet their provincial requirements in addition to the national ones.

According to national law, a music therapist who wishes to practice must present their university diploma to the corresponding government authorities and request a number for registration. Healthcare professionals are not allowed to work with clients without this number (Pensa and Godetti 2017). If the music therapist has studied in another country, after transferring their degree, they must also obtain this registration number before they can begin practicing.

Nowadays the scope of the laws has expanded, influencing job placement for music therapists. For example, there are institutions called Therapeutic Educational Centers (Centros Educativos Terapéuticos, CETs) that offer educational and therapeutic services to children and adolescents who, for one reason or another, cannot enter the school system. Currently, no CET can legally operate if its professional team does not include at least one registered music therapist with a university diploma.

These requirements are similar to those that other professions in the country must meet. This degree of national and provincial regulation reflects the status that music therapy has established in Argentinian society. Attaining this level of acknowledgement has not been easy, and was only possible through countless collective efforts by therapists and colleagues across multiple decades.

Research

As in other scientific disciplines, research is crucial for the evolution of music therapy, and can generate or update ideas within the field that impact not only the therapeutic community but also broader society (Godetti *et al.* 2023). In order to carry out effective research, however, music therapists must be sufficiently trained in research methodologies. So once again we find a link between robust professional training and precipitous growth in the music therapy community in Argentina.

In a 2019 interview with Franco Rolleti, researcher Nadia Justel remarked that any professional in a field can carry out research, stating that there was no need for specialized skills. In the undergraduate Music Therapy degree programs at UBA and Maza University (Universidad Juan Agustín Maza, UMAZA), research training is built into the curriculum to equip all therapists with research methodology and academic writing skills from the start of their careers.

Research in music therapy has increased in the last half century in Argentina. This has been driven partly by music therapists entering official science and technology research institutions such as the National Council for Scientific and Technical Research (Consejo Nacional de Investigaciones Científicas y Técnicas, CONICET) (Godetti *et al.* 2023). This represents an important step forward for the profession, opening up new developments through research, and conferring additional prestige and legitimacy to the profession by placing it in the same circles as other more established and recognized scientific disciplines.

Research also allows the music therapy community to establish a higher standard of practice and accountability. At the same time, the rest of the hospital teams' disciplines demand specific knowledge from music therapy, different from that of other disciplines, and it is expected that this knowledge will be of high quality (Tosto 2016). The fact that in Argentina music therapists study an undergraduate degree program makes this knowledge completely independent from that of other professions.

In a 2023 inquiry into the current state of music therapy research in Argentina, Godetti, López, and Diaz Abrahan found that the majority of music therapists in Argentina were not conducting research. When asked to explain why, many of the therapists' answers pointed toward a lack of sufficient training in methodology, or lack of time. This might be improving—the authors learned that there are students who join research teams during their undergraduate study, often at the invitation of their professors (Godetti *et al.* 2023).

There remains a question as to which types of research music therapists should prioritize. What is most valuable for the functional practice of the discipline? What sort of research would help to further establish the legitimacy of music therapy as a scientific discipline? Virginia Tosto explores these questions in a 2016 publication in *ECOS*, outlining areas of interest including the need to validate the effectiveness of treatment interventions, the instruments used for data collection, and the communication of results, both to music therapists and to the broader scientific community (Tosto 2016).

In other countries, where training may be received as a postgraduate degree, music therapists may already have training in another discipline. This prior knowledge can enrich music therapy (Eslava Mejía 2019), as we see valuable research on specific therapeutic objectives such as motor skills or language (primary concerns for physiotherapists and speech therapists, respectively) carried out in the context of music therapy by practitioners with prior training in those disciplines.

These types of interventions cannot always be easily implemented by other music therapists who do not have the right prior training. And this knowledge does not always represent specific knowledge of music therapy, but rather transdisciplinary knowledge. This is why it is essential to increase research in Argentina that takes into account these local specificities that the profession presents in the territory.

Conclusion

The weak Argentinian national economy has greatly hindered access to academic texts and training published or hosted in other nations for music therapists practicing in the country. This has pushed Argentinian therapists and researchers to become prolific publishers, teachers, and organizers, creating the necessary resources to nurture the development of their profession locally. It also means that the fruits of these labors are extremely affordable for members of the broader music therapy community to access.

Argentina maintains options for its inhabitants to both study and receive music therapy for free. This access to free education and treatment extends to individuals living in Argentina, even non-citizens. Because music therapy training in Argentina is conducted at undergraduate level, there are postgraduate update courses in Music Therapy that adhere to high academic standards. Many of these courses are also taught remotely, enabling therapists around the world to access this training.

Since the 1960s, when Dr. Benenzon and other pioneers began establishing the discipline in Argentina, a large volume of research has been conducted. Access to many of these studies is free for anyone anywhere in the world, making Argentina a major resource for music therapy research for the broader global therapeutic community. The research carried out in Argentina also allows us to constantly improve interventions and establish the same rigorous scientific standards for music therapy that apply for other professions. While much of the research begins with regional or local needs, many of these studies' results have the potential to be applied abroad due to broad similarities between patient populations across the world (e.g., patients with autism spectrum disorder or cerebral palsy).

Beyond research, education, and access, the legal achievements of the music therapy community in Argentina have also been instrumental in spurring on the broad development of the discipline. Both the national law and provincial laws on professional practice and access to treatment represent examples and models that can be followed by nations still fighting for policies that allow music therapy to be applied to its best effect for their people. The unique challenges facing Argentinian music therapy throughout its long development have created an academic and therapeutic community with much to offer the rest of the world. Communicating these possibilities is part of our professional responsibility to aid the global growth of our beloved profession.

LA EVOLUCIÓN DE LA MUSICOTERAPIA EN ARGENTINA

Benenzon y más allá

GRACIELA BROQUA

Introducción

Si bien muchas historias sitúan el origen de la musicoterapia moderna en el trabajo en Europa y Estados Unidos con las víctimas de la Primera y Segunda Guerra Mundial (Bright 1991; Ferreira 2015), los argentinos tenemos una visión diferente. Los pueblos originarios de Argentina mantuvieron tradiciones chamánicas. Los chamanes no sólo lidiaban con dolencias físicas, sino también con dificultades emocionales y personales (Ferreira 2015). Ellos empleaban sonido, silencio, ritmo, canto, baile, música e instrumentos musicales para aliviar el sufrimiento del pueblo. Por ende, los terapeutas argentinos no necesitamos mirar más allá de la historia de nuestra propia tierra y las personas que vivieron aquí para encontrar las raíces de nuestra disciplina.

Quizás por eso el desarrollo académico de nuestra profesión comenzó tan temprano en relación con el resto del mundo. En 1966 en Buenos Aires un grupo multidisciplinario de profesionales (docentes de Música, profesionales de la salud, especialistas en trabajo corporal o en expresión corporal) fundaron la primera asociación de Musicoterapia, ASAM (Asociación Argentina de Musicoterapia) la cual aún hoy opera (Cárdenas *et al.* 2008; Tosto 2016).

En aquella época había pocas carreras académicas de Musicoterapia en el mundo. Y su alcance era limitado ya que no se contaba con una forma efectiva de impartir educación a distancia (Broqua 2023a, c). Países vecinos como Uruguay, Chile, Paraguay y Bolivia no habían desarrollado carreras todavía (Broqua 2023c), y según Rejane Méndez Barcellos y Carvalho Santos (2021) el primer programa de Musicoterapia en Brasil no se fundó hasta 1969 en Paraná. También encontramos registros de una carrera de Musicoterapia desarrollada posteriormente, en 1972, en Rio de Janeiro (Ferreira 2015; Rejane Méndez Barcellos y Carvalho Santos 2021). De modo que no era posible para esos pioneros argentinos ser musicoterapeutas con títulos universitarios, por lo que el equipo de trabajo en Argentina tuvo que desarrollar su carrera sin un modelo directo, al carecer ellos mismos de títulos en Musicoterapia.

Las leyes argentinas de educación superior exigen que las profesiones vinculadas a los campos de la salud o la educación no pueden ejercerse sin un diploma de una carrera de grado (en otros países llamada de pregrado). Según la ley argentina, los títulos de posgrado certifican estudios académicos, pero no confieren el derecho a practicar una disciplina. En otras palabras, los fundadores de ASAM sabían que tendría que haber una carrera de grado en Musicoterapia para poder tener musicoterapeutas en ejercicio en Argentina. Así, en 1966, fundaron la primera carrera de Musicoterapia en la Facultad de Medicina de la Universidad del Salvador, una institución privada en Buenos Aires. La carrera se lanzó en 1967 y abrió la puerta al establecimiento de la Musicoterapia como profesión en Argentina (Cárdenas *et al.* 2008; UBA 2013).

Posteriormente, en 1973, la Universidad del Museo Social Argentino (también privada) sostuvo una segunda carrera de Musicoterapia por poco tiempo hasta el fallecimiento de su fundador, el Decano Dr. Julio Bernaldo de Quirós (Elencwajg 2020; UBA 2013). A pesar de su lamentable duración, este programa obtuvo el respaldo internacional de destacados músicos, educadores, musicoterapeutas y psicólogos como Juliette Alvin, Edgar Willems y Julián de Ajuriaguerra (UBA 2013).

Uno de los argentinos que propulsó el desarrollo temprano de la profesión fue Rolando Benenzon, quien había estudiado Medicina y estaba enfocando su atención en los efectos de la música en pacientes con diversas patologías (Benenzon 1976; Benenzon y Yepes 1972). Benenzon fue responsable de dar a conocer conceptos, como el principio del ISO o la identidad sonora de un sujeto o un grupo (Benenzon 1976), en varios rincones de la Argentina a través de su trabajo en diferentes ciudades.

Muchos docentes de Música estuvieron también entre los pioneros iniciales de la Musicoterapia en Argentina, y demostraron cómo diversas actividades con música (la ejecución de ritmos, la práctica instrumental, el movimiento al tempo de la música escuchada) mejoraban las habilidades motrices de sus estudiantes, incluso de quienes tenían discapacidades. Así, ideas desarrolladas por pedagogos musicales como Carl Orff, Zoltán Kodály o Émile Jacques-Dalcroze, fueron adaptadas para lograr objetivos terapéuticos (Benenzon y Yepes 1972; Elencwajg 2020; Sabbatella 2004).

Benenzon continuó desarrollando sus propias ideas y las difundió no solo a lo largo del resto de Argentina, sino del mundo (Rejane Méndez Barcellos y Carvalho Santos 2021). Y él no fue el único. Argentina se estaba transformando en el hogar de un número cada vez mayor de musicoterapeutas con títulos legalmente autorizados para aplicar la profesión. Después de ASAM, surgió otra asociación, AMURA (Asociación de Musicoterapeutas de la República Argentina) y, aunque fue disuelta más tarde, sentó las bases para una mayor y más activa participación de musicoterapeutas que trabajaban en Argentina.

Poco a poco, más instituciones y profesionales de la educación y de la salud comenzaron a apreciar los resultados de las intervenciones musicoterapéuticas, y el interés por la disciplina creció. En 1993, con la ayuda de Vida Brenner de Aisenwaser (Chuchuy 2023; Elencwajg 2020), una carrera de Musicoterapia fue agregada en la Facultad de Psicología de la Universidad de Buenos Aires (UBA), una institución nacional y pública. La primera cohorte comenzó en 1994, inaugurando el recorrido para una nueva ola de estudiantes en Argentina que realizó estudios de pregrado en Musicoterapia en una institución pública, sin costo de matrícula (Chuchuy 2023).

Musicoterapia gratis

Además de la matrícula universitaria gratuita, las universidades públicas de Argentina ofrecen otros servicios sin costo para toda la población en el territorio nacional. Esto surge de la idea que la educación es un bien público y social, y que el acceso a este beneficio es un derecho del que debería gozar cualquier habitante de la Argentina (Cannarozzo 2020b). Al momento de escribir este capítulo (2024), la Universidad de Buenos Aires (una institución importante y reconocida internacionalmente) sigue siendo la primera y única universidad pública en las Américas que ofrece una carrera universitaria gratuita de Musicoterapia en español, programa que comenzó en 1994 (Broqua 2023a). Carreras con estas características son también poco comunes en el extranjero, lo que hace que la oferta en Argentina sea pertinente para la comunidad musicoterapéutica internacional también.

Inicialmente en 1994 a los postulantes a la carrera de Musicoterapia de la Universidad de Buenos Aires (UBA) se les exigía ser Profesores de Música. Sin embargo, si no tenían ese título previo, pero sí poseían un conocimiento musical equivalente, podían rendir un examen de ingreso (UBA 2013). Estos requisitos indicaban que la universidad demandaba altos niveles de musicalidad y aptitud académica entre los aspirantes. Actualmente los postulantes a la carrera de grado de la UBA no necesitan un título de Profesor, pero deben aprobar un examen de ingreso que evalúa su base previa de conocimientos musicales.

La carrera se dicta presencialmente en Avellaneda, provincia de Buenos Aires (aunque durante la pandemia de COVID-19 hubo asignaturas dictadas remotamente de manera excepcional). Cuando la carrera de grado fue lanzada en 1994 el plan de estudio aprobado consistía en 2652 horas de clases presenciales que, al completarse, entregaba un diploma de Musicoterapeuta (UBA 2013). Este título fue expedido hasta el 31 de diciembre de 2014 (Ministerio de Educación Nacional 2014). Más tarde este plan de estudio fue actualizado y consistió en 3046 horas de clases presenciales realizadas durante un período de al menos cinco años y, desde 2004 hasta hoy, otorga el diploma de Licenciado en Musicoterapia (Chuchuy 2023). Durante varios años, ambos planes coexistieron y el estudiantado tenía la opción de elegir por continuar la carrera con uno u otro plan, y recibir uno u otro título.

Argentina no utiliza los créditos académicos ECTS (Sistema Europeo de Transferencia y Acumulación de Créditos). En cambio, cada carrera registra el número de horas de clases dictadas. Esto incluye solo el tiempo que los estudiantes pasan con sus docentes, en su práctica supervisada y (en el caso de la carrera de Musicoterapia de la UBA) un número de horas estándares adjudicadas a la elaboración de la tesis. Las horas de estudio, lectura, ejercicios, tareas, investigación, participación en proyectos de extensión universitaria o voluntariado y prácticas no están incluidas en este número.

Después de cursar todas las asignaturas y aprobar todos los exámenes, al estudiantado se le requería (y aún se le requiere) escribir una tesis antes de recibir su diploma o título (UBA 2013). En 1994 esto agregaba a la carrera de grado de Musicoterapia una exigencia más que a la de Psicología, cuyos estudiantes no tenían que escribir una tesis para recibir su título (aunque ahora sí deben hacerlo). Esto nos indica qué tanto había aumentado la exigencia académica en Musicoterapia comparada a otras profesiones (Chuchuy 2023).

Un título universitario gratuito en una universidad pública amplió enormemente la posible base de aspirantes. La UBA también ofrece matrícula gratuita a estudiantes extranjeros y continúa recibiendo postulantes de todo el mundo hoy en día, aumentando considerablemente el número de musicoterapeutas capacitados en Argentina.

Pero la educación pública no fue el único factor que impulsó el desarrollo de la profesión. En Argentina también existe un sistema de salud público, con hospitales públicos que ofrecen servicios de salud gratuitos a los ciudadanos. A medida que esos hospitales comenzaron a incorporar musicoterapeutas a sus equipos, y los pacientes pudieron recibir tratamientos de musicoterapia gratuitos, más personas comenzaron a ver el valor potencial de la Musicoterapia, y la profesión se consolidó cada vez más (Berenstecher *et al.* 2022; Cannarozzo 2020a; Cannarozzo *et al.* 2021; Díaz 2023; Gaiada 2020; Lanzoni y Gómez 2020; Reibel 2022; Rodríguez 2017; Vesco y Marasco 2021).

Algunos hospitales ofrecen residencias para ciertas profesiones. Estas son carreras de posgrado e investigación para profesionales que ya poseen su título de grado. Los aspirantes deben pasar un examen de ingreso para ser considerados y durante su residencia los musicoterapeutas trabajarán de lunes a viernes en los hospitales aportando intervenciones a pacientes además de estudiar, escribir y publicar. Cada terapeuta recibe un pequeño beneficio económico para complementar sus ingresos y ayudar a sostener la exigente carga de trabajo. Aunque todavía hay pocas residencias disponibles para musicoterapeutas, el número ha crecido en los últimos años (Carrizo 2021; Uzal 2016).

Estas residencias suponen un importante salto hacia una mejor formación y calidad asistencial en los hospitales públicos argentinos, y ayudan a seguir legitimando la Musicoterapia al mismo nivel de especialización y rigor de otras profesiones terapéuticas.

El tratamiento de la discapacidad representa otro factor importante en el desarrollo de la Musicoterapia en Argentina. En 1981 se sancionó la Ley Nacional 22.431 para proteger los derechos de las personas con discapacidades. Desde entonces, el gobierno argentino ha prestado especial atención a las necesidades de esta población y los tratamientos que requieren (Poder Ejecutivo Nacional 1981a, b). La ley ha sido actualizada a lo largo de los años, y en 2016 una nueva ley, y un decreto posterior en 2018, creó una gran oportunidad para los musicoterapeutas que trabajan en los campos de la discapacidad o la diversidad funcional (Congreso de la Nación Argentina 2016).

La ley de 2016 establece que cada persona con discapacidad o diversidad funcional tiene el derecho de obtener un Certificado Único de Discapacidad que le garantiza el acceso a numerosos derechos en la Argentina (Congreso de la Nación Argentina 2016). Uno de esos derechos es recibir cualquier tratamiento que su médico considere necesario, sin cargo, a lo largo de toda su vida. Esto incluye musicoterapia, expandiendo ampliamente la población de pacientes y clientes que pueden acceder al servicio y creando un gran potencial de trabajo para los musicoterapeutas en Argentina.

Acceso abierto

En términos de acceso al conocimiento académico, la situación en Argentina es muy diferente al resto del mundo. A pesar de lo expresado por Barbara Wheeler en el Prefacio de *Music Therapy Methods in Neurorehabilitation:*

A Clinician's Manual (Wheeler 2006) los musicoterapeutas que trabajaban en rehabilitación en los 90 en Argentina tenían dificultades para obtener recursos, artículos académicos o libros de países extranjeros. La traducción y el desarrollo de su propia literatura fueron esenciales.

Pero las traducciones no eran fácilmente accesibles. Sólo un puñado de libros de musicoterapia publicados en el extranjero fueron traducidos al español y llegaron al mercado argentino. Estos incluyeron *Music in Geriatric Care: A Second Look* (Bright 1991) o *Music Therapy and its Relationship to Current Treatment Theories* (Ruud 1990), ambos traducidos por Gregorio Tisera López, y un texto de Edith Lecourt traducido por Violeta Hemsy de Gainza (Lecourt 2006). Se han logrado avances, pero aún queda trabajo por hacer en este frente (Broqua 2023d; Sokolov y Curcio 2021).

Pero si las traducciones eran difíciles de conseguir, las prolíficas publicaciones en torno a las ricas prácticas regionales ayudaron a equilibrar la situación. Hay abundantes textos de diversos autores, eventos e instituciones argentinos que registran el trabajo, las ideas y los desafíos de la comunidad local de practicantes (Broqua 2022; Federico 2016; Federico y Tosto 2018; Ferrari 2013; Gallardo 1998; Gauna *et al.* 2008; Papalia 1998; Pfeiffer y Zamani 2017; Rodríguez Espada 2020; Satinosky 2006; Schapira *et al.* 2007; Zaín 2014). Los autores de estos textos hicieron grandes esfuerzos para obtener tiradas, aunque sólo pudieran conseguir unos pocos ejemplares, para poder difundir sus hallazgos dentro de la comunidad terapéutica argentina.

En Argentina está ampliamente aceptado que el conocimiento pertenece a toda la humanidad y como resultado, existen numerosas oportunidades de educación continua y redes de intercambio abiertas para musicoterapeutas, estudiantes y profesionales de otras disciplinas. A numerosos eventos, conferencias, talleres e incluso congresos se pueden asistir gratuitamente y en línea. Las prácticas de publicación académica también siguen este principio, por ejemplo, el Congreso Internacional de la Facultad de Psicología de la Universidad de Buenos Aires publica cada año sus actas en línea de forma gratuita, incluyendo trabajos sobre musicoterapia, con indexación internacional para facilitar la búsqueda de textos.

En cuanto a la Musicoterapia concretamente, la revista *ECOS* (lanzada en 2016) es la principal productora de conocimiento académico de acceso abierto. Hasta la fecha, *ECOS* se puede encontrar en más de diez índices académicos, bases de datos o catálogos. *ECOS* utiliza un proceso de revisión por pares doble ciego, pone su contenido completo a disposición en línea y no cobra tarifas a sus lectores o autores (Godetti *et al.* 2020).

ECOS es editada por la Cátedra Libre de Musicoterapia de la Universidad Nacional de La Plata, universidad pública de la provincia de Buenos

Aires. Como no hay licenciatura en Musicoterapia en esa universidad, la Cátedra Libre está formada por musicoterapeutas voluntarios y estudiantes que organizan charlas de musicoterapia, conferencias y eventos académicos, y publicaciones, entrevistas y proyectos difunden investigaciones e información útiles sobre la profesión para la comunidad estudiantil de la universidad (Cannarozzo y Diaz Abrahan 2023).

Hasta aquí hemos mencionado dos universidades (una pública y otra privada, porque la carrera de la Universidad del Museo Social Argentino ya no existe) donde la gente puede formarse para practicar la Musicoterapia en Argentina; hospitales en los que musicoterapeutas pueden trabajar y continuar su educación después de recibir su diploma; y la Cátedra Libre de la Universidad Nacional de La Plata, que difunde conceptos y prácticas de la Musicoterapia. Pero esto es sólo la base para la formación continua, la forma de trabajo y la investigación que hacen los musicoterapeutas en Argentina.

Formación y actualizaciones

Formarse en Musicoterapia en el exterior no es realista para la mayoría de los profesionales en Argentina debido a la situación económica del país en comparación con el resto del mundo. Por eso, para los argentinos, el establecimiento de espacios de formación de calidad dentro de la propia Argentina es crucial. Además, como mencionamos antes, solo las personas con un título universitario de grado avalado pueden practicar Musicoterapia en Argentina, lo que significa que a gran parte de los terapeutas con diplomas extranjeros con frecuencia no se le consideran cualificados.

Antes de que las carreras de Musicoterapia universitarias fueran comunes, el Dr. Rolando Benenzon y otros dictaban cursos en varios países para difundir conocimiento de la profesión (Rejane Méndez Barcellos y Carvalho Santos 2021). Ahora, en 2024, solo Argentina tiene siete carreras donde el estudiantado puede obtener un título de Licenciado en Musicoterapia (CLAM 2021). Una de ellas es ofrecida por una universidad pública, como mencionamos antes, mientras que las otras seis funcionan en universidades privadas. Cuatro de ellas están en la ciudad de Buenos Aires, la carrera pública está en la provincia de Buenos Aires, otra está ubicada en la ciudad de Rosario (provincia de Santa Fe) y la séptima es dictada por una universidad en la provincia de Mendoza (Broqua 2023a, c; Elencwajg 2020). Para un estudiante es posible completar cualquiera de las carreras privadas en cuatro años, mientras que la universidad pública requiere un mínimo de cinco años de estudio. Cada carrera requiere que los estudiantes participen de un período de práctica supervisada antes de recibir el diploma.

Como los musicoterapeutas en Argentina deben pasar a través de carreras de grado, la Musicoterapia en el país es practicada con un nivel de exigencia similar al de la Kinesiología, la Psicología o la Fonoaudiología, cuyos profesionales estudiaron carreras que en sus universidades duran una cantidad similar de años. La exigencia de la educación universitaria permite a los musicoterapeutas participar en intercambios interdisciplinarios con sus colegas, aportando a la evolución de la Musicoterapia como una profesión y ayudando a legitimarla en instituciones de salud (Broqua 2020).

Los títulos de Licenciatura en Musicoterapia proveen de un amplio espectro de conocimiento general que prepara a sus graduados para comenzar a practicar la profesión en cualquier contexto, aunque el extenso desarrollo de la disciplina en Argentina demanda que los terapeutas se especialicen y sigan educándose continuamente. Así, varias asociaciones y terapeutas individuales han desarrollado cursos para centrarse en aplicaciones específicas de la Musicoterapia, destinados a profesionales que ya obtuvieron su diploma (Broqua 2023b).

La considerable extensión territorial de la Argentina plantea un obstáculo para diseminar la formación de musicoterapeutas a lo largo del país, y la distancia o los formatos de aprendizaje híbrido se han vuelto populares entre profesionales en Argentina. Las capacitaciones en línea también permiten a musicoterapeutas de todo el mundo acceder a este conocimiento especializado, un detalle significativo considerando que existen pocos países en el mundo con opciones sólidas de educación continua para musicoterapeutas que ya tienen sus títulos de grado (Broqua 2023a, b, c).

En los últimos años, algunas universidades han comenzado a ofrecer capacitaciones de posgrado de Musicoterapia específicas para profesionales que ya tienen un título de grado en Musicoterapia. Para diferenciar estos de los posgrados que buscan diseminar los avances de la Musicoterapia entre otras disciplinas o los que se enfocan en entrenar profesionales de diferentes disciplinas para ejercer la Musicoterapia, los llamaremos "cursos de posgrado de actualización" (Broqua 2023a, b, c).

Entre los "cursos de posgrado de actualización" universitarios en Musicoterapia se encuentran la Diplomatura en Musicoterapia Comunitaria de la Universidad Favaloro (Isla y Demkura 2023) y el Curso de Accesibilidad en Musicoterapia con Tecnología Asistiva de la UBA (Broqua 2023b, c). Ambos ofrecen la posibilidad de estudio a distancia para terapeutas que no viven en Argentina.

Al día de hoy no hay carreras de especialización de posgrado, maestrías ni doctorados en Musicoterapia en Argentina. En el sistema universitario argentino estos tres tipos de carreras de posgrado duran habitualmente entre uno y tres años (o más, dependiendo de la naturaleza del estudio) y el estudiantado recibe sus diplomas después de aprobar una tesis o trabajo final académico. Estas son cuentas pendientes que involucrarían especializaciones de muy alto nivel a las cuales, en este país, los profesionales de otras disciplinas no podrían postularse, sino solo musicoterapeutas con diplomas universitarios. Es importante recordar que los títulos de posgrado en Argentina son considerados solo como académicos. Por lo tanto, cursos de especialización, maestrías y doctorados otorgan diplomas, pero no autorizan el ejercicio de ninguna profesión determinada en Argentina.

Todos los factores mencionados han contribuido mucho al amplio desarrollo que la musicoterapia argentina ha visto en las últimas décadas; sin embargo, uno de los más cruciales momentos en el desarrollo de la profesión no fue en el ámbito de la formación sino en el jurídico: la sanción de la Ley de Ejercicio Profesional (Congreso de la Nación Argentina 2015).

La ley

Como mencioné en la primera Conferencia Internacional del Programa CRE sobre Rehabilitación Neuro-Socio-Psico en la Universidad Rayat-Bahra en Punjab, a medida que tenemos más derechos, debemos hacernos cargo de más responsabilidades (Broqua 2021).

En 1995, el Artículo 43 de la Ley de Educación Superior Argentina estableció que existen profesiones consideradas "de riesgo" porque implican el interés público y la salud o los derechos de las personas a las que sirven (Congreso de la Nación Argentina 1995; Marquina 2004). La Musicoterapia cumple con los criterios para ser considerada una profesión de este tipo, lo que significa que los musicoterapeutas en Argentina tienen mayores responsabilidades que muchas otras profesiones.

En 2015, se aprobó la Ley Nacional 27153 para regular el ejercicio profesional de la Musicoterapia en Argentina. Su texto dicta las cualificaciones que debe tener una persona para ejercer la profesión en cualquier parte de Argentina (Congreso de la Nación Argentina 2015). Estas exigencias regulatorias son incluso mayores que las que ya se cumplían en todo el país antes de que se aprobara la legislación. Esto implica que, para garantizar una profesión adecuadamente desarrollada, al igual que otras disciplinas deben respetar (Marquina 2004), absolutamente todos los musicoterapeutas deben cumplir con todas las normas: las anteriores, las implícitas y las nuevas.

La ley aprobada en 2015 estipula que cualquier persona que quiera ejercer la Musicoterapia en Argentina debe tener un título de grado en el campo (Broqua 2023a, c). Este título debe cumplir con los estándares requeridos en el país: debe ser emitido por una universidad autorizada en el territorio, debe estar regulado, y los estudiantes deben tomar un mínimo de 2600 horas de clases y prácticas (sin incluir tareas) durante un período de al menos cuatro años (Marquina 2004). Esto significó que los diplomas de Musicoterapia otorgados por cursos más cortos ya no autorizaban el ejercicio de la profesión, y quienes tenían títulos de esos programas debían someterse a educación adicional para poner sus calificaciones profesionales en cumplimiento con la ley. En el lado positivo, esto elevó los estándares académicos de la disciplina, pero también impuso mayores demandas a los terapeutas.

Esta ley también introdujo un requisito para quienes han estudiado Musicoterapia en el extranjero, obligándolos a homologar sus títulos en Argentina para trabajar como musicoterapeutas. Esta homologación confirma que los contenidos y habilidades que alguien aprendió en su carrera en una universidad extranjera son equivalentes a los programas autorizados dentro del país. Este es un punto crucial y crea un problema, teniendo en cuenta la disparidad entre la formación en Musicoterapia en Argentina frente a la de otros países, donde los musicoterapeutas a menudo reciben su formación en carreras de posgrado.

El problema es que una maestría en Musicoterapia con 60 créditos del Sistema Europeo de Transferencia y Acumulación de Créditos (ECTS) no es igual a un título argentino. Un crédito europeo representa entre 25 y 30 horas de estudio y trabajo (Palacios Picos 2004), por lo que una carrera de posgrado de 60 ECTS abarcaría alrededor de 1800 horas tanto de clases como de tiempo de estudio, una cifra mucho menor que el requisito argentino de 2600 horas de clases únicamente. Esto crea dificultades potenciales para alguien con una maestría en Musicoterapia que desee ejercer en Argentina, mientras que aquellos que han estudiado en carreras de grado en el extranjero con una exigencia similar a las de Argentina tienen un camino más directo para que sus diplomas de Musicoterapia sean aprobados por el gobierno argentino. Sin embargo, los requisitos federales no siempre son la única barrera.

Bajo la Ley Nacional 27153, cada provincia del país debe decidir si desarrolla su propia ley provincial sobre la práctica de la Musicoterapia, o si se adhiere al texto de la ley nacional (Congreso de la Nación Argentina 2015). Algunas provincias, como Buenos Aires y Entre Ríos (Gobierno de la Provincia de Buenos Aires 2006; Poder Legislativo Provincial de Entre Ríos 2012), han promulgado sus propias leyes provinciales, lo que obliga a cada musicoterapeuta que quiera trabajar en esos territorios a cumplir con sus requisitos provinciales además de los nacionales.

De acuerdo con la ley nacional, cada musicoterapeuta que desee ejercer debe presentar su título universitario a las autoridades gubernamentales correspondientes y solicitar un número de matrícula. A los profesionales de la salud no se les permite trabajar con pacientes sin este número (Pensa y Godetti 2017). Si el musicoterapeuta ha estudiado en otro país, después de homologar su título, también debe obtener este número de matrícula antes de poder comenzar a ejercer.

Hoy en día, el alcance de las leyes ha crecido, influyendo en la ubicación laboral de los musicoterapeutas. Por ejemplo, existen instituciones llamadas Centros Educativos Terapéuticos (CETs) que ofrecen servicios educativos y terapéuticos a infantes y adolescentes que, por una razón u otra, no pueden ingresar al sistema escolar. Actualmente, ningún CET puede operar legalmente si su equipo profesional no incluye al menos un musicoterapeuta registrado con un título universitario.

Estos requisitos son similares a los que deben cumplir otras profesiones en el país. Este grado de regulación nacional y provincial refleja el estatus que la Musicoterapia ha establecido en la sociedad argentina. Alcanzar este nivel de reconocimiento no ha sido fácil y solo fue posible a través de incontables esfuerzos colectivos de terapeutas y colegas a lo largo de múltiples décadas.

Investigación

Como en otras disciplinas científicas, la investigación es crucial para la evolución de la Musicoterapia y puede generar o actualizar ideas dentro del campo, que impacten no solo a la comunidad terapéutica, sino también a la sociedad en general (Godetti *et al.* 2023). Para llevar a cabo investigaciones efectivas, sin embargo, los musicoterapeutas deben adquirir formación y metodologías que les permitan alcanzar estos logros. Así que, una vez más, encontramos un vínculo entre una formación profesional sólida y el crecimiento precipitado de la comunidad musicoterapéutica en Argentina.

En una entrevista de 2019 con Franco Rolleti, la investigadora Nadia Justel comentó que cualquier profesional en un campo puede realizar investigaciones, afirmando que no se necesitan habilidades especializadas. En las Licenciaturas en Musicoterapia de la UBA y de la Universidad Maza, la formación en investigación está incorporada en el plan de estudios para equipar a todos los terapeutas con habilidades de metodología de investigación y redacción académica desde el inicio de sus carreras.

En Argentina, la investigación en Musicoterapia ha aumentado en el último medio siglo. Este incremento ha sido impulsado en parte por musicoterapeutas que ingresan a instituciones oficiales de investigación científica y tecnológica, como el Consejo Nacional de Investigaciones Científicas y Técnicas (CONICET) (Godetti *et al.* 2023). Esto representa un paso importante hacia adelante para la disciplina, abriendo nuevos desarrollos a través de la investigación y confiriendo prestigio y legitimidad adicionales a la profesión al ubicarla en los mismos círculos que otras disciplinas científicas más establecidas y reconocidas.

La investigación también permite a la comunidad musicoterapéutica establecer un estándar más alto de práctica y responsabilidad. Al mismo tiempo, los equipos interdisciplinarios demandan un conocimiento específico de la Musicoterapia, diferente al de otras disciplinas, y se espera que este conocimiento sea de calidad (Tosto 2016). El hecho de que en Argentina los musicoterapeutas estudien en una carrera de grado hace que este conocimiento de la Musicoterapia en el país sea completamente independiente del de otras profesiones.

En una investigación de 2023 sobre el estado actual de la investigación en Musicoterapia en Argentina, Godetti, López y Diaz Abrahan encontraron que la mayoría de los musicoterapeutas en Argentina no estaban realizando investigaciones. Cuando se les preguntó por qué, muchas de las respuestas de los terapeutas señalaron la falta de suficiente formación en metodología o la falta de tiempo. Esto podría estar mejorando: los autores descubrieron que hay estudiantes que se unen a equipos de investigación durante sus estudios de grado, a menudo por invitación de sus profesores (Godetti *et al.* 2023).

Esto nos deja la pregunta de qué tipos de investigación deberían priorizar los musicoterapeutas. ¿Qué es lo más valioso para la práctica funcional de la disciplina? ¿Qué tipo de investigación ayudaría a establecer aún más la legitimidad de la Musicoterapia como disciplina científica? Virginia Tosto explora estas preguntas en una publicación de 2016 en *ECOS*, delineando áreas de interés que incluyen la necesidad de validar la efectividad de las intervenciones terapéuticas; los instrumentos utilizados para la recopilación de datos, y la comunicación de los resultados tanto a los musicoterapeutas como a la comunidad científica en general (Tosto 2016).

En otros países, donde la formación puede recibirse como un título de posgrado, los musicoterapeutas pueden haber completado su formación previa en otra disciplina. Este conocimiento previo puede enriquecer la Musicoterapia (Eslava Mejía 2019), ya que vemos investigaciones valiosas sobre objetivos terapéuticos específicos como las habilidades motoras o el lenguaje (preocupaciones principales de kinesiólogos y fonoaudiólogos, respectivamente) llevadas a cabo en el contexto de la Musicoterapia por profesionales con formación previa en esas disciplinas.

Este tipo de intervenciones no siempre puede ser implementado fácilmente por otros musicoterapeutas que no tienen la formación previa adecuada. Y este conocimiento no siempre representa un conocimiento específico de la Musicoterapia, sino un conocimiento transdisciplinario. Por eso, es esencial aumentar la investigación en Argentina que tenga en cuenta estas especificidades locales que la profesión presenta en el territorio.

Conclusión

La débil economía nacional argentina ha obstaculizado en gran medida el acceso a textos académicos y formación publicados o impartidos en otros países para musicoterapeutas que ejercen en el país. Esto ha empujado a terapeutas e investigadores argentinos a convertirse en prolíficos editores, docentes y organizadores, creando los recursos necesarios para nutrir el desarrollo de su profesión a nivel local. También significa que los frutos de estos esfuerzos son extremadamente asequibles para los miembros de la comunidad de musicoterapia a nivel global.

Argentina mantiene opciones para que sus habitantes estudien y reciban Musicoterapia de forma gratuita. Este acceso a la educación y tratamiento gratuito se extiende a las personas que viven en Argentina, incluso a los no ciudadanos. Debido a que la formación en Musicoterapia en Argentina se lleva a cabo a nivel de licenciatura, existen cursos de actualización de posgrado en Musicoterapia que se adhieren a altos estándares académicos. Muchos de estos cursos también se imparten de manera remota, lo que permite que terapeutas de todo el mundo accedan a estas formaciones.

Desde la década de 1960, cuando el Dr. Rolando Benenzon y otros pioneros comenzaron a establecer la disciplina en Argentina, se ha llevado a cabo una gran cantidad de investigaciones. El acceso a muchos de estos estudios es gratuito para cualquier persona en cualquier parte del mundo, lo que convierte a Argentina en un recurso importante para la investigación en Musicoterapia a nivel global.

La investigación realizada en Argentina también nos permite mejorar constantemente las intervenciones y establecer los mismos rigurosos estándares científicos para la Musicoterapia que se aplican a otras profesiones. Si bien gran parte de las investigaciones surgen desde necesidades regionales o locales, muchos de los resultados de estos estudios tienen el potencial de ser aplicados en el extranjero debido a las amplias similitudes entre las poblaciones de pacientes en todo el mundo (por ejemplo, pacientes con trastorno del espectro autista o parálisis cerebral).

Más allá de la investigación, la educación y el acceso, los logros jurídicos de la comunidad musicoterapéutica en Argentina también han sido fundamentales para impulsar el amplio desarrollo de la disciplina. Tanto la ley nacional como las leyes provinciales sobre la práctica profesional y el acceso a los tratamientos representan ejemplos y modelos que pueden ser seguidos por naciones que aún luchan por políticas que permitan que la

Musicoterapia se aplique de la mejor manera posible para sus pueblos. Los desafíos únicos que ha enfrentado la Musicoterapia argentina a lo largo de su extenso desarrollo han creado una comunidad académica y terapéutica con mucho que ofrecer al resto del mundo. Comunicar estas posibilidades es parte de nuestra responsabilidad profesional para ayudar al crecimiento global de nuestra amada profesión.

CHAPTER 8

OVERVIEW OF MUSIC THERAPY TRAINING IN LATIN AMERICA

PATRICIA ZARATE DE PEREZ

Introduction

This chapter will present a summary of music therapy training in Latin America and the Caribbean. The data presented comes from a research project from the Latin American Music Therapy Committee (Comité Latinoamericano de Musicoterapia, CLAM). I started working virtually with CLAM during the 2020 COVID-19 pandemic as part of the Training Process Committee (Comisión de Procesos de Formación Profesional). In 2023 I was elected to serve as Vice-President of the organization with Lorena Buenseñor of Uruguay as President-elect and Flor Ruva of Argentina as Secretary-elect.

As stated on the organization's website:

> The Latin American Music Therapy Committee (CLAM) is a non-profit organization, established since 1993 by organizations linked to different fields of research, theory and practice of music therapy in Latin America. The CLAM aims to bring together, integrate, link and represent participating entities in the area of music therapy, based in Latin American countries, as well as promote communication and integration of their scientific, academic, theoretical and professional activities. Since its creation, each country has determined the form of participation in the committee, including representation through a delegate, being respectful of the process experienced in each country, and understanding that the professional reality is different, according to each context. CLAM does not receive financial contributions of any kind, understanding that the delegates fulfill their role voluntarily with

the sole purpose of making a contribution to the professional development of Music Therapy in Latin America.

This summary of music therapy training in the region was organized during 2020 and 2021; at the time, the President of CLAM was Mariane Oselame. The goal of the study was to collect data about music therapy training in Latin America via a digital questionnaire that was later transformed into a system map available on the organization's website.

In this chapter, I will discuss various programs, to contextualize the current state of music therapy training in Latin America. It is important to recognize the fact that Latin American music therapists are always adapting to rapid shifts in their socioeconomic and political realities, as is the profession as a whole. As such, it is expected that this report will be revised at least once every three to five years.

Latin American music therapy training has a rich history and consists of training created by therapists in the region mixed with resources drawn from abroad. New training is increasingly diverse in terms of how it is presented. Especially since the COVID-19 pandemic, it is more common to see both asynchronous and synchronous virtual training, hybrid models, and what I refer to as hyper-hybrid, which blends all the above elements with in-person training.

This report shows that Latin American training in music therapy is also informed by international training creating a diverse disciplinary space. Students from countries that do not have formal music therapy training return from studies abroad in the United States, Europe, and other regions of the world to build programs in their countries of origin. Even within Latin America there is a great deal of movement and cross-pollination of ideas—students from all over the region study in countries like Argentina, Brazil, Chile, or Colombia, which host affordable Spanish-language courses. After the data was collected, two system maps were created via the app kumu.io, one reflecting the Music Therapy curricula of the Master's degree programs, and the other covering the Bachelor's degree programs. The maps show all the classes that are included in most Latin American music therapy programs.[1]

This final report is an introductory study of the music therapy training processes in Latin America, and it only includes formal university training and what we consider education within Western Eurocentric epistemologies. It shows the complexity and diversity of the region, as well as its potential for development; however, it does not include Indigenous

---

1   View these maps at www.musicoterapiaclam.com/mapa-de-sistemas

epistemologies or any other non-standard systems. Most importantly, it shows how Latin America is involved in the making and re-making of music therapy as a discipline, and what is considered important for the profession in each country.

The members of the CLAM Training Commission (Comisión de Formación) who carried out the investigation and wrote the report include: Karin Biegun (Argentina), Mayara Ribeiro (Brazil), Patricia Lallana (Chile), Diego Torres (Colombia), Patricia Zarate de Perez (Panama), Ana María Passadore (Uruguay), and Lorena Buenseñor (Coordinator, Uruguay).

In December 2021, the Commission on Training Process Committee (Comisión de Procesos de Formación Profesional) created by CLAM published a report with updated information on the academic institutions that provide university-level professional training in music therapy in various countries. To collect the information, the Committee designed a questionnaire to obtain both qualitative and quantitative data that could be used and presented in a precise and accurate fashion.

The questions included:

- Does your country have training in music therapy?
- Is this professional training?
- Is your institution public or private?
- How many professional music therapists does your institution graduate annually?
- How many people have graduated since the training first started?
- Which ministry recognizes your music therapy training?
- What are the requisites to enter training?
- How many hours does the training require to graduate?
- How many hours of practice does the training include?

Data collection was carried out in two stages. The first, during 2020, focused on preparing a questionnaire to be filled out by universities, educational institutions, and other associations in the 36 countries of Latin America and the Caribbean. We received 19 responses in 2020 and another 4 in 2021. In the second stage, during 2021, the questionnaire was improved in order to collect more data and prepare the final report, which was then published in December of that year.

For each country, the data indicates the existence of any music therapy training programs, the number of years the programs have run and their historical background, the type of degree awarded to students, the number of academic hours, and entry and exit requirements, among other things. This report was produced to further develop the work of several authors who are frequently cited in music therapy research, such as Juanita Eslava Mejía (2019), Patricia Sabbatella (2004), Lia Rejane Mendes Barcellos (1999), and Karina Ferrari (n.d.), among others, who made early efforts to catalog the educational environment for practitioners in Latin America.

I will now provide a synthesis of the information presented in the report, starting with the general background of each country with regard to music therapy training. The data is then presented in table format, and I will close the chapter by sharing the reflections of the team in charge of the research along with my own conclusions.

Music therapy training in Latin America, according to the questionnaire

Eleven Latin American countries present training in music therapy associated with a university: Argentina, Bolivia, Brazil, Chile, Colombia, Cuba, Mexico, Panama, Paraguay, Uruguay, and Venezuela.

Argentina

In the 1940s, Dr. Carolina Tobar García, together with music professor María Laura Nardelli, began to work with music in schools for children with special needs to improve their physical and mental health. Other music teachers who represented different specialties joined the project—Helga Lancy de Epstein, focusing on the study of the voice; Frances Wolff, focusing on the blind; Lidia Penovi, on hearing loss; Violeta Hemsy de Gainza and Viviana Brenner de Aisenwasser, in the area of learning disabilities—along with a number of doctors, psychologists, and speech therapists. At the same time, Dr. Rolando Benenzon, a psychiatrist and musician, and Dr. Bernaldo de Quirós, a pioneer of speech therapy in Argentina, began to investigate the effects of music on different pathologies.

On July 23, 1966, in the Magna classroom of the Faculty of Medicine of the University of Buenos Aires (Facultad de Medicina de la Universidad de Buenos Aires, UBA), the Argentine Association of Music Therapy (Asociación Argentina de Musicoterapia, ASAM) was formed. That year, its members presented the proposal to create a degree program at the University of Salvador (Universidad del Salvador, USAL), thus establishing the first university training in music therapy in Latin America. On December 16, 1966, the music therapy department was created, with the music therapy course consisting of three years and a total of 26 subjects. In 1967, under the direction of Dr. Benenzon, the program commenced at the School of Otoneuro Phoniatrics of the Faculty of Medicine of El Salvador (Escuela de Otoneuro Foniatría de la Facultad de Medicina de El Salvador), dedicated to disturbances in human communication. The pioneering music educators dedicated to this specialty made up the first teaching staff of the program. Its first graduates between 1969 and 1970 were Amelia Ferraggina, Nora Moyano, Elena Flores, Susana Dato, María Rosa Alfonsin, and María Celia Pérez, all music teachers.

Over the following decades, the course has been taught in other Argentinian schools, which has enriched and complexified professional training for music therapists in the region. Music therapy is currently taught as a Bachelor's degree in six universities located in various areas of Argentina. The courses, all recognized by the Ministry of Education (Ministerio de Educación), were included from their creation in the following institutions: University of Salvador (Universidad del Salvador, USAL) (1966, City of Buenos Aires), University of Buenos Aires (Universidad de Buenos Aires, UBA) (1993, Avellaneda headquarters, province of Buenos Aires), Interamerican Open University (Universidad Abierta Interamericana) (1995, Rosario Headquarters and 1996, City of Buenos Aires headquarters), Maimónides University (Universidad Maimónides) (2006, City of Buenos Aires), Juan Agustín Maza University (Universidad Juan Agustín Maza) (2016, City of Mendoza), and University of Business and Social Sciences (Universidad de Ciencias Empresariales y Sociales) (2019, City of Buenos Aires).

Bolivia

Starting in 2009, there were diploma programs teaching about the music therapy field. In 2019 a four-month diploma program, titled "Introduction to Clinical, Social-Communal, and Educational Music Therapy," was offered thanks to the collaboration of the International Institute of Educational Sciences (Instituto Internacional de Ciencias de la Educación), the Specialized Continuing Education Department (Unidad de Formación Continua Especializada), and the Association of Music Therapists from Bolivia (Asociación de Musicoterapeutas de Bolivia). There were five versions of the Introduction to Music Therapy courses in La Paz and two versions of the Diploma in Children's Music Therapy thanks to a collaboration with the University of Murcia (Universidad de Murcia).

Since 2022, Bolivia has had a diploma program that is carried out thanks to the alliance of the Bolivian Evangelical University (Universidad Evangélica Boliviana) with the Music Therapy and Health Foundation (Fundación Musicoterapia y Salud) through the Autonomous University of Madrid (Universidad Autónoma de Madrid, UAM) in Spain.[2] As of 2024, Bolivia is organizing a Master's degree program with a local university.

---

2   See www.musicoterapiaysalud.org for further information.

Brazil

The first steps of music therapy in Brazil were taken in the 1960s in the state of Rio de Janeiro, where the Brazilian Music Therapy Association (Asociación Brasileña de Musicoterapia, ABMT) was founded (COSTA 2020). Given the growing need for training in the area, courses were being developed, and in 1970 the first graduate training in music therapy in Brazil began. Initially it was offered at the Faculty of Musical Education of Paraná (Facultad de Educación Musical de Paraná), today, Faculties of Arts of Paraná (Facultades de Artes de Paraná, FAP). In 1972, the Brazilian Conservatory of Music of Rio de Janeiro (Conservatorio Brasileño de Música de Río de Janeiro, CBM – CEU) offered the first graduate course in music therapy (COSTA 2020), which was recognized by the Federal Council of Education (Consejo Federal de Educación) in 1978 (SITE AMT-RJ).

The state of Rio de Janeiro played a key role in creating courses in other Brazilian states including Goiás and Paraná, often sending teachers to run courses or help with their organization. From there, new courses emerged, initially, as graduate courses and later, in some states, as undergraduate courses. The first graduation course in a federal public institution was started in 1999 by the School of Music and Performing Arts of the Federal University of Goiás (Escuela de Música y Artes Escénicas de la Universidad Federal de Goiás).

Music therapy training in Brazil began through extension courses, which later became graduate courses and in some cases, undergraduate courses. Currently, music therapy training in Brazil can be done in two ways: through postgraduate studies (two years) or through undergraduate studies (three or four years).

Undergraduate training is offered by the following public institutions: Federal University of Goiás (Universidad Federal de Goiás) (implemented in 1999), the State University of Paraná (Universidad Estatal de Paraná) (implemented in 1983), the Federal University of Minas Gerais (Universidad Federal de Minas Gerais) (implemented in 2009), or the Federal University of Rio de Janeiro (Universidad Federal de Río de Janeiro) (implemented in 2019). In the private system, the options are United Metropolitan Colleges (Faculdades Metropolitanas Unidas) (implemented in 2001) and Faculdades EST (implemented in 2003). Regarding graduate courses, there are several institutions, including the Fenix Institute (Instituto Fenix) and Faculdade Censupeg, among others, that train professionals in different places, currently reaching almost all Brazilian states.

Training courses must be recognized by the Ministry of Education (Ministerio de Educación). To verify the quality of the music therapist's training, the Brazilian Union of Music Therapy Associations (União Brasileira das

Associações de Musicoterapia, UBAM) carries out a consultative evaluation of the graduate courses. This allows those interested in pursuing a postgraduate degree to consult UBAM regarding a program's compliance with government regulations on professional training.

Chile
Music therapy training in Chile was created in 1999 by music therapist Susanne Bauer with the support of academics from the University of Chile (Universidad de Chile), including Dr. Luis Merino, dean of the faculty at that time, along with Professor Mimi Marinovic and music therapists Valeska Sigren, Patricia Ubilla, and Patricia Lallana. It is a Specialization course taught by the Graduate School of Arts of the University of Chile (Escuela Superior de Artes de la Universidad de Chile), under the title "Postgraduate Course in Art Therapies with a Focus in Music Therapy." As the only program in Chile that trains specialists in music therapy, the stated objective of the postgraduate degree is to train highly qualified and well-rounded practitioners who are prepared to work in education, health, communities, or organizations.

In 2005, the Chilean Association of Music Therapy (Asociación Chilena de Musicoterapia, ACHIM) was created, which brings together music therapists from different training programs, both national and foreign, whose main objective is to "contribute to the development of a professional community of music therapists, provide ethical guidance regarding their work. Professionalize, promote and disseminate music therapy in Chile, through outreach, training, and research activities in this area."[3]

Colombia
Colombian music therapy training began with Professor Carmen Barbosa Luna, Dr. Miguel Ángel Suarez, Professor Álvaro Ramírez, and Dr. Juanita Eslava, at the National University of Colombia (Universidad Nacional de Colombia) in 2006. It was initially assigned a Specialization program in the Faculty of Arts (Facultad de Artes), and the following year it transitioned from Specialization to a Master's degree and was redesignated.

In Colombia, the National University of Colombia is the only university that has formal training at university level in music therapy. In recent years, some universities have begun to set up music therapy diplomas, courses, and workshops for dissemination of specific knowledge for both music therapists and the general community.

---

3   https://achim.cl/musicoterapia-definicion/ser-musicoterapeuta

Cuba

Between 2008 and 2010, Dr. Fernández de Juan coordinated the Specialization in Music Therapy (with a Master's degree) as a joint program of the Faculty of Psychology of the University of Havana (Facultad de Psicología de la Universidad de La Habana) and the Faculty of Music of the Higher Institute of Art (Facultad de Música del Instituto Superior de Arte). The Master's program was taught by professors from Canada, Argentina, Uruguay, and Colombia.

The Association of Cuban Music Therapists (Asociación de Musicoterapeutas de Cuba, AMC) is the main entity that organizes the country's practitioners. Currently there is no professional training in music therapy in Cuba; however, there are online courses, introductory classes on music therapy as part of other programs, individualized training, informal mentoring, and annual events on music therapy. As of 2024 Cuban music therapists have been organizing events such as Histamed International Colloquium (History, Art and Medicine) (Coloquio Internacional Histamed (Historia, Arte y Medicina)) focused on celebrating "20 years of interdisciplinarity in pursuit of human improvement." Some of the events include the XIII International Colloquium of Integrating History, Art and Medicine (XIII Coloquio Internacional Integrador de Historia, Arte y Medicina), the IV HistArtMed Meeting between cultures (IV Encuentro HistArtMed entre culturas), the IV International Music and Health Workshop "Dr. Antonio M. Gordon" (IV Taller Internacional de Música y Salud "Dr. Antonio M. Gordon"), among others (private message to author, with poster and explanation of the events).

Mexico

Music therapy training in Mexico has as its precursor Dr. Víctor Muñoz Pólit who, through the Mexican Institute of Humanist Music Therapy (Instituto Mexicano de Musicoterapia Humanista), began, in 1996, accompanying a team of professionals with specialty training in humanist music therapy. The Diploma in Humanist Music Therapy was also taught at the National Autonomous University of Mexico (Universidad Nacional Autónoma de México, UNAM) in 1998 and 2002. In 2012, the Master's degree in Humanistic Psychomusical Theories and Techniques was launched (with official endorsement from the Ministry of Public Education (Ministerio de Educación Pública), 2013–15), and subsequently, from 2015 until the current date, the Master's degree in Humanistic Music Therapy has been taught.

As of the date of this report (2024), other training is offered at diploma level and there are courses in other institutions, among which the Diploma in Clinical and Psychosocial Music Therapy stands out, as it is taught by UNAM in its Faculty of Music.

Panama

Music therapy training in Panama is marked by the work of women, and begins in the early 1990s with Mariela Correa, a pioneer of music therapy in Panama, who studied the therapeutic effects of music in Peru and Argentina and worked with children at the Panamanian Institute for Special Habilitation (Instituto Panameño de Habilitación Especial, IPHE). Later, in 1994, Vilma Esquivel graduated from the Catholic University of America in Washington, DC as a music therapist. After graduation, she returned to Panama and founded the "In Harmony" Music Therapy Center (Centro de Musicoterapia "En Armonía") in Panama City, where she offered music therapy courses and services until 2004. Melanie Taylor, who graduated with a Master's degree in Music Therapy from Drexel University College of Medicine in the United States in 1999, has offered music therapy courses, services, and a diploma program with the University of the Americas (Universidad Especializada de las Américas, UDELAS).

Also notable are Paola Casal, who graduated in 2007 with a Master's degree in Communication and Non-Verbal Language: Psychomotor Skills, Music Therapy and Performance from the Ca' Foscari University in Venice, Italy; Sarah Muñoz, who graduated from the University of Salvador (Universidad del Salvador, USAL) in Argentina in 2020 as a music therapist; and Ekaterina Zúñiga, who graduated with a Master's degree in Music Therapy from the University of Derby, England, in 2023.

Patricia Zarate de Perez, Chilean by birth and nationalized Panamanian, obtained her music therapy degree at Berklee College of Music (Boston, US) in 1999, beginning her work in Panama in 2003 with classes, mentoring, formal and informal events at the Panama Jazz Festival and the Danilo Pérez Foundation. In January 2013, Patricia founded the Latin American Music Therapy Symposium and in 2015 the Music Therapy Center of Panama. In 2020, all the aforementioned music therapists came together to form the Panamanian Association of Music Therapy (Asociación Panameña de Musicoterapia, APAMU), which, since its inception, has led a campaign to approve a music therapy law to regulate the practice of the profession in Panama. This policy was approved by the Panamanian congress and the President of Panama in October 2022.

Paraguay

Paraguay has offered university training since 2019, based at Nuestra Señora de la Asunción Catholic University, within the framework of private education. The degree to be accredited is a Bachelor's or Baccalaureate degree (Bachelor's in Music Therapy). This professional training is recognized by the Ministry of Education (Ministerio de Educación), with national scope under the responsibility of the National Council of Higher Education (Consejo Nacional de Educación Superior).

Uruguay

Music therapy training in Uruguay began in 1967, with the help of Lyda Florez, a specialist teacher who developed her work in the educational field working with disabled students. She trained with Dr. Rolando Benenzon in Argentina, and together they coordinated the first music therapy training at the Center for the Arts (Centro de las Artes). The First School of Music Therapy (Primera Escuela de Musicoterapia, PEMU) was then created, where the first generation of Uruguayan music therapists graduated following Dr. Benenzon's approach and model.

In 2004, Uruguay organized and hosted the Congress for the Latin American Music Therapy Committee (Comité Latinoamericano de Musicoterapia, CLAM), in Montevideo, with Clive Robbins as a special guest. This event constituted an even greater boost for the official qualification of the Music Therapy degree in Uruguay.

In 2010, the CEDIIAP University Center (Centro Universitario CEDIIAP) established a Music Therapy degree, and the corresponding qualification process began. It is worth mentioning that, given the lack of previous academic training in the country in this area of study, the university relied on expert music therapists from abroad with experience in teaching and training to design and configure the new degree, which culminated in 2016 in an official qualification and recognition process.

Uruguay now offers undergraduate training at a private university (CEDIIAP), recognized by the Ministry of Education and Culture (Ministerio de Educación y Cultura, MEC) and the Ministry of Public Health (Ministerio de Salud Pública, MSP). It should be noted that the Association of Uruguayan Music Therapists (Asociación de Musicoterapeutas Uruguayos, AMU) is currently processing the approval of the degree to be taught at the Public University of the Eastern Republic of Uruguay (Universidad Pública de la República Oriental del Uruguay, UDELAR).

Venezuela

Dr. Yadira Albornoz is the first academically credentialed person in charge of music therapy training in Venezuela. She created the Venezuelan Music Therapy Foundation (Fundación Venezolana de Musicoterapia, FUNVE-MUST) in 2010. Dr. Albornoz is a clarinetist, singer, composer, and professor at the School of Music of the University of the Andes (Escuela de Música de la Universidad de los Andes), holding a doctorate in Philosophy of Music Therapy and a Master's degree in Music.

In 2015 Dr. Albornoz managed to implement a five-semester postgraduate program of Specialization in Music Therapy that ran at the University of the Andes based in Mérida until 2017, from which a total of 23 music therapy specialists graduated. This course is not currently being taught.

Countries without university training programs in music therapy
Barbados
Foreign training has been carried out in Barbados. Thanks to the Commonwealth of Learning and Canada/STARR Bajan, classes have been offered on the Berklee College of Music virtual platform taught by music therapist Suzanne Hanser. Introductory courses have also been held at Barbados Community College by music therapist Tamara Adams. Likewise, the University of the West Indies, St. Augustine, currently has an introductory class in music therapy.

Cayman Islands
Music therapist Julianne Parolisi, a professor at Lesley University in Boston, MA, founder and director of Music Therapy Without Borders – Cayman Music Therapy, points out that in the Cayman Islands there is neither a professional association of music therapists nor a music therapy career track, but there is individual training and informal mentoring, including classes at two local universities. Having established the first music therapy practice in the Cayman Islands in 2010, Parolisi has undertaken multiple informal training to integrate music therapy principles into education and health. She has additionally conducted mentorships including shadowing opportunities, volunteering, and finding international training programs for people interested in the profession.

Costa Rica
Despite the lack of university training in music therapy, in Costa Rica there is some access to knowledge about various music therapy approaches through complementary courses in traditional health or artistic degree programs. Specifically, music therapy is taught through introductory classes (as part of a health or artistic career), certificates or diplomas from other non-university institutions, personalized individual training, informal mentoring, and annual events such as symposiums, conferences, clubs, etc.

According to information collected through the research study, the absence of a music therapy association makes establishing the presence of the discipline in the higher education system difficult. It is held that neither the public nor private educational bureaucratic system is flexible enough to develop or incorporate a university training program at this point.

Dominican Republic

In the Dominican Republic there is no professional training in music therapy, although introductory classes have been held as part of some artistic or healthcare career tracks, along with annual music therapy events. Several music therapists from the Dominican Republic have graduated from Berklee College of Music music therapy department, and have worked nationally and internationally as music therapists and educators.

Ecuador

According to the data from the research study, music therapy is still a new profession in Ecuador. Education is marred by misinformation, however, and the courses taught are not endorsed for professional practice. The majority of professional music therapists are trained abroad. Non-university training is framed within the course format of other disciplines, such as the Master's in Psychotherapy at the Technical University of Ambato (Universidad Técnica de Ambato, UTA).

Among the private training one is focused on acquiring music therapy tools, with a duration of between 500 and 1000 hours. However, it is not recognized by any ministry or secretary of state, but only as an introductory class as part of a health or artistic career. In addition, some certificates or diplomas are taught by other non-university institutions. As of September 2024, Ecuador has organized the Ecuadorian Association of Music Therapists (Asociación Ecuatoriana de Musicoterapeutas) and is in the process of applying to be part of the Latin American Music Therapy Committee (Comité Latinoamericano de Musicoterapia, CLAM).

El Salvador

El Salvador does not yet offer professional training at university level. Current options include online courses, introductory classes as part of a career in health or the arts, personalized individual training, informal mentoring, and annual events such as symposiums, conferences, clubs, and others. As of September 2024, Rocio Moreno, Katherine Zelaya, and Estella Zelaya have combined their efforts to open the Music Therapy Center of El Salvador (Centro de Musicoterapia de El Salvador), the first of its kind in the country.

Guatemala

Educational training in Guatemala is currently carried out by a therapeutic duo, which, with the "Music Therapy Guatemala" initiative, teaches introductory experiential workshops in music therapy and individual treatment. According to information collected through the questionnaire, there is interest in creating a professional training program. A curriculum for a diploma or specialization is currently being prepared for presentation to different universities in the country.

Haiti

In Haiti there is no professional training in music therapy, but there are some music therapists from Haiti who study and work in the US.

Honduras

Honduras does not have university professional training in music therapy, and nor does it have any association of music therapists. We only know of one person interested in training who is pursuing a Bachelor's degree in Uruguay.

Peru

In Peru there is still no university training program in music therapy, but rather, some presentations, diplomas, and certificates from various national and international institutions. There is currently a research and development center that has dedicated itself to raising awareness of the need for professional training in music therapy. The Peruvian Music Therapy Association (Asociación Peruana de Musicoterapia) was established in 2022, and organized the first congress of music therapy in the country in February 2024.

Puerto Rico

Puerto Rico hosts the Puerto Rico Music Therapy Association (Asociación de Musicoterapia de Puerto Rico), founded in 2021. As reported through the questionnaire, it is held that the public and private educational bureaucratic systems do not have the flexibility required to incorporate university training. This results in a number of diverse undergraduate professional training offers in Puerto Rico associated with other careers, such as introductory classes in health or arts careers and professional internships for those who need an internship to complete their academic degree and/or achieve certification from the examining board in the US. Likewise, there are other alternatives, such as online degree courses that do not require any logged hours of practice, other degree courses that require approximately

200 hours, and finally, courses in the US that have a total of 1200 hours of practice as a requirement.

As of August 2024, Puerto Rico is working closely with the American Music Therapy Association® (AMTA) to open the Bachelor's of Music Therapy at Puerto Rico Conservatory (Bachillerato en Musicoterapia en el Conservatorio de Puerto Rico) in 2025. We also know that music therapists from Puerto Rico are working to pass a law that will regulate the profession on the island.

Trinidad and Tobago

In Trinidad and Tobago there is a professional music therapy association called the Music Therapy Association of Trinidad and Tobago, but there is no professional music therapy training. Academic training is given through introductory classes that are part of a health or arts career, specifically a three-month exposure class in a Bachelor's degree in Music.

Summary of pre- and post-degree university training processes in Latin America and the Caribbean

Country/ training institution	General characteristics of the training	Curriculum
Argentina: University of Salvador (Universidad del Salvador, USAL)	Degree training at a private university Started in 1967 First clinical practices in Braulio Moyano Hospital (Hospital Braulio Aurelio Moyano), the Municipal Hospital of José Tiburcio Borda, and the Vitra Foundation (La fundación VITRA) Latest study plan: 1995 Average number of annual graduates: 50–55 Total graduates since its inception: 2000	Degree awarded: Bachelor's in Music Therapy Entry requirement: General admission course and musical leveling course, musical audition/personal interview Four-year course Total number of hours: 3240, of which 648 are supervised practice Graduation requirement: Final written integrative work with oral defense

Argentina: University of Buenos Aires (Universidad de Buenos Aires, UBA)	Degree training at a public university Average number of graduates per year: approx. 35 Total graduates since its inception: approx. 1000	Degree awarded: Bachelor's in Music Therapy Entry requirement: Audition or preparatory course Five-year course (four years plus common basic cycle) Total number of hours: 3228, of which 540 are internships Graduation requirement: Written presentation of thesis and oral defense of thesis in front of a jury
Argentina: Interamerican Open University (Universidad Abierta Interamericana, UAI)	Degree training at a private university Average number of graduates per year: UAI Rosario: 8, UAI Buenos Aires: 3–5 Total graduates since its inception: UAI Rosario: 106, UAI Buenos Aires: 174	Degree awarded: Bachelor's in Music Therapy Entry requirement: Musical audition/personal interview Four-year course Total number of hours: 3408, of which 162 are supervised pre-professional practice Graduation requirement: Written presentation of the thesis and presentation of the thesis in front of a jury
Argentina: Maimónides University (Universidad Maimónides)	No information	Degree awarded: Bachelor's in Music Therapy Four-year course Total number of hours: 2712
Argentina: Maza University (Universidad Juan Agustín Maza, UMAZA)	Degree training at a private university Number of graduates: No graduates to date (2021). First cohort was in the process of professional internships and thesis preparation	Degree awarded: Bachelor's in Music Therapy Entry requirement: Personal interview Four-year course Total number of hours: 2845, of which 600 are supervised practice Graduation requirement: Written presentation of the thesis and oral defense of the thesis

cont.

159

Country/ training institution	General characteristics of the training	Curriculum
Argentina: University of Business and Social Sciences (Universidad de Ciencias Empresariales y Sociales, UCES)	Degree training at a private university Number of graduates: They were not registered as of the date of the report (2021)	Degree awarded: Bachelor's in Music Therapy Entry requirement: Musical audition and personal interview Four-year course Total number of hours: 2672, of which 576 are pre-professional practice Graduation requirement: Written presentation of the final work and oral defense of the thesis
Barbados	No programs or institutions provide training in music therapy	Does not apply
Bolivia: Bolivian Evangelical University (Universidad Evangélica Boliviana)	Diploma program carried out in alliance with the Music Therapy and Health Foundation (Fundación Musicoterapia y Salud) through the Autonomous University of Madrid (Universidad Autónoma de Madrid, UAM)	No information

Brazil: Public institutions: Federal University of Goiás (Universidad Federal de Goiás); Paraná State University (Universidad Estatal de Paraná); Federal University of Minas Gerais (Universidad Federal de Minas Gerais); Federal University of Rio de Janeiro (Universidad Federal de Río de Janeiro)	There are two training routes: undergraduate studies, lasting three to four years; postgraduate specialization studies, lasting two years All training must be recognized by the Ministry of Education	Degree awarded (pre-degree): Bachelor's in Music Therapy Entry requirements: Through academic writing and/or proof of musical knowledge Four-year course Total number of hours: between 3000 and 4000, of which approximately 300 are internships and at least 60 hours supervised Graduation requirement: Complete and comply with all the requirements of the degree, with presentation of the final thesis and oral defense of the same Degree awarded (postgraduate): Music Therapy Specialist Entry requirements: Certificate of tertiary training and/or proof of musical knowledge
Private institutions: United Metropolitan Faculties; EST Faculties Specialization courses: Fenix Institute, Faculdade Censupeg, among others		Two-year course Total hours: Minimum of 360 hours, of which 60 are practical and internship and 20 supervised Graduation requirement: Complete and comply with all postgraduate requirements, with presentation of the final thesis
Cayman Islands	No university training	Does not apply

cont.

Country/ training institution	General characteristics of the training	Curriculum
Chile: University of Chile (Universidad de Chile)	Postgraduate specialization course in Art Therapies, a mention in Music Therapy Started in 1999 Graduates by 2021: approximately 500	Degree awarded: Postgraduate in Music Therapy Duration: Three semesters Total hours: 477 contact hours, of which the first two semesters are theoretical classes and the third a professional practice of six hours per week Entry requirements: An academic degree or professional title in the areas of Music, Health, Education, or another related area. If the professional title is not in the area of Music, the applicant must have mastery of a musical instrument, which will be evaluated during the application process Graduation requirements: Write a report and take a final exam
Colombia: National University of Colombia (Universidad Nacional de Colombia)	Postgraduate program Began in 2007 Graduates by 2021: 154 Music Therapy Master's, average of 10 graduates per year	Degree awarded: Master's in Music Therapy Admission: Personal interview, musical aptitude test, and academic writing (proposal and work intention essay) Program duration: Two years Total hours: 3216 hours of work, of which 1056 are internships and internships under supervision Graduation requirement: Complete the Master's subjects, culminating in the presentation of the final work and oral defense of the same
Costa Rica	No university education	Does not apply

Cuba: University of Havana and Higher Institute of Art (Universidad de La Habana e Instituto Superior de Arte)	Joint specialization program of the Faculty of Psychology of the University of Havana and the Faculty of Music of the Higher Institute of Art, with the rank of Master's degree Taught between 2008 and 2010 Graduates: 15 professionals	Degree awarded: No information Total hours: Between 1000 and 2000, of which 50 to 100 were professional practice
Cuba: Havana University of Medical Sciences (Universidad de Ciencias Médicas de La Habana)	Music and Health Diploma program at the National Council of Scientific Health Societies Carried out between 2020 and 2021	Degree awarded: No information 95 academic credits Duration 1410 hours, part-time in-person modality Curriculum: Module I: Introduction to music therapy Module II: Music and medicine Module III: Musical skills and competencies necessary for musical-therapeutic exercise
Dominican Republic	No university education	Does not apply
Ecuador	No university education	Does not apply
El Salvador	No university education	Does not apply
Guatemala	No university education	Does not apply
Haiti	No university education	Does not apply
Honduras	No university education	Does not apply
Mexico: Mexican Institute of Humanist Music Therapy (Instituto Mexicano de Musicoterapia Humanista, IMH)	Master's program in Humanistic Music Therapy Started in 2015	Duration: 570 total hours, of which 195 are practical work

cont.

Country/ training institution	General characteristics of the training	Curriculum
Mexico: National Autonomous University of Mexico (Universidad Nacional Autónoma de México, UNAM)	Diploma program in Clinical and Psychosocial Music Therapy	Degree awarded: Diploma in Clinical and Psychosocial Music Therapy Duration: 117 hours in blended mode
Panama: University of the Americas (Universidad Especializada de las Américas, UDELAS)	Diploma program in Music Therapy (postgraduate) (2017–18: 20 graduates) (Master's in Music Therapy started in 2024)	Diploma awarded: Diploma in Music Therapy Admission: Personal interview, musical aptitude test, and academic writing Duration: Six months Five study modules Total hours: 240 of teaching, of which 80 are of practice Grants 15 university credits Graduation requirement: Complete and comply with all the subjects of the diploma, presentation of final work and a written piece of research work
Paraguay: Catholic University of Asunción (Universidad Católica "Nuestra Señora de la Asunción" (private university)	Bachelor's or Baccalaureate pre-degree program Begun in 2019 No graduates to date	Degree awarded: Bachelor's in Music Therapy Entry: Academic writing Duration: Four years Total number of hours: 3000 to 4000, of which 250 to 500 are dedicated to internships and practicums Graduation requirement: Complete the entire curriculum of classes and a written thesis Final presentation of thesis in front of a jury or public. Oral thesis defense

Peru	No university education	Does not apply
Puerto Rico	No university education	Does not apply
Trinidad and Tobago	No university education	Does not apply
Uruguay CEDIIAP University Center (Centro Universitario CEDIIAP)	Undergraduate program: Bachelor's in Music Therapy Started in 2010 Graduates: 11	Degree awarded: Bachelor's in Music Therapy Admission: Personal interview and academic writing Duration: Four years Total hours: 2000 to 3000, of which 100 to 250 are practical and internships and approximately 100 supervised Graduation requirement: Complete and comply with all the requirements of the degree, culminating in the presentation of the final thesis and oral defense of the same
Venezuela University of the Andes (Universidad de los Andes, Mérida)	Postgraduate specialization in Music Therapy Taught between 2015 and 2017 Graduates: 23	Degree awarded: Music Therapy Specialists Duration: Five semesters Entry: Bachelor's in Music or Art/Bachelor's in any area, demonstrating aptitude in music/musical audition (theoretical/practical) demonstrating solid musical training, verifiable via credentials and musical audition Music therapists accredited with Bachelor's degrees from another country are admitted to the specialization directly

Conclusion

The report was published on November 23, 2021. CLAM wanted the format and content to serve as a resource or reference guide for those interested in knowing the academic options that different countries offer for training music therapists and for teaching music therapy concepts. Likewise, it was hoped that more accurate quantitative and qualitative data would continue to be generated in future updates. Although the report was updated in February 2024, the rapid development of music therapy in the region calls for another update, not only incorporating the countries that did not participate originally, but also obtaining new data and relevant information regarding music therapy training. This means that it will be possible to have a more complete view of the situation, which will allow agreement on some general criteria and/or guidelines for all of Latin America and the Caribbean, with the aim of the discipline continuing to grow in terms of professional training.

On the other hand, the historical background revealed by the study shows the high diversity in the training processes investigated. There are countries in Latin America that have had established university training for more than 40 years, as well as others that have only started introductory music therapy courses in recent years. The same phenomenon happens with associations, where a plurality of situations is exposed, with countries that have associations but that do not have training, and others that have training but do not have an association. The countries that have both present the most heterogeneity in terms of preparation possibilities in professional music therapy training.

Likewise, analysis of the data revealed a multiplicity of training programs in music therapy in Latin America, ranging from public and private university institutions to non-university courses. There is complexity, however, regarding the origin of the training, where there are music therapists who lived and studied abroad and then practice the profession in their country of origin, and in other cases, music therapists train in their country and then work abroad.

Regarding the general characteristics of the training, the countries that have more history and expertise also offer solid Bachelor's and Baccalaureate programs (four years' training or more). In these cases, and as an entry requirement, musical listening is also considered fundamental in training music therapists. The necessary requirements for graduation include bibliographic research processes, thesis writing, and oral defense before a tribunal, reflecting a rigorous academic process.

Observation and analysis of the findings has allowed CLAM to identify other topics that are relevant to training music therapists in Latin America, which can be addressed in future updates. The following stand out: the limits and scope of online education; the diversity of perspectives and theoretical-practical models in training; modalities and frameworks for internships and practicums; analysis of the study plans; and minimum required contents.

Finally, I would like to remind you that the mission of the CLAM is to support and inform the music therapy community about the current situation and how this is being navigated and transformed in the region, considering the particular needs and realities of each country in Latin America and the Caribbean. The original document that contains the report that has been synthesized here continues to be available to the entire music therapy community.[4]

---

4   www.musicoterapiaclam.com/comisiones [in Spanish].

PANORAMA DE LA FORMACIÓN EN MUSICOTERAPIA EN AMÉRICA LATINA

PATRICIA ZARATE DE PEREZ

Introducción

En este capítulo se presentará un resumen de la formación en musicoterapia en América Latina y el Caribe. Los datos que se presentan aquí provienen de un proyecto de investigación del Comité Latinoamericano de Musicoterapia (CLAM). Comencé a trabajar virtualmente con el CLAM durante la pandemia de COVID-19 de 2020 como parte del Comité de Procesos de Formación Profesional. En 2023 fui elegida para desempeñarme como Vicepresidenta de la organización junto con Lorena Buenseñor de Uruguay como Presidenta electa y Flor Ruva de Argentina como Secretaria electa. Como se indica en el sitio web de la organización:

> El Comité Latinoamericano de Musicoterapia (CLAM) es una organización sin fines de lucro, constituida desde 1993 por organizaciones vinculadas a diferentes campos de investigación, teoría y práctica de la musicoterapia en América Latina. El CLAM tiene como objetivo agrupar, integrar, vincular y representar a las entidades participantes en el área de la musicoterapia, con sede en países de América Latina, así como promover la comunicación e integración de sus actividades científicas, académicas, teóricas y profesionales. Desde su creación, cada país ha determinado la forma de participación en el comité, incluyendo la representación a través de un delegado, siendo respetuoso del proceso vivido en cada país, y entendiendo que la realidad profesional es diferente, según cada contexto. El CLAM no recibe aportes económicos de ningún tipo, entendiendo que los delegados cumplen su rol

de manera voluntaria con el único fin de realizar un aporte al desarrollo profesional de la Musicoterapia en América Latina.

Este resumen de la formación en musicoterapia en la región se organizó durante 2020–2021; en ese momento, la presidenta del CLAM era Mariane Oselame. El objetivo de este estudio fue recopilar datos sobre la formación en musicoterapia en América Latina a través de un cuestionario digital que luego se transformó en un mapa de sistema disponible en el sitio web de la organización. En este capítulo, analizaré varios programas, para contextualizar el estado actual de la formación en musicoterapia en América Latina. Es importante reconocer el hecho de que los musicoterapeutas latinoamericanos siempre se están adaptando a cambios rápidos en sus realidades socioeconómicas y políticas, al igual que la profesión en su conjunto. Como tal, se espera que este documento se revise al menos una vez cada tres a cinco años. La formación en musicoterapia en América Latina tiene una rica historia y consiste en capacitaciones creadas por terapeutas de la región combinadas con recursos extraídos del extranjero. La nueva formación es cada vez más diversa en términos de cómo se presenta. Especialmente desde la pandemia de COVID-19, es más común ver capacitación virtual tanto asincrónica como sincrónica, modelos híbridos y lo que yo llamo hiperhíbrido, que combina todos los elementos anteriores con capacitación en persona.

Este proyecto de investigación muestra que la formación latinoamericana en musicoterapia también se nutre de la formación internacional, lo que crea un espacio disciplinar diverso. Estudiantes de países que no cuentan con formación formal en musicoterapia regresan de estudios en el extranjero en Estados Unidos, Europa y otras regiones del mundo para crear programas en sus países de origen. Incluso dentro de América Latina hay mucho movimiento y polinización cruzada de ideas: estudiantes de toda la región estudian en países como Argentina, Brasil, Chile o Colombia, que ofrecen cursos de estudio en español a precios asequibles. Después de recopilar los datos, se crearon dos mapas de sistema en la aplicación kumu. io, uno que refleja los planes de estudio de musicoterapia de los programas de maestría y el otro que cubre los programas de licenciatura. Los mapas muestran todas las clases que se incluyen en la mayoría de los programas de musicoterapia latinoamericanos.

Este informe es un estudio introductorio de los procesos de formación en musicoterapia en América Latina y sólo incluye la formación universitaria formal y lo que consideramos educación dentro de las epistemologías eurocéntricas occidentales. Muestra la complejidad y diversidad de la región, así como su potencial de desarrollo, sin embargo, no incluye epistemologías indígenas ni ningún otro sistema no estándar. Lo más importante es que muestra cómo América Latina está involucrada en la creación y reconstrucción de la musicoterapia como disciplina y lo que se considera importante en relación con la profesión en cada país.

Los miembros de la Comisión de Formación del CLAM que llevaron a cabo la investigación y redactaron el informe incluyen: Karin Biegun (Argentina), Mayara Ribeiro (Brasil), Patricia Lallana (Chile), Diego Torres (Colombia), Patricia Zárate de Perez (Panamá), Ana María Passadore (Uruguay), Lorena Buenseñor (Coordinadora – Uruguay).

En diciembre de 2021, la Comisión de Procesos de Formación Profesional creada por el Comité Latinoamericano de Musicoterapia (CLAM) publicó un informe con información actualizada sobre las instituciones académicas que imparten formación profesional universitaria en musicoterapia en diversos países. Para recolectar la información, el Comité diseñó un cuestionario con el que buscó obtener datos tanto cualitativos como cuantitativos que pudieran ser utilizados y presentados de manera precisa y exacta. Las preguntas incluyeron las siguientes:

- ¿Su país cuenta con formación en musicoterapia?
- ¿Se trata de una formación profesional?
- ¿Su institución es pública o privada?
- ¿Cuántos musicoterapeutas profesionales gradúa anualmente su institución?
- ¿Cuántas personas se han graduado desde que inició la formación?
- ¿Qué ministerio reconoce su formación en musicoterapia?
- ¿Cuáles son los requisitos para ingresar a la formación?
- ¿Cuántas horas requiere la formación para graduarse?
- ¿Cuántas horas de práctica incluye la formación?

La recolección de datos se realizó en dos etapas. La primera, durante 2020, se centró en la elaboración de un cuestionario para ser llenado por universidades, instituciones educativas y otras asociaciones de los 36 países de América Latina y el Caribe. Recibimos 19 respuestas en 2020 y otras cuatro en 2021. En la segunda etapa, durante 2021, se mejoró el formulario con el fin de recopilar más datos y elaborar el informe final, que se publicó en diciembre de ese año.

Para cada país, los datos indican la existencia de programas de formación en musicoterapia, el número de años de duración de los programas y su trayectoria histórica, el tipo de titulación otorgada a los estudiantes, el número de horas académicas y los requisitos de ingreso y egreso, entre otros. Este informe fue un esfuerzo por desarrollar el trabajo de varios autores que son frecuentemente citados en la investigación en musicoterapia, como Juanita Eslava Mejía (2019), Patricia Sabbatella (2004), Lia Rejane Mendes Barcellos (1999) y Karina Ferrari (s.f.), entre otros, quienes hicieron esfuerzos tempranos por catalogar el entorno educativo de los profesionales en América Latina.

A continuación, proporcionaré una síntesis de la información presentada en el informe, comenzando con los antecedentes generales de cada país en lo que respecta a la formación en musicoterapia. Los datos se presentarán en tablas y cerraré compartiendo las reflexiones del equipo a cargo de la investigación junto con mis propias conclusiones.

Formación en musicoterapia en América Latina según el cuestionario

Once países de América Latina cuentan con capacitaciones en musicoterapia asociadas a una universidad. Entre estos países se encuentran Argentina, Bolivia, Brasil, Chile, Colombia, Cuba, México, Panamá, Paraguay, Uruguay y Venezuela.

Argentina

En la década de 1940, la doctora Carolina Tobar García, junto a la profesora de música María Laura Nardelli, comenzaron a trabajar con la música en escuelas para niños con necesidades especiales con el objetivo de mejorar la salud física y mental de los niños que asistían a esas instituciones. Al proyecto se sumaron otros profesores de música que representaban distintas especialidades: H. Epstein, que se enfoca en el estudio de la voz; F. Wolff que se enfoca en los ciegos; L. Penovi en la hipoacusia; V. de Gainza y V. Brenner de Aisenwaser en el área de las discapacidades del aprendizaje, junto a una serie de médicos, psicólogos y fonoaudiólogos. Al mismo tiempo, el doctor Rolando Benenzon, médico psiquiatra y músico, y el doctor Bernaldo de Quirós, pionero de la fonoaudiología en Argentina, comenzaron a investigar los efectos de la música en distintas patologías.

El 23 de julio de 1966, en el aula Magna de la Facultad de Medicina de la Universidad de Buenos Aires (UBA), se formó la Asociación Argentina de Musicoterapia (ASAM). Ese año, sus integrantes presentaron la propuesta de crear una carrera de grado en la Universidad del Salvador, estableciéndose así la primera formación universitaria en musicoterapia en América Latina. El 16 de diciembre de 1966 se creó el departamento de Musicoterapia, que constaba de tres años de duración y un total de 26 asignaturas.

En 1967, bajo la dirección del Dr. Rolando Benenzon, la carrera comenzó a impartirse en la Escuela de Otoneuro Foniatría de la Facultad de Medicina de El Salvador, dedicada a los trastornos de la comunicación humana. Los pioneros pedagogos musicales dedicados a esta especialidad conformaron el primer cuerpo docente de la carrera. Sus primeras egresadas entre 1969 y 1970 fueron Amelia Ferraggina, Nora Moyano, Elena Flores, Susana Dato, María Rosa Alfonsin y María Celia Pérez, todas profesoras de música.

En las décadas siguientes, la carrera se ha impartido en otras escuelas argentinas, lo que ha enriquecido y complejizado la formación profesional de los musicoterapeutas de la región. Actualmente la musicoterapia se imparte como carrera de grado en seis universidades ubicadas en diversas zonas de Argentina. Las carreras, todas reconocidas por el Ministerio de Educación, estuvieron comprendidas desde su creación en las siguientes instituciones: Universidad del Salvador (1966, Ciudad de Buenos Aires), Universidad de Buenos Aires (1993, sede Avellaneda, provincia de Buenos Aires), Universidad Abierta Interamericana (1995, sede Rosario y 1996, sede Ciudad de Buenos Aires), Universidad Maimónides (2006, Ciudad de Buenos Aires), Universidad Juan Agustín Maza (2016, Ciudad de Mendoza) y Universidad de Ciencias Empresariales y Sociales (2019, Ciudad de Buenos Aires).

Bolivia

A partir de 2009, Bolivia cuenta con un diplomado para profesionales que imparte docencia sobre el campo de la musicoterapia. En 2019 se impartió un diplomado de cuatro meses de duración titulado Introducción a la Musicoterapia Clínica, Sociocomunitaria y Educativa gracias a la colaboración del Instituto Internacional de Ciencias de la Educación, la Unidad de Formación Continua Especializada y la Asociación de Musicoterapeutas de Bolivia. Se realizaron cinco versiones de los cursos de Introducción a la Musicoterapia en La Paz y dos versiones del Diplomado en Musicoterapia Infantil gracias a una colaboración con la Universidad de Murcia.

Desde 2022, Bolivia cuenta con un diplomado que se lleva a cabo gracias a la alianza de la Universidad Evangélica Boliviana, con la Fundación Musicoterapia y Salud a través de la Universidad Autónoma de Madrid (UAM), en España. A partir de 2024, Bolivia organiza un Programa de Maestría con una universidad local.

Brasil

Los primeros pasos de la musicoterapia en Brasil se dieron en la década de 1960 en el estado de Río de Janeiro, donde se fundó la Asociación Brasileña de Musicoterapia (ABMT) (COSTA, 2020). Dada la creciente necesidad de formación en el área, se fueron desarrollando cursos y en 1970 se inició la primera formación de posgrado en musicoterapia en Brasil. Inicialmente se ofreció en la Facultad de Educación Musical de Paraná, hoy Facultades de Artes de Paraná (FAP). En 1972, el Conservatorio Brasileño de Música de Río de Janeiro (CBM – CEU) ofreció el primer curso de posgrado en musicoterapia (COSTA, 2020), que fue reconocido por el Consejo Federal de Educación en 1978 (SITE AMT-RJ).

El estado de Río de Janeiro jugó un papel clave en la creación de cursos en otros estados brasileños, incluidos Goiás y Paraná, a menudo enviando profesores para impartir cursos o ayudar con la organización. A partir de ahí, surgieron nuevos cursos inicialmente como cursos de posgrado y más tarde, en algunos estados, cursos de pregrado. El primer curso de graduación en una institución pública federal fue iniciado en 1999 por la Escuela de Música y Artes Escénicas de la Universidad Federal de Goiás.

La formación en musicoterapia en Brasil comenzó a través de cursos de extensión, que luego se transformaron en cursos de posgrado y en algunos casos en cursos de pregrado. Actualmente, la formación en musicoterapia en Brasil puede realizarse de dos formas: a través de estudios de posgrado (de dos años de duración) o a través de estudios de pregrado (de tres o cuatro años de duración).

La formación de pregrado es ofrecida por las siguientes instituciones públicas: Universidad Federal de Goiás (implementada en 1999), Universidad Estatal de Paraná (implementada en 1983), Universidad Federal de Minas Gerais (implementada en 2009) o Universidad Federal de Río de Janeiro (implementada en 2019). En el sistema privado, las opciones son las Facultades Metropolitanas Unidas (implementada en 2001) y las Facultades EST (implementadas en 2003). En cuanto a los cursos de posgrado, existen diversas instituciones, entre ellas el Instituto Fenix, Faculdade Censupeg, entre otras, que forman profesionales en diferentes lugares, llegando actualmente a casi todos los estados brasileños.

Los cursos de formación deben ser reconocidos por el Ministerio de Educación. Para verificar la calidad de la formación del musicoterapeuta, la União Brasileira das Associações de Musicoterapia (UBAM) realiza una evaluación consultiva de los cursos de posgrado. Esto permite que los interesados en realizar un posgrado consulten a la UBAM sobre la adecuación del programa a las normas gubernamentales sobre formación profesional.

Chile

La formación en musicoterapia en Chile fue creada en 1999 por la musicoterapeuta Susanne Bauer con el apoyo de académicos de la Universidad de Chile, entre ellos el Dr. Luis Merino, decano de la facultad en ese entonces, junto a la profesora Mimi Marinovic y las musicoterapeutas Valeska Sigren,

Patricia Ubilla y Patricia Lallana. Se trata de una carrera de especialización impartida por la Escuela Superior de Artes de la Universidad de Chile, bajo el título Curso de Postgrado en Arteterapias con Mención en Musicoterapia. Siendo el único programa en Chile que forma especialistas en musicoterapia, el objetivo declarado del postgrado es formar profesionales altamente calificados e integrales, preparados para trabajar en educación, salud, comunidades u organizaciones.

En 2005 se creó la Asociación Chilena de Musicoterapia (ACHIM), que agrupa a musicoterapeutas de distintos programas de formación, tanto nacionales como extranjeros, cuyo principal objetivo es "contribuir al desarrollo de una comunidad profesional de musicoterapeutas, brindar orientación ética respecto de su trabajo. Profesionalizar y promover y difundir la musicoterapia en Chile, a través de actividades de extensión, formacióne investigación en esta área".[1]

Colombia

La formación en musicoterapia colombiana se inició con la Maestra Carmen Barbosa Luna, el Dr. Miguel Ángel Suárez, el Maestro Álvaro Ramírez y la Dra. Juanita Eslava, en la Universidad Nacional de Colombia en el año 2006. Inicialmente fue un programa de especialización adscrito a la Facultad de Artes, al año siguiente pasó de especialización a maestría y se reestructuró.

En Colombia, la Universidad Nacional de Colombia es la única universidad que cuenta con formación formal a nivel universitario en musicoterapia. En los últimos años, algunas universidades han comenzado a abrir diplomados, cursos y talleres de musicoterapia para la difusión de conocimientos específicos tanto para musicoterapeutas como para la comunidad en general.

Cuba

Entre 2008 y 2010, el Dr. Fernández de Juan coordinó la especialización en musicoterapia (con título de maestría) como programa conjunto de la Facultad de Psicología de la Universidad de La Habana y la Facultad de Música del Instituto Superior de Arte. El programa de maestría fue impartido por profesores de Canadá, Argentina, Uruguay y Colombia.

La Asociación de Musicoterapeutas de Cuba (AMC) es la principal entidad que organiza a los practicantes del país. Actualmente no existe una formación profesional en musicoterapia en Cuba, sin embargo, existen cursos en línea, clases introductorias sobre musicoterapia como parte de otros programas, entrenamientos individualizados, mentorías informales y eventos

---

1   https://achim.cl/musicoterapia-definicion/ser-musicoterapeuta

anuales sobre musicoterapia. A partir de 2024 los musicoterapeutas cubanos organizan eventos como el Coloquio Internacional Histamed (Historia, Arte y Medicina) enfocado a celebrar "20 años de interdisciplinariedad en pos del mejoramiento humano". Algunos de los eventos que producen incluyen el XIII Coloquio Internacional Integrador de Historia, Arte y Medicina, el IV Encuentro HistArtMed entre culturas, el IV Taller Internacional de Música y Salud "Dr. Antonio M. Gordon", entre otros eventos.

México

El website de la asociación de Musicoterapia de Mexico dice que

> Las primeras actividades de Musicoterapia en México se remontan a prin-
> cipios de los años 80. Un hito muy importante es la creación de la pri-
> mera fundación en utilizar musicoterapia en México "Terapia y Educación
> I.A.P.", a cargo de Consuelo Deschamps y José Guillermo Villegas, quienes
> comenzaron a atender discapacidad a través de técnicas de musicoterapia,
> y además ofrecieron los primeros cursos de psicomúsica en el país. México
> se hace presente en la constitución del Comité Latinoamericano de Musi-
> coterapia (antes Secretariado Latinoamericano de Musicoterapia) a través
> de la musicoterapeuta mexicana, Mariela Petraglia, quién también impartió
> talleres y cursos en México desde los años 80.

En el país se desarrolla un modelo de musicoterapia, hoy reconocido por la Federación Mundial de Musicoterapia, a través del maestro Víctor Muñoz, quien comenzó a impartir talleres de musicoterapia humanista a mediados de los años 80. Con la fundación del Instituto Mexicano de Musicoterapia Humanista en 1995, se fue dando cauce a las necesidades de entrenamiento y formación alrededor de la psicoterapia musical, se crearon relaciones con importantes Musicoterapeutas de otros países, se hizo presencia en insti-tuciones de salud y también abrió la puerta a entrenamientos en el modelo GIM y en el Modelo de Musicoterapia Plurimodal.

El modelo GIM llega a México en 1996, a través de la musicoterapeuta Ginger Clarkson, formada en Estados Unidos, quien impartió formaciones en colaboración con el Instituto Mexicano de Musicoterapia Humanista y posteriormente colaboraría como académica de la Universidad de las Améri-cas. Destaca también el desarrollo de investigación en musicoterapia a través de la musicoterapeuta Esther Murow, entrenada por Ken Bruscia en Estados Unidos y quien a su regreso a nuestro país, realiza trabajo en diversas áreas, hacia finales de los años 80, incluyendo la práctica privada con niños con discapacidad. Inició el primer programa de musicoterapia en un sistema hospitalario, siendo la primera musicoterapeuta de tiempo completo en el

Instituto Nacional de Psiquiatría. En este mismo lugar, desarrolló gran parte de sus investigaciones en conjunto con el instituto, lo que permitió fortalecer la presencia de la musicoterapia para otros profesionales de la salud.

Otro hito importante es la inscripción en el Registro Nacional de Instituciones y Empresas Científicas y Tecnológicas (RENIECYT) del Consejo Nacional de Ciencia y Tecnología (CONACYT) de la primera organización de Musicoterapia (MusiCura S.C) por parte de la musicoterapeuta mexicana Dra. Eugenia Hernández Ruiz, quien se desempeña ahora como docente e investigadora de musicoterapia en los Estados Unidos, y colabora para importantes revistas de investigación en Musicoterapia. A través de su agencia, se han proporcionado servicios musicoterapia en práctica privada y en organizaciones como Fortaleza, Centro de Atención Integral a la Mujer y la Familia, A.C. y la Clínica Mexicana de Autismo y Alteraciones del Desarrollo, A.C. Otro acontecimiento sobresaliente en la historia de la musicoterapia en México, fue la visita del Dr. Rolando Benenzon a nuestro país en 2009, lo que derivó en la creación del Centro Benenzon de Musicoterapia de México, con sede en la Facultad de Música de la Universidad Autónoma de Nuevo León, por parte de María Teresa Gómez Huerta y Juan Francisco Gómez Villalobos. Gracias a todos estos esfuerzos se empezaron a impartir entrenamientos en la Terapia Benenzon en México.

Se han impartido cursos y diplomados de musicoterapia en la Universidad Autónoma de México (UNAM), Destaca el esfuerzo de más de 25 años de la musicoterapeuta Adriana Sepúlveda, con su proyecto permanente para apoyar la formación musical profesional de alumnos ciegos y/o débiles visuales así como para personas con discapacidad, a través de la Facultad de Música de la UNAM. También se han impartido talleres y cursos de musicoterapia en la Facultad de Estudios Superiores de Iztacala de la UNAM, por parte del Maestro Horacio Hernández. De igual forma es importante mencionar el reciente lanzamiento del Diplomado en Musicoterapia en la Facultad de Música de la UNAM, iniciado por la musicoterapeuta danesa Elske de Jong y actualmente coordinado por el musicoterapeuta mexicano Daniel Torres.

Un hito importante en la historia de la Musicoterapia en México es la creación de la primera asociación de musicoterapia, la AMME (Asociación de Musicoterapeutas en México), fundada por el maestro Juan Carlos Camarena en 2018, a través de la cual México participa por primera vez en la Federación Mundial de Musicoterapia como miembro con derecho a voto y de igual manera, se integra como delegación al Comité Latinoamericano de Musicoterapia. La AMME inicia gestión a fines del 2020, y desde entonces ha trabajado en la difusión de la disciplina de forma gratuita a través de entrevistas con profesionales de diferentes países, así como en la definición de criterios para la regulación profesional y el establecimiento de categorías de afiliación que contemplen la diversidad de formaciones en el país. Se tiene también registro de un primer Congreso de Musicoterapia en México, organizado por el Instituto Mexicano de Musicoterapia Interdisciplinaria, en 2018. De igual forma se organizó el primer Encuentro Internacional de Musicoterapeutas por parte de la Asociación de Musicoterapeutas en México en 2021 y posteriormente en el mismo año, un primer Simposio de Musicoterapia, organizado por el Centro Mexicano de Musicoterapia. A la fecha de este resumen, México ha sido elegido a través de la AMME como sede del Congreso Latinoamericano de Musicoterapia, el cual se celebrará en 2025.

Panamá

La formación en musicoterapia de Panamá está marcada por el trabajo de las mujeres y se inicia a principios de los años 90 con la señora Mariela Correa, pionera de la musicoterapia en Panamá, quien estudió los efectos terapéuticos de la música en Perú y Argentina y trabajó con niños en el Instituto Panameño de Habilitación Especial (IPHE). Posteriormente, en 1994, Vilma Esquivel se graduó de la Universidad Católica de América en Estados Unidos como musicoterapeuta. Luego de graduarse, regresó a Panamá y fundó el Centro de Musicoterapia "En Armonía" en la Ciudad de Panamá, donde ofreció cursos y servicios de musicoterapia hasta el año 2004. Melanie Taylor, quien se graduó con una maestría en musicoterapia de la Facultad de Medicina de la Universidad de Drexel en Estados Unidos en 1999, ha ofrecido cursos, servicios y un diplomado en musicoterapia con la Universidad de las Américas (UDELAS).

También destacan Paola Casal, quien se graduó en 2007 con una maestría en Comunicación y Lenguaje No Verbal: Habilidades Psicomotrices, Musicoterapia y Performance de la Universidad Ca' Foscari de Venecia, Italia; Sarah Muñoz, quien se graduó de la Universidad del Salvador en Argentina en 2020 como musicoterapeuta; y Ekaterina Zúñiga, quien se graduó con una maestría en musicoterapia de la Universidad de Derby, Inglaterra en 2023.

Patricia Zarate de Pérez, chilena de nacimiento y nacionalizada panameña, obtuvo su título de musicoterapia en Berklee College of Music (Boston, EE.UU.) en 1999, iniciando su trabajo en Panamá en 2003 con clases, mentorías, eventos formales e informales en el Festival de Jazz de Panamá y la Fundación Danilo Pérez. En enero de 2013, Patricia fundó el Simposio Latinoamericano de Musicoterapia y en 2015 el Centro de Musicoterapia de Panamá. En el año 2020, todos los musicoterapeutas antes mencionados se unieron para formar la Asociación Panameña de Musicoterapia (APAMU), que desde sus inicios lideró una campaña para aprobar una ley de musicoterapia que regulara el ejercicio de la profesión en Panamá. Esta política fue aprobada por el congreso panameño y el presidente de Panamá en octubre de 2022.

Paraguay

Paraguay ofrece formación universitaria desde el año 2019, con sede en la Universidad Católica "Nuestra Señora de la Asunción," en el marco de la educación privada. El Título a acreditar es el de Licenciado o Bachiller (Licenciatura en Musicoterapia). Esta formación profesional es reconocida por el Ministerio de Educación, con alcance nacional a cargo del Consejo Nacional de Educación Superior.

Uruguay

La formación en musicoterapia en Uruguay se inició en 1967, de la mano de Lyda Florez, docente especializada que desarrolló su labor en el ámbito educativo trabajando con alumnos discapacitados. Se formó con Rolando Benenzon en Argentina y juntos coordinaron la primera formación en musicoterapia en el Centro de las Artes. Luego se creó la PEMU (Primera Escuela de Musicoterapia), donde se graduó la primera generación de musicoterapeutas uruguayos siguiendo el enfoque y modelo de Benenzon.

En 2004, Uruguay organizó y fue sede del Congreso del Comité Latinoamericano de Musicoterapia (CLAM), en Montevideo, con Clive Robbins como invitado especial. Este evento constituyó un impulso aún mayor para la titulación oficial de la carrera de musicoterapia en Uruguay.

En 2010, el Centro Universitario CEDIIAP estableció la carrera de musicoterapia, y se inició el proceso de titulación correspondiente. Cabe mencionar que, dada la falta de formación académica previa en el país en esta área de estudio, la universidad se apoyó en musicoterapeutas expertos del exterior con experiencia en docencia y formación para el diseño y configuración de la nueva titulación, que culminó en 2016 con el proceso de titulación y reconocimiento oficial.

Uruguay ofrece ahora formación de grado en una universidad privada (CEDIIAP), reconocida por el Ministerio de Educación y Cultura (MEC) y el Ministerio de Salud Pública (MSP). Cabe señalar que la Asociación de Musicoterapeutas Uruguayos (AMU) se encuentra actualmente tramitando la homologación de la titulación que se impartirá en la Universidad Pública de la República Oriental del Uruguay (UDELAR).

Venezuela

Yadira Albornoz es la primera persona con credenciales académicas a cargo de la formación en musicoterapia en Venezuela. Creó la Fundación

Venezolana de Musicoterapia FUNVEMUST en el año 2010. La Dra. Albornoz es clarinetista, cantante, compositora y profesora de la Escuela de Música de la Universidad de los Andes, doctora en Filosofía de la Musicoterapia y magíster en música.

En el año 2015 logró implementar un programa de posgrado de cinco semestres de Especialización en Musicoterapia que funcionó en la Universidad de los Andes con sede en Mérida hasta el año 2017, del cual egresaron un total de 23 Especialistas en Musicoterapia. Actualmente esta carrera no se imparte.

Países sin programas de formación universitaria en musicoterapia
Barbados
En este país se han realizado formaciones internacionales. Gracias a la Commonwealth of Learning y Canadá/STARR Bajan, se han impartido clases en la plataforma virtual del Berklee College of Music impartidas por la musicoterapeuta Suzanne Hanser. También se han realizado cursos introductorios en el Barbados Community College a cargo de la musicoterapeuta Tamara Adams. Asimismo, la Universidad de las Indias Occidentales, St. Augustine, cuenta actualmente con una clase introductoria de musicoterapia.

Costa Rica
A pesar de no contar con formación universitaria en musicoterapia, en Costa Rica existe cierto grado de acceso al conocimiento sobre la disciplina vía propuestas de abordaje o cursos complementarios en carreras tradicionales de salud o artísticas. En concreto, la enseñanza de la musicoterapia se realiza a través de clases introductorias (como parte de una carrera de salud o artística), certificados o diplomas de otras instituciones no universitarias, formación individual personalizada, mentorías informales y eventos anuales como simposios, congresos, clubes, etc.

Según información recabada a través del estudio, la ausencia de una asociación de musicoterapia dificulta establecer la presencia de la disciplina en el sistema de educación superior. Se sostiene que ni el sistema burocrático educativo público ni privado es lo suficientemente flexible como para desarrollar o incorporar un programa de formación universitaria en este momento.

Ecuador
Según los datos de este estudio, la musicoterapia es aún una profesión nueva en Ecuador. La educación está empañada por la desinformación y los cursos que se imparten no están avalados para el ejercicio profesional. La

mayoría de los musicoterapeutas profesionales se forman en el extranjero. La formación no universitaria se enmarca dentro del formato de cursos de otras disciplinas, como la Maestría en Psicoterapia de la UTA (Universidad Técnica de Ambato).

Entre los cursos de formación privados hay uno enfocado en la adquisición de herramientas de musicoterapia, cuya duración es de entre 500 y 1000 horas. Sin embargo, no está reconocido por ningún Ministerio o Secretaría de Estado sino solo como una clase introductoria como parte de una carrera de salud o artística. Además, hay algunos certificados o diplomas impartidos por otras instituciones no universitarias.

En septiembre de 2024, Ecuador organizó la Asociación Ecuatoriana de Musicoterapeutas y está en proceso de postulación para ser parte del Comité de Musicoterapia de Latinoamérica (CLAM).

El Salvador

El Salvador aún no ofrece formación profesional a nivel universitario. Las opciones actuales incluyen cursos en línea, clases introductorias como parte de una carrera en salud o artes, entrenamientos individuales personalizados, mentorías informales y eventos anuales como simposios, conferencias, clubes y otros. A partir de septiembre de 2024, Rocio Moreno, Katherine Zelaya y Estella Zelaya unieron sus esfuerzos para abrir el Centro de Musicoterapia de El Salvador, el primero de su tipo en el país.

Guatemala

Actualmente, la formación educativa en Guatemala la lleva a cabo un dúo terapéutico, que con la iniciativa "Musicoterapia Guatemala" imparte talleres vivenciales introductorios en MT y tratamiento individual.

De acuerdo con la información recabada a través del formulario, existe interés en crear un programa de formación profesional. Actualmente, se está elaborando un plan de estudios para un diplomado o especialización para presentarlo en diferentes universidades del país.

Haití

En Haití no existe formación profesional en musicoterapia, pero hay algunos musicoterapeutas de este país que estudian y trabajan en Estados Unidos.

Honduras

Honduras no cuenta con formación profesional universitaria en musicoterapia ni cuenta con ninguna asociación de musicoterapeutas. Solo conocemos una persona interesada en formarse que está cursando una licenciatura en Uruguay.

Islas Caimán

La musicoterapeuta Julianne Parolisi, profesora de la Universidad Lesley en Boston, MA, fundadora y directora de Music Therapy Without Borders – Cayman Music Therapy, señala que en las Islas Caimán no existe una asociación profesional de musicoterapeutas ni una carrera en musicoterapia, pero sí hay formación individual y tutoría informal, incluidas clases en dos universidades locales. Tras establecer la primera práctica de musicoterapia en las Islas Caimán en 2010, Parolisi ha realizado múltiples capacitaciones informales para integrar los principios de la musicoterapia en la educación y la salud. Además, ha realizado tutorías que incluyen oportunidades de observación, voluntariado y búsqueda de programas de formación internacionales para personas interesadas en la profesión.

Perú

En el Perú aún no existe un programa de formación universitaria en musicoterapia, sino algunas ponencias, diplomados y certificados de diversas instituciones nacionales e internacionales. Actualmente existe un Centro de Investigación y Desarrollo que se ha dedicado a generar conciencia sobre la necesidad de formación profesional en musicoterapia para el país. La Asociación Peruana de Musicoterapia fue creada en 2022 y organizó el primer congreso de musicoterapia en el país en febrero de 2024.

Puerto Rico

Puerto Rico acoge la Asociación de Musicoterapia de Puerto Rico, fundada en 2021. Según se informa a través del formulario, se sostiene que los sistemas burocráticos educativos públicos y privados no cuentan con la flexibilidad requerida para incorporar la formación universitaria. Esto resulta en una cantidad diversa de ofertas de formación profesional subgraduada en Puerto Rico asociadas a otras carreras, como clases introductorias en carreras de la salud o las artes y pasantías profesionales. Asimismo, existen otras alternativas, como cursos de grado en línea que no requieren horas de práctica registradas, otros cursos de grado que requieren aproximadamente 200 horas y, por último, cursos en los EE.UU., que requieren un total de 1200 horas de práctica como requisito.

A partir de agosto de 2024, Puerto Rico está trabajando estrechamente con la Asociación Americana de Musicoterapia (AMTA) para abrir el Bachillerato en Musicoterapia en el Conservatorio de Puerto Rico en 2025. También sabemos que los musicoterapeutas de Puerto Rico están trabajando para aprobar una ley que regule la profesión en la isla.

República Dominicana

En República Dominicana no existe una formación profesional en musicoterapia, aunque se han impartido clases introductorias en el marco de algunas carreras artísticas, de la salud, y en eventos anuales de musicoterapia. Varios musicoterapeutas de República Dominicana se han graduado en el Departamento de Musicoterapia del Berklee College of Music y han trabajado a nivel nacional e internacional como musicoterapeutas y educadores.

Trinidad y Tobago

En Trinidad y Tobago existe una asociación profesional de musicoterapia llamada Music Therapy Association of Trinidad and Tobago, pero no existe una formación profesional en musicoterapia. La formación académica en musicoterapia se imparte a través de clases introductorias que forman parte de una carrera de salud o de arte, específicamente una clase de exposición de tres meses en una licenciatura en música.

**Resumen de los procesos de formación universitaria
pre y post grado en América Latina y el Caribe**

País/ institución de formación	Características generales de la formación	Currículo
Argentina: Universidad del Salvador (USAL)	Formación de grado en universidad privada Iniciada en 1967 Primeras prácticas clínicas en los hospitales psiquiátricos Braulio Moyano, Borda y Fundación Vitra Último plan de estudios: 1995 Número medio de egresados anuales: 50-55 Total de egresados desde su creación: 2000	Título otorgado: Licenciatura en Musicoterapia Requisito de ingreso: Curso de admisión general y curso de nivelación musical, audición musical/entrevista personal Carrera de 4 años Horas totales: 3240, de las cuales 648 son prácticas supervisadas Requisito de graduación: Trabajo final escrito integrador con defensa oral

cont.

País/ institución de formación	Características generales de la formación	Currículo
Argentina: Universidad de Buenos Aires (UBA)	Formación de grado en universidad pública Número medio de egresados al año: 35 aprox. Total de egresados desde su creación: 1000 aprox.	Título otorgado: Licenciado en Musicoterapia Requisitos de ingreso: Audición o curso propedéutico Duración del curso: 5 años (4 años más ciclo básico común) Número total de horas: 3228, de las cuales 540 son prácticas Requisito de graduación: Presentación escrita de la tesis y defensa oral de la misma ante un tribunal
Argentina: Universidad Abierta Interamericana (UAI)	Formación de grado en universidad privada Promedio de graduados/as anuales: UAI Rosario: 8. UAI Buenos Aires: 3–5 Total de graduados/as desde sus inicios: UAI Rosario: 106. UAI Buenos Aires: 174	Título otorgado: Licenciado en Musicoterapia Requisito de ingreso: Audición musical/entrevista personal Carrera de 4 años Total de horas: 3408, de las cuales 162 son prácticas preprofesionales supervisadas Requisito de graduación: Presentación escrita de la tesis y exposición de la misma ante un jurado
Argentina: Universidad Maimónides	No hay información	Título otorgado: Licenciado en Musicoterapia Carrera de 4 años de duración Cantidad de horas totales: 2712
Argentina: Universidad Juan Agustín Maza (UMAZA)	Formación de grado en universidad privada Número de egresados: No hay egresados a la fecha (2021). Primera cohorte en proceso de prácticas profesionales y elaboración de tesis	Título otorgado: Licenciado en Musicoterapia Requisito de ingreso: Entrevista personal Carrera de 4 años Total de horas: 2845, de las cuales 600 son prácticas tuteladas Requisito de graduación: Presentación escrita de la tesis y defensa oral de la misma

Argentina: Universidad de Ciencias Empresariales y Sociales (UCES)	Formación de Grado en Universidad Privada Número de egresados: No se encuentran registrados a la fecha del informe (2021)	Título otorgado: Licenciado en Musicoterapia Requisito de ingreso: Audición musical y entrevista personal Carrera de cuatro años Total de horas: 2672, de las cuales 576 son prácticas preprofesionales Requisito de graduación: Presentación escrita del trabajo final y defensa oral del mismo
Barbados	No existen programas o instituciones que brinden formación en musicoterapia	No aplica
Bolivia: Universidad Evangélica Boliviana	Programa de diplomado realizado en alianza con la Fundación Musicoterapia y Salud, a través de la Universidad Autónoma de Madrid (UAM)	No hay información
Brasil: Instituciones públicas: Universidad Federal de Goiás; Universidad del Estado de Paraná; Universidad Federal de Minas Gerais; Universidad Federal de Río de Janeiro Instituciones privadas: Facultades Metropolitanas Unidas; Facultades EST	Existen 2 rutas de formación: estudios de grado con una duración de 3–4 años; estudios de especialización de posgrado con una duración de 2 años Toda formación debe ser reconocida por el Ministerio de Educación 163	Título otorgado (pre-grado): Licenciatura en Musicoterapia Requisitos de ingreso: Mediante escrito académico y/o constancia de conocimientos musicales 4 años de carrera Número total de horas: entre 3000 a 4000, de las cuales aproximadamente 300 son de prácticas y al menos 60 de supervisión Requisito de graduación: Completar y cumplir con todos los requisitos de la carrera, con presentación de la monografía final y defensa oral de la misma Título otorgado (posgrado): Especialista en Musicoterapia Requisitos de ingreso: Certificado de formación terciaria y/o constancia de conocimientos musicales

cont.

País/ institución de formación	Características generales de la formación	Currículo
Cursos de especialización: Instituto Fenix, Faculdade Censupeg, entre otros		Cursos de 2 años Horas totales: Mínimo de 360, de las cuales 60 son prácticas y de prácticas y 20 de supervisión Requisito de graduación: Completar y cumplir con todos los requisitos de posgrado, con presentación de la monografía final
Chile: Universidad de Chile	Curso de Especialización de postgrado en Arteterapias, mención Musicoterapia Iniciado en 1999 Egresados al 2021: aproximadamente 500	Título otorgado: Posgrado en Musicoterapia Duración: 3 semestres Horas totales: 477 horas contacto, de las cuales los dos primeros semestres son de clases teóricas y el tercero de práctica profesional de seis horas semanales Requisitos de ingreso: Poseer grado académico o título profesional en las áreas de Música, Salud, Educación u otra afín. Si el título profesional no es en el área de Música, el aspirante deberá tener dominio de un instrumento musical, lo cual será evaluado durante el proceso de postulación Requisitos de graduación: Redactar un informe y presentar un examen final

Colombia: Universidad Nacional de Colombia	Programa de posgrado de la Universidad Nacional de Colombia Inicia el año 2007 Graduados al 2021: 154 Másteres en Musicoterapia, promedio de 10 graduados por año	Título que se otorga: Máster en Musicoterapia Admisión: Entrevista personal, prueba de aptitud musical y redacción académica (propuesta y ensayo de intención de trabajo) Duración del programa: 2 años Horas totales: 3216 de trabajo, de las que 1056 son prácticas y prácticas supervisadas Requisito de graduación: Cursar y completar las asignaturas del Máster, culminando con la presentación del trabajo final y defensa oral del mismo
Costa Rica	No tiene estudios universitarios	No aplica
Cuba: Universidad de La Habana e Instituto Superior de Arte	Programa de especialización conjunto de la Facultad de Psicología de la Universidad de La Habana y la Facultad de Música del Instituto Superior de Arte, con rango de Máster Dictado entre 2008 y 2010 Graduados: 15 profesionales	Título otorgado: No hay información Horas totales: Entre 1000 y 2000, de las cuales entre 50 y 100 fueron de práctica profesional
Cuba: Universidad de Ciencias Médicas de La Habana	Programa de diplomado en Música y Salud del Consejo Nacional de Sociedades Científicas de la Salud Realizado entre 2020-21	Título otorgado: Sin información 95 créditos académicos Duración 1410 horas, modalidad presencial a tiempo parcial Plan de estudios: Módulo I: Introducción a la musicoterapia Módulo II: Música y medicina Módulo III: Habilidades y competencias musicales necesarias para el ejercicio musicoterapéutico

cont.

País/ institución de formación	Características generales de la formación	Currículo
Ecuador	No tiene estudios universitarios	No aplica
El Salvador	No tiene estudios universitarios	No aplica
Guatemala	No tiene estudios universitarios	No aplica
Haití	No tiene estudios universitarios	No aplica
Honduras	No tiene estudios universitarios	No aplica
Islas Caimán	No hay formación universitaria	No aplica
México: Instituto Mexicano de Musicoterapia Humanista	Programa de Maestría en Musicoterapia Humanística Inicio 2015	Duración: 570 horas totales, de las cuales 195 son de prácticas
México: Universidad Nacional Autónoma de México	Programa de Diplomado en Musicoterapia Clínica y Psicosocial	Título obtenido: Diplomado en Musicoterapia Clínica y Psicosocial Duración: 117 horas en modalidad semipresencial
Panamá: Universidad Especializada de las Américas (UDELAS)	Programa de Diplomado en Musicoterapia (posgrado). (2017–18, 20 graduados) (Máster en Musicoterapia inicia en 2024)	Título que se obtiene: Diplomatura en Musicoterapia Admisión: Entrevista personal, prueba de aptitud musical y redacción académica Duración: 6 meses 5 módulos de estudio Horas totales: 240 horas lectivas, de las cuales 80 son prácticas Otorga 15 créditos universitarios Requisito de graduación: cursar y cumplir con todas las materias de la diplomatura, presentación de trabajo final y trabajo de investigación escrito

Paraguay Universidad Católica "Nuestra Señora de la Asunción" (universidad privada)	Programa de pregrado de licenciatura o bachillerato Iniciado en 2019	Título otorgado: Licenciado en Musicoterapia Modalidad de ingreso: Escritura académica Duración: 4 años Total de horas: 3000 a 4000, de las cuales 250 a 500 se dedican a prácticas y pasantías Requisito de graduación: Completar todo el plan de estudios de clases y tesis escrita Presentación final ante jurado o público. Defensa oral de tesis
Perú	No tiene estudios universitarios	No aplica
Puerto Rico	No tiene estudios universitarios	No aplica
República Dominicana	No tiene estudios universitarios	No aplica
Trinidad y Tobago	No tiene estudios universitarios	No aplica
Uruguay Centro Universitario CEDIIAP	Programa de pregrado: Licenciatura en Musicoterapia Inicio en 2010 Graduados: 11 (en el 2022)	Título otorgado: Licenciatura en Musicoterapia Admisión: Entrevista personal y redacción académica Duración: 4 años Horas totales: 2000 a 3000, de las cuales 100 a 250 son prácticas y pasantías y aproximadamente 100 de supervisión Requisito de graduación: Completar y cumplir con todos los requisitos de la titulación, culminando con la presentación de la monografía final y defensa oral de la misma

cont.

País/institución de formación	Características generales de la formación	Currículo
Venezuela Universidad de los Andes, Mérida	Postgrado de especialización en Musicoterapia Dictado entre 2015 y 2017 Graduados: 23	Título otorgado: Especialistas en Musicoterapia Duración: 5 semestres Ingreso: Licenciatura en Música o Arte/Licenciatura en cualquier área, que demuestre aptitud en música/Audición musical (teórica/práctica) que demuestre sólida formación musical, comprobable mediante credencial y audición musical Los musicoterapeutas acreditados con Licenciatura de otro país son admitidos directamente a la Especialización

Conclusión

Este informe fue publicado el 23 de noviembre de 2021. El CLAM buscó que el formato y contenido de dicho documento sirviera como recurso o guía de referencia para las partes interesadas en conocer las opciones académicas que ofrecen los distintos países para la formación de musicoterapeutas, o la enseñanza de conceptos musicoterapéuticos. Asimismo, se esperaba seguir generando datos cuantitativos y cualitativos más precisos en futuras actualizaciones. Este informe fue actualizado en febrero de 2024, sin embargo, el rápido desarrollo de la musicoterapia en la región hace necesario una actualización de los datos, no solo incorporando a los países que no participaron originalmente, sino también obteniendo nuevos datos e información relevante respecto de la formación en musicoterapia. De esta manera, será posible tener una visión más completa de la situación, que permita consensuar algunos criterios y/o lineamientos generales para toda América Latina y el Caribe, con el objetivo de que la disciplina siga creciendo en términos de formación profesional.

Por otra parte, los antecedentes históricos que revela el estudio dan cuenta de la alta diversidad en los procesos de formación investigados. Latinoamérica presenta países que cuentan con formación universitaria establecida desde hace más de 40 años, así como otros que vienen realizando cursos introductorios de musicoterapia solo en los últimos años. El mismo fenómeno sucede con las asociaciones, donde se expone una pluralidad de situaciones, con países que cuentan con asociaciones pero no cuentan con formación, y otros que cuentan con formación y no cuentan con asociación. Se confirma que los países que presentan ambas son los que presentan mayor heterogeneidad, en cuanto a posibilidades de preparación en formación profesional en musicoterapia.

Asimismo, el análisis de los datos reveló una multiplicidad de programas de formación en musicoterapia en Latinoamérica, que abarcan desde instituciones universitarias públicas y privadas hasta cursos no universitarios. Existe complejidad en cuanto al origen de la formación, donde vemos que hay musicoterapeutas que vivieron y estudiaron en el extranjero y ejercen la profesión en su país de origen. En otros casos, los musicoterapeutas se forman en su país y luego trabajan en el extranjero.

En cuanto a las características generales de la formación, los países que cuentan con mayor trayectoria y antigüedad también ofrecen programas sólidos de licenciatura y bachillerato (cuatro años de formación o más). En estos casos, y como requisito de ingreso, la escucha musical también se considera un eje fundamental en la formación del musicoterapeuta. En el caso del perfil de egreso, son condiciones necesarias los procesos de investigación bibliográfica, la redacción de tesis y la defensa oral ante tribunal, reflejando un riguroso proceso académico.

La observación y análisis de los hallazgos permitió al CLAM identificar otros temas relevantes para la formación de musicoterapeutas en América Latina, que pueden ser abordados en futuras actualizaciones. Entre los ejes temáticos propuestos, se destacan: límites y alcances de la educación en línea; diversidad de perspectivas y modelos teórico-prácticos en la formación; modalidades y marcos de prácticas/pasantías; y análisis de los planes de estudio y contenidos mínimos requeridos.

Por último, quisiera recordarles que la Comisión de Procesos de Formación Profesional del CLAM tiene como misión apoyar e informar a la comunidad musicoterapéutica sobre la situación actual de dichos procesos y cómo se está navegando y transformando dicha situación en la región, considerando las necesidades y realidades particulares de cada país de América Latina y el Caribe. El documento original que contiene el informe aquí sintetizado continúa a disposición de toda la comunidad musicoterapéutica.[2]

---

2   www.musicoterapiaclam.com/comisiones

CHAPTER 9

PERSPECTIVES ON BRAZILIAN MUSIC THERAPY IN THE EUROPEAN CONTEXT

An Understanding of the Present and the Future

GUSTAVO SCHULZ GATTINO

Introduction

Music therapy emerged in Brazil in the 1960s and was directly influenced by existing mental health and music education practices in the country (UBAM 2024a). Formal Brazilian music therapy has its origins at the "Latin American Music Therapy Days" in Argentina, where influential Brazilians who were interested in the therapeutic effect of music fostered a national movement. I would like to highlight music therapists Di Pinto Pâncaro, Cecília Conde, and Clotilde Leinig among the leaders of these pioneering music therapists.

Brazil has seven Bachelor's degree courses in Music Therapy and several Specialization courses (which, until 2026, also qualify graduates to practice the profession) (Law No. 14,842, 2024). Four of the courses are at entirely tuition-free public universities (UBAM 2024b). At the moment, Brazil has more than 3000 music therapists working in various areas of practice, including autism, mental health, hospitals, business organizations, and social and community music therapy (UBAM 2020).

Music therapists in Brazil are accredited via different spheres of public power, such as the Brazilian Occupation Code (Classificação Brasileira de Ocupações, CBO), and public policies, such as the Unified Health System (Sistema Único de Saúde, SUS) and the Unified Social Assistance System (Sistema Único de Assistência Social, SUAS) (UBAM 2024a). In 2024, the music therapy profession was officially regulated through Law 14,842 (2024). This defines how music therapists must be trained, where they may work, and what music therapy practice consists of.

Brazil has a strong tradition in music therapy research, with different Master's and doctoral programs each focusing on specific specialties. Music therapy papers written by Brazilian professionals are published in renowned national and international scientific journals. Brazilian music therapists and researchers appear at national and international scientific events, and serve in important international political organizations such as the World Federation of Music Therapy (WFMT) and the Latin American Music Therapy Committee (Comité Latinoamericano de Musicoterapia, CLAM).

This introduction might give the impression that Brazilian music therapy occupies significant space on the world stage, yet what happens in Brazil is actually little known in other countries due to various factors. One of the main obstacles is that most Brazilian professionals only speak Brazil's official language of Portuguese, so most Brazilian music therapy publications are written in Portuguese and fail to reach the most-read scientific journals of the international music therapy community.

I decided to write this chapter not just to talk about Brazilian music therapy, but to also talk about my experience as a music therapist, teacher, and researcher in music therapy in different European countries, where I have worked directly and indirectly for the last 14 years. My aim is to describe my professional experiences in Europe, and to provide some reflections on these experiences from my point of view, and also from concepts derived from music therapy from a multicultural perspective (Kim 2021) and colonialism in music therapy (Gilman 2022), which allow for a broader and more critical view from the accounts presented here.

In addition, I also seek to point out future directions for the work of Brazilian music therapists within Europe and other parts of the world. I don't present absolute truths here, but rather thoughts resulting from many years of work on the European continent. It is my hope that this will create some space in the Global Music Therapy conversation for the knowledge that has emerged from the unique context of Brazilian music therapy.

The chapter is organized into sections where I discuss my professional and personal background, and then report on my experiences in practice, teaching, and research in the European context. The chapter concludes with reflections on Brazilian music therapy's future in Europe and the world, along with some final considerations.

My professional and personal career

I was born in Brazil in 1985 and studied from kindergarten through the end of my Bachelor's degree in Music Therapy in private Lutheran schools following the German educational tradition. I began practicing music at the age of 12, playing in samba schools, rock and reggae bands, and orchestras, and did some formal musical training at a conservatory. I also learned a great deal about music in the Lutheran church, playing in ceremonies and being part of the church's youth group.

When I finished my Bachelor's degree, I went straight into a Master's and then a doctorate at a public university in the faculty of medicine, carrying out specific research into music therapy in child and adolescent health. I worked as a music therapist in Brazil for eight years, attended various events, and actively participated in international research, such as the TIME-A international study of music therapy and autism (from 2012 to 2017) (Bieleninik *et al.* 2017). By the time I moved to Europe, I had been published in books and scientific journals, and had been a board member for various music therapy-centric political organizations in the country—in other words, I arrived in Portugal with some meaningful experience in my profession.

In 2013, I married a Portuguese woman, and our son was born in Portugal in 2022. As such, I have been immersed in Portuguese culture and family dynamics for a long time. I have worked as a music therapist in the north of Portugal and have been a professor and researcher at the University of Aalborg (Denmark) since 2017. I have been teaching in different Master's programs in Music Therapy in Spain since 2016. I have also recently begun teaching in Italy and the Netherlands. I have been Denmark's representative on the European Music Therapy Confederation (EMTC) since 2021 and a member of the WFMT board as chair of the publications committee since 2023.

This short summary of my initial journey in Brazil and Europe should give an idea of my familiarity with both environments, and allow for a more dynamic flow in comparing the realities of Brazil and Europe.

Some reflections on my practice as a music therapist in Portugal

I had my first music therapy sessions in Portugal in 2011, before I moved there permanently. These took place in an institution for young people and adults with disabilities, where I held individual sessions, and in an anthroposophical institution for adults with disabilities. Although we share the same language, the Portuguese accent sounds different from the Brazilian accent. This means that music therapists working in Portugal not only need to learn the country's music, but must also sing with a European Portuguese accent so that the lyrics are easier for patients and clients to understand. From my first day at work, I realized that Brazilians generally seem more interested in the culture and news of the United States than of Portugal

(Motta, Alcadipani, and Bresler 2001), and that it is more common in Brazil to listen to music from the US than to songs from Portugal, even though we share the same language. I felt powerless, and I struggled to understand why we weren't more connected with a country that shares not only a language but also rhythms and songs in common, as well as dealing with some similar socioeconomic challenges (Sardo, Almeida, and Godinho 2012).

I also noticed that the manner of communication in music therapy sessions in Portugal felt more formal than back in Brazil, where we are looser with body language and facial expressions. I had to adapt in particular with regard to physical contact when working with patients in Portugal, and in terms of verbal communication I had to take extra care with pronouns.

In my search for professional contacts in Portugal, I also had my first surprises about the relational dynamics between music therapists in the country. Unlike Brazil, which has several professional associations due to its continental dimensions, Portugal has only one professional music therapy association, the Portuguese Music Therapy Association (Associação Portuguesa de Musicoterapia, APMT), which has around 50 associated professionals.[1] In Brazil, it is common for professionals to interact on a daily basis and exchange information in WhatsApp and Facebook groups to foster mutual professional growth. The dynamics in Portugal are different. There isn't such direct communication, and people tend not to share so much about their work (this is not a value judgment, just an observation about differences in practice).

Just as I was surprised at how little I knew about Portuguese music, I was surprised to learn that music therapists in Portugal know little about Brazilian music therapy. In fact, during their training, students in Portugal read more texts from the United States than from Brazil. This is curious, since Brazil has a large collection of texts in Portuguese, has had a consolidated practice for longer than Portugal,[2] and has more cultural and socioeconomic similarities with Portugal (Sardo et al. 2012) than the US.

This is my first reflection on the relational dynamics of the practice of a Brazilian music therapist in Portugal. This is only my perspective—it does not represent an absolute truth that cannot be contested. In Portugal, there is a strong feeling of nationalism, a drive not to lose one's roots and traditions. Adopting concepts and practices from Brazil could be felt as a significant loss of identity for colleagues in the country. Although I understand this kind of dynamic, I believe that Brazilian music therapy has a lot to contribute, precisely because the theoretical constructions of Brazilian

---

1   https://emtc-eu.com/portugal
2   https://emtc-eu.com/portugal

music therapy models and concepts are closer to Portuguese music therapy than to the publications from the US and the UK, which are commonly used in Portugal. The way of understanding community music therapy in Brazil, for example (Arndt and Maheirie 2021), is much closer to the way of thinking in Portugal than the models that have been established in the UK (Ansdell and DeNora 2016) and Norway (Stige 2014). Portugal has similar problems to Brazil regarding violence and social vulnerability, issues that are less pronounced in most other European countries—one of the few writings on community music therapy in Portugal addresses the challenges faced by refugees. Social vulnerability is a main topic in the paper, and is addressed using the music therapy theory of Rosemyriam Cunha, a Brazilian music therapist focused on community music therapy in social situations (Cunha 2016).

The issue of maintaining roots and traditions is even more evident in the case of language use in music therapy practice. Portuguese parents are extremely concerned about their children speaking Brazilian Portuguese rather than European Portuguese (Nunes 2021). It's much easier to find videos of people speaking Brazilian Portuguese than European Portuguese, which can lead to a feeling of cultural "invasion" that is difficult to control. This concern about cultural "invasion" even appears when I'm conducting my music therapy sessions. From an optimum of cultural sensitivity (Kim 2021), I know that my way of acting within the language will have a direct impact on the people I work with, especially in the case of children. This causes an internal conflict, because if I completely change the way I speak and sing in Portuguese, I undermine my authenticity as a Brazilian music therapist.

In a publication on authenticity in music therapy, Bøtker and Jacobsen (2023) state that authenticity is related to being "true (to oneself)," "reliable," "genuine," "real," "honest," and "sincere." The solution to this conundrum is not easy, because I believe that I need to value my voice and my way of being in the world, even when I act in service to others. At the moment, I try to speak with my Brazilian accent, but use the words and phrases a Portuguese person would. When I sing Portuguese songs, I try to emulate the European accent from a perspective of cultural humility, because I recognize that as a therapist I am also in a position of power where I need to value and give space to the voice of the other as it presents itself.

Being a Brazilian music therapist in another country means that I need to be aware of who I am, but at the same time be aware of who the person I'm treating is, which implies an in-depth knowledge and study of cultural competence in music therapy. According to Sue and Sue (2013), cultural competence is formed by the therapist's cultural self-awareness, their knowledge and understanding of the culture of the person being assessed (in a technical and empathic way), and the therapeutic skills to deal with different cultural contexts. This understanding of cultural competence has led me to better navigate not only how I use my voice in music therapy, but also the choice of repertoire in the sessions. I play the songs that are important to the country's culture, but I also bring songs and rhythms from Brazil to expand the patient's horizons and connect with a core part of my own identity, not as a countertransference, but as a way of being authentic and encouraging a positive perspective on the process.

Some reflections on my practice as a music therapy teacher in Europe

One of my most enjoyable and challenging practices is facilitating education in music therapy in Europe. This includes training future music therapists as well as teaching practice for music therapists who have already graduated. The act of teaching in music therapy directly incorporates the teacher's sociocultural constructions and expressions, which go far beyond the content being taught (Gombert 2022). From my first class in Spain in 2016, on music therapy research, I felt that I needed to teach about the proposed content, but that I also had to be authentic (Bøtker and Jacobsen 2024) when talking about what music therapy research existed in Brazil, and try to show my teaching style, which was the result of the experiences I'd had working in Brazil.

Another element that emerged from that first lesson was that I had achieved a great feat in my career, because I was teaching in Europe, which at that time meant "a better place than Brazil." My childhood and adolescence in Brazil took place in the 1980s and 1990s. During this period, it was always very clear that Brazil was a "fifth-rate" country (as they say in Brazil), which had much to learn from more "developed" nations. This cultural view, with its colonialist undercurrent, was always present in what I saw on TV or the conversations I had with people. When a footballer went to Europe, it meant that he was very good and deserved to play with the best. When a relative went to Europe, it meant that they had more money and could go to a better place where "everything worked out." When I was eight years old, my school teacher went to Europe for vacation. She told us about beauty when she came back, but also about some of the problems, and so I began to understand that not everything about this far-off place was perfect.

However, it's very difficult to get it out of a Latin American's mind that being in Europe means status, that Europe is a better place to be than Latin America. Since that first lesson in Spain, this idea has evolved. I've noticed in parts of Europe that there is a dynamic in which the models, approaches, and orientations that come from certain European countries are dominant, and that teachers and professionals wish to perpetuate these theories and practices without investigating models that come from other regions of the world. In other words, there is a movement to maintain certain knowledge as European traditions, since these proposals represent some people in their identity as a way of thinking and teaching others. Here, there is a colonialist ideology that is still difficult to change, since many of the teaching collaborations between programs only take place between European countries. It becomes increasingly difficult to make space for other voices concerning the educational practices of other countries, as is the case in Brazil.

I am currently a teacher in a music therapy education program that has a psychodynamic matrix (De Backer and Sutton 2014) and is centered on the Guided Imagery and Music (GIM) proposals (Grocke and Moe 2015). Based on the processes and dynamics already created in this program, it is difficult to add anything new or that deviates from these perspectives, as I would be changing the identity of the place or the context of teaching and learning. Within this context, there is also a different cultural dynamic, as I am the only non-European teacher in the program. This means that every time I explain or present an idea about possible new ways of understanding teaching and learning processes, I need to explain and contextualize the origins of these ideas and my point of view. Because the cultural dynamics are so different from my place of origin, it can become difficult for my colleagues or students to understand the meaning of these proposals, and this can lead to rejection or a sense of estrangement from the ideas I am offering.

So that my perspectives as a music therapist and teacher in Brazil are not ultimately invalidated in the different places where I teach, I try to gradually suggest texts from Brazil (and other places in the world besides Europe) in each institution's official documents. When this isn't possible, I try to include this content during my lessons and leave my students with some reading suggestions. One of the great challenges of being a minority in the music therapy programs in Europe where I teach is attempting to express my perspective on the theories and concepts that permeate my experience as a Brazilian music therapist coherently, without disrespecting or contradicting what is already taught in each program. This can be almost impossible, as some of these views are completely antagonistic.

In Brazil, there is a great tradition of behavioral music therapy, mainly through Applied Behavior Analysis (ABA), either by a discreet attempt or from a naturalistic perspective (Gattino 2022). In most European countries, there is a great tradition of psychodynamic music therapy, which clashes with behavioral music therapy mainly over the understanding of the music therapy process, the role of music in music therapy, and the role of the therapist in the process. I remember the first few times I talked about behavioral music therapy in teaching contexts with some music therapist colleagues, and their facial expressions as I spoke. I often felt as if I was talking about something that was forbidden. Over time, I realized that I needed to do my best to expand my students' understanding of the different ways of thinking that exist about music therapy in the world. It does no good to withhold my perspective simply because others think differently or struggle to understand my line of reasoning because my experience (having spent most of my life in Brazil) is so different from theirs. Navigating the intellectual and ideological conflicts that may arise is an essential skill for students if they find themselves, like me, traveling far from home to practice.

One of the biggest differences I've found between being a teacher in Brazil and the places I've taught in Europe is the way students behave in relation to what is required of them in class. In Brazil, I noticed a great appreciation of what is taught and an understanding of what is required in the different courses. In the places where I have taught in Europe, I've noticed a greater tendency to complain or challenge what is required, as well as the way of teaching, the number of hours per class, and the format of the practical and theoretical exams. Once again, let me make it clear that this is a perception based on my experiences and that it is not a generalization about all the countries on the European continent.

One of the great joys of being a music therapy teacher in Europe is being able to teach Brazilian and Latin American rhythms in practical music classes for students. Certainly one of the biggest bridges I see between Brazil and my practice as a teacher is being able to facilitate students experimenting with composition, improvisation, songs, and percussion techniques based on rhythms from Brazil. Given the complexity of Brazilian rhythms, I end up teaching rhythms from other parts of Latin America such as merengue, chamamé, and guarania (all of which can be heard in Brazil) to help contextualize the music for students (da Silva 2021). Because of the authenticity I can lend to these practical experiences, these are the ones that are most remembered and valued by my students. I am inclined to invest more and more energy into this fundamental bridge between myself and my students because of its significance for all of us in the process of teaching and learning. I believe that the way I can best communicate with my students and make my contribution to their training or continuing education is when the music of my roots, be it samba, bossa nova, maracatu, baiao, or chamamé, is present in every musical moment I share with them.

After many years as a Brazilian music therapy teacher in Europe, I have developed a lightness and flexibility in my approach to my practice (allowing me to adapt to the various realities I work with), and I see many changes in the European landscape as well. In the last two years there has been a strong movement to discuss issues such as social justice, social equality, giving everyone a voice, power struggles, inclusivity, respecting differences, and representation. These themes were the focus of the 2022 European Music Therapy Congress (QMU 2022) and the 2024 British Music Therapy Conference (BAMT 2024). Likewise, the publication of the book *Colonialism and Music Therapy* in 2022 has also contributed to a more critical understanding of music therapy in the world, encouraging greater openness toward other ways of thinking within education.

During that same time, I've noticed a more open attitude toward dialogue between different voices in Europe, including the voices of Brazilian music therapists with regard to our theories and concepts, which are becoming more valued by the broader music therapy community. In 2023, music therapist Lia Rejane Mendes Barcellos received an award from the WFMT in recognition of her career in clinical practice. She was responsible for creating interactive music therapy, a model now recognized by the WFMT (McFerran *et al.* 2023), and the author of "Music, meaning and music therapy under the light of the Molino/Nattiez Tripartite Model" (Barcellos 2012), an interpretation model taught in music therapy assessment courses at Aalborg University (Denmark), Codarts University (Netherlands), Pablo Olavide University (Spain), and the University of Barcelona (Spain).

Some reflections on my practice as a music therapy researcher in Europe

My experiences with music therapy research in Europe are perhaps the most complex and at the same time the most remarkable I've had in my career so far. Here I want to offer reflections on the complex interactions and movements that shape the practice of a Brazilian researcher and music therapist in Europe. To begin with, it is necessary to understand the origin of most of the conflicts and difficulties in the relationships that will be presented here by understanding some things about how science works in Europe.

Initially a European cultural practice, Western science quickly spread across the globe through colonialism and imperialism (Held 2023). Over centuries, it has become a universally applicable and legitimate means of generating new knowledge, capable of making valuable contributions to many fields of study including music therapy. Early on in the development of scientific journals, most publications were founded in North America (Reschke-Hernández 2011), but since the 1980s there has been a significant growth in the creation of music therapy-centered scientific journals in Europe, as well as the founding of doctoral programs in music therapy in countries such as Belgium, Denmark, Finland, Norway, and the UK.

The influence of these journals and doctoral programs has directly impacted the practice of research both inside and outside Europe, as well as the dynamics for forming research consortia either to carry out specific research or to share information with different colleagues. I am currently part of two consortia in Europe: the International Music Therapy Assessment Consortium (IMTAC)[3] and a consortium of universities with doctoral programs in music therapy (International Consortium of Music Therapy Research).[4] Neither of these consortia include a Latin American university.

Although I am a member of these consortia, I don't feel that the voice of Brazilian music therapy is adequately represented. To achieve that, we'd need someone who is living in Brazil currently and can give real-time insight into the dynamics of research there. This would allow Brazilian music therapy to be more present in Europe as a research institution. Although I am optimistic that power relations are changing within the profession, there is a long way to go for Latin American (and, in turn, Brazilian) universities to be recognized for their achievements and accomplishments and to win a place within the major research initiatives of the world.

My first experience as a Brazilian researcher in Europe came just after I finished my doctorate in 2012, when I worked in the TIME-A international study on music therapy and autism. At the time, I was living in Brazil, but I traveled to Europe to take part in some of the project's activities. I was reminded of childhood memories of the Brazilian footballers who went to play for clubs in Europe: in my mind, this was a step up from any work I could be doing in Brazil. When the project started, I had my first big surprise: I had the space to speak and suggest ideas from my point of view. I was assuming that I would simply be expected to follow instructions, not anticipating that I would also be asked to collaborate in the construction of the project. I was soon faced with the need to think from a decolonial perspective. Decoloniality is a concept that arose from the need to overcome the view that colonization was a completed event (de Souza Oliveira and Lucini 2021). It is an understanding that colonization is an ongoing process, which persists today in new forms. I realized that in my mind I was still perpetuating a view I had internalized during my basic training in music therapy in Brazil: that it was scientists abroad who carried out the

---

3 www.communication.aau.dk/research/music-therapy-research/imtac#9c3a43ab-fafb-4cb3-92d6-efcbf38b5f0f
4 www.aru.ac.uk/cambridge-institute-for-music-therapy-research/about/links-and-partnerships

real research, and that I should learn from them so that one day I could become as important as they were.

The reality I witnessed was exactly the opposite. The group followed some principles based on peer learning (with direct and indirect influences from the problem-based learning model and *Pedagogy of the Oppressed*) (de Carvalho and Pio 2017; Wood 2003), where everyone has something to teach and learn. Thus, I understood that in some places, my voice carries the same weight as the voice of others. The experience of this project not only transformed my life as a music therapy researcher, but also gave me the strength to understand that everyone can be heard and can listen. That early experience was empowering, but I have also faced discrimination, especially at scientific music therapy events where myself or other colleagues from Brazil have presented work developed in our country. At a world congress, I went to present a vision of "evidence-based music therapy" and a colleague criticized my work by suggesting I read another researcher's book, claiming she was the one who knew the subject best. In another situation, a Brazilian colleague was giving a presentation on her ongoing research projects, and another colleague raised concern that she hadn't had her projects approved by a research ethics committee. My colleague calmly replied that all her projects had been approved, but I doubt she would have been questioned in this manner had she been from Europe. There is often an assumption in Europe that science in Latin America is not as well-regulated or rigorous as it is in Europe or the US.

These two incidents are just a few of many I have witnessed in my career. To explain behaviors like these and others I will relate here, it is necessary to talk about the mechanisms that perpetuate the dominance of the colonizer's voice over that of the colonized (Higgins and Kim 2019). These directly influenced my practice as a Brazilian music therapy researcher, both when I was still living in Brazil and in Europe.

First is the *devaluation of local knowledge* (Nicholls 2011). I had many difficulties as a researcher in the field of psychometrics in music therapy in communicating that Brazil is one of the countries that publishes the most on psychometrics (mainly on validation studies and cross-cultural adaptation of assessment tools), and that its methodologies are among the most advanced in the world. As I spoke about this, many colleagues appeared surprised. The looks on some faces seemed to indicate that I must be mistaken. Even today, most music therapists do not look to publications from Brazil as a first resource, even when Brazilian studies might be one of their best options on a given topic. This is a manifestation of the colonialist attitude that the knowledge of the colonized is inferior to that of the colonizers, which discourages many people from colonizing nations from being curious about the intellectual activity of people in their colonies, even many generations and decades or centuries of development down the line.

The second mechanism for perpetuating the voice of the colonizer is *control over historical narratives* (Bhambra 2023). In music therapy, this manifests mainly as a habit most therapists and researchers have of consulting references solely from English-language publications, meaning they might miss key ideas from papers that have not yet been translated as they are conducting their research. This came up often when mentioning Brazilian researchers who had done essential and well-recognized work in Latin America to colleagues in Europe. For many years, only the work of Lia Rejane Mendes Barcellos was known here, and when Brazilian research was cited, it was almost always hers. Although one would logically assume that if one has found an excellent researcher from a country of 200 million that there would be more where she came from, it was as if people here assumed that they need not look any further into research in Brazil. While doing so might take work, especially in the sense that it might challenge some European professionals to update their perspectives, there could be much to gain from pulling that thread. But this might also risk diluting or undermining the authority of European music therapy institutions, and this is why institutions of all stripes in this part of the world have historically ignored or suppressed the knowledge of others. This is another deeply entrenched aspect of colonialism, one which many people in colonizing nations remain unconscious of.

The third mechanism for perpetuating the colonizer's voice is maintaining *institutional barriers* (Abdul-Jabbar 2019). When I started working as a researcher in Europe, I was shocked by the amount of material I could not access simply because of financial barriers or exclusive access to only one major university's database. Over the years, I realized that it was essential to write reviews and theoretical chapters where the themes of publications little known to Brazilians could be exposed to them through texts in Portuguese. In the book *Fundamentos de Avaliação em Musicoterapia [Essentials of Music Therapy Assessment]*, which had its Portuguese version published in 2020 (Gattino 2020), I tried to compile various music therapy assessment concepts and practices only available in English.

The last mechanism for perpetuating the colonizer's voice that I want to address here is the *hegemony of the English language* (Nicholls 2011). This mechanism seems evident since it is necessary to know English to participate in the scientific community in Europe and worldwide. However, the point I want to make here is not about the necessity of speaking English but about the difficulties some European researchers have in accepting a term that does not exist in English and which, when translated into English, may lose some of its meaning. In Portuguese (the language of Brazil), we have *saudade*. This word names a certain feeling where you miss something or someone (Freitas, Lourenço, and Pitta 2014). Explaining how this single word describes a complex emotional and mental state can be difficult, since the roundabout ways of describing it in other languages never quite seem to capture the essence of *saudade*. Because of words like this, sometimes key points in a research paper are rendered almost meaningless in the process of translating them, which seems to necessitate that if one wanted to publish a translation, the paper should be published in its original language as well to maintain accurate meaning, and that the translation should note the potential misunderstandings that could occur.

This difficulty came up for a colleague who was reporting on her music therapy work at a corporation. Her English-speaking colleagues translated her description of the nature of her work as "team-building," but this does not accurately reflect her or her clients' perception of the work and its role, as it is a common practice in Brazil and other Latin American countries for music therapists to work within companies, whereas it would be unusual or "special" in the dynamics of many corporate environments elsewhere in the world (de Castro, Valentin, and de Sá 2015). This is an example of how important context and subtleties of meaning can be lost in translation, even when attempting to translate a simple summary of a researcher's or therapist's work, and gives an idea of the degradation of information that is occurring as non-English-speaking researchers attempt to share their discoveries with the global scientific community.

Today, I see myself as someone who can make his voice heard as a Brazilian in different research environments. Likewise, the regulation of the music therapy profession in Brazil in 2024 (Law No. 14,842, 2024) has elevated our status in the scientific community, and people are showing more curiosity about research in Brazil.

Some critical reflections on the future of Brazilian music therapists in Europe and around the world

Throughout my training and career, I've seen the complexity of developing therapeutic, teaching, and research practices as a Brazilian music therapist in Europe. The challenge has been to adapt and maintain authenticity within these practices, especially regarding the ways of thinking and expressing oneself that originate in Brazilian reality.

As with other Latin American music therapists who have had to leave their country to become immigrants in Europe and other parts of the world, it is increasingly common to find Brazilian music therapists abroad.

According to Lee (2020), immigrants experience isolation, frustration, fatigue, and dissatisfaction, which can lead to burnout, and in the future, I hope to be able to create some community or a network between us, for my colleagues scattered across the globe, as our stories are similar and resonate with those in publications about being an immigrant and working as a music therapist (Grimmer and Schwantes 2018; Lee 2020; Maeda 2020).

Since I arrived in Europe, I have undergone therapy to help deal with situations related to burnout as a result of constantly adapting to the challenges of working outside Brazil. I believe that in the future, we should organize and offer music therapy to music therapists working and living abroad so that they can connect with their origins and have a space where they can express their authentic voices and their music of origin, and replenish their energy to meet the challenges of everyday life in a foreign place.

Being a music therapist is complex; being an immigrant music therapist is even more so. While we all encounter similar challenges, how they are characterized and how the individual experiences them will depend very much on the country and region where the person is from. As I write this text, I believe that Andeline dos Santos's (2022) work on music therapy and empathy is one of the models best suited to understanding the difficulties immigrant music therapists face. This proposal is not specific to immigrants, but offers a flexible means of understanding the inner worlds of others.

Final considerations

A common phrase in Brazil is that we are Brazilians, and "nós nunca desistimos" [we never give up]. This simple notion is the core message I carry with me after many years of working in Europe. I have accumulated (and continue to develop) effective coping skills, emotional regulation techniques, and a great deal of resilience. These allow me to reflect on being a Latin American music therapist from a country of continental dimensions in Europe, a place where many people do not pay much attention to the world outside, where you must decolonize your own thinking even once you feel you have "arrived." The more I work in Europe, the more deeply Brazilian I feel, and the more I want to be in Brazil and collaborate with my colleagues there. I may return to my homeland one day, but for the moment I'm happy with the life I have chosen here, on the other side of the ocean, where I might build bridges between Brazil and Europe in music therapy. My hope is that we can reach a point where our similarities unite us, and our differences strengthen us.

CONCLUSIONS

PATRICIA ZARATE DE PEREZ

The cultural and musical contexts of music therapy in Latin America are diverse and at times divergent. There is no singular "Latin American" experience, and music therapy practices in the region are shaped by the social, economic, cultural, and epistemological circumstances of each locale. Latin America is best understood as a diaspora. Peoples from Latin America bring their traditions to the places to which they migrate, or at times maintain those traditions after their land has been lost to colonization. Their musical traditions are important in any effort to contextualize and learn about the differences between countries and the specificity of different groups living in precise regions of Latin America. The region presents immense diversity—Indigenous, European, and African peoples have migrated for different reasons, mixed and transformed their cultural and musical contexts since the 16th century. The music therapy profession in Latin America has a solid tradition based on decades of praxis in countries like Argentina, Brazil, Colombia, and Chile. In other countries, music therapy is a young but growing profession that may not have professional/academic associations or educational programs, but there is always someone, or some group, working on advancing the music therapy profession.

Music therapists work with Latin American clients in many parts of the world, including the United States, where almost 20 percent of the population is of Latin American descent. When working with the diaspora, music therapists may encounter numerous disparate cultural and musical contexts: one country in the region can be very different from another, and even within the borders of one nation people may speak different languages and trace their ancestry from any number of different ethnic groups including various Indigenous lineages. The music therapist–client relationship is important in Latin American contexts for music therapy, as family, friends, and community relationships are an important part of the culture. The connections between music and other forms of expression such as dance, art, and poetry are important to understand when working with Latin American clients. Within each locale in the region we may experience several different cultural and musical contexts depending on the community in which we live. Music therapists working with Latin American people can easily find themselves serving clients who might speak an Indigenous language, Spanish, English, Creole, Portuguese, or any combination of these and others.

The work with Indigenous populations of the Americas is especially interesting as the relationship between music and healing in those communities is much older than the music therapy profession itself. Many Indigenous groups challenge the Eurocentric epistemologies in which the music therapy profession was created, and question its practice in cultural contexts that have different, at times contrasting, epistemologies. To better understand the cultural and social contexts of Latin America, it is important to understand the history of colonization and the development of theories like Aníbal Quijano's "coloniality of power." Using philosophical, sociological, and cultural theories in Latin America, we can understand the immense gulf between Indigenous epistemologies and Eurocentric thought, both living in constant struggle within the music therapy profession.

REFERENCES

Abdul-Jabbar, W.K. (2019) "The Theoretical and Methodological Framework: Post-colonial Theory, Double Consciousness, and Study Design." In *Negotiating Diasporic Identity in Arab-Canadian Students* (pp.47–74). Palgrave Studies in Educational Futures. Cham, Switzerland: Palgrave Macmillan. https://doi.org/10.1007/978-3-030-16283-2_4

Academy of Neurologic Music Therapy, The (2015) "Locate current affiliates in your area." https://nmtacademy.co/findannmt

Albornoz, Y. (2022). Musical spiritual experiences through the Indigenous voice. *Colonialism and Music Therapy Interlocutors (CAMTI) Collective* (Ed.), *Colonialism and Music Therapy* (pp. 137–162). Barcelona Publishers.

Almerud, S. and Petersson, K. (2003) "Music therapy—A complementary treatment for mechanically ventilated intensive care patients." *Intensive and Critical Care Nursing 19*, 1, 21–30. https://doi.org/10.1016/S0964-3397(02)00118-0

Álvarez-Trutié, J.A., Fernández-Fernández, L., Lahite-Savón, Y., and Rivo-Sayoux, B.N. (2020) "La musicoterapia como alternativa para el control de la agitación y sedación de pacientes con ventilación mecánica invasiva." *Revista Información Científica 99*, 5, 442–451. www.scielo.sld.cu/scielo.php?script=sci_arttext&pid=S1028-99332020000500442

AMME (Asociación de Musicoterapeutas en México) (no date) "Musicoterapia." www.musicoterapiamexico.org/musicoterapia.html

AMTA (American Music Therapy Association) (2021) "Standards for education and clinical training." www.musictherapy.org/members/edctstan

Ansdell, G. and DeNora, T. (2016) *Musical Pathways in Recovery: Community Music Therapy and Mental Wellbeing.* Abingdon: Routledge.

Anzaldúa, G. (1987) *Borderlands/La Frontera: The New Mestiza.* San Francisco, CA: Aunt Lute Books.

Anzaldúa, G., Vivancos Pérez, R.F., and Cantú, N.E. (2021) *Borderlands/La Frontera: The New Mestiza.* The Critical Edition. San Francisco, CA: Aunt Lute Books.

Arndt, A.D. and Maheirie, K. (2021) "Musicoterapia social e comunitária e processos de subjetivação política" ["Social and community music therapy and processes of political subjectivation"]. *Psychology & Society 33.* https://doi.org/10.1590/1807-0310/2021v33235846

Ayllón Garrido, N., Álvarez González, M., and González García, M. (2007) "Factores ambientales estresantes percibidos por los pacientes de una Unidad de Cuidados Intensivos." *Enfermería intensiva 18*, 4, 159–167.

Ayón, C., Marsiglia, F., and Bermudez-Parsai, M. (2010) "Latino family mental health: Exploring the role of discrimination and familismo." *Journal of Community Psychology 38*, 6, 742–756. doi: 10.1002/jcop.20392.

BAMT (British Association for Music Therapy) (2024) "BAMT Conference. 2024." www.bamt.org/DB/events-view/bamt-conference-2024

Barcellos, L.R. (1999) *Musicoterapia: Transferência, contratransferência e resistência.* Rio de Janeiro, Brasil: Enelivros.

Barcellos, L.R. (2012) "Music, meaning, and music therapy under the light of the Molino/Nattiez Tripartite Model." *Voices: A World Forum for Music Therapy 12*, 3. https://doi.org/10.15845/voices.v12i3.677

Baum, S., Ma, J. and Payea, K. (2013) *Education Pays, 2013: The Benefits of Higher Education for Individuals and Society.* Trends in Higher Education Series. College Board. https://eric.ed.gov/?id=eD572537

Benenzon, R.O. (1976) *Musicoterapia en la psicosis infantil.* Buenos Aires: Editorial Paidós.

Benenzon, R.O. and Yepes, A. (1972) *Musicoterapia en psiquiatría.* Buenos Aires: Editorial Barry.

Berenstecher, M., Biegun, K., Ciai, S., and Riccomini, M.E. (2022) "Práctica musicoterapéutica y población migrante: Aspectos culturales en el ámbito hospitalario público de la Ciudad de Buenos Aires." *ECOS – Revista Científica De Musicoterapia Y Disciplinas Afines 7*, 31. https://doi.org/10.24215/27186199e031

Bhambra, G.K. (2023) "Modernity, Colonialism, and Postcolonial Critique." In G.K. Bhambra, *Rethinking Modernity: Postcolonialism and the Sociological Imagination* (pp.3–28). Basingstoke: Palgrave Macmillan. https://doi.org/10.1007/978-3-031-21537-7_1

Bieleninik, L., Geretsegger, M., Mössler, K., Assmus, J., *et al.* (2017) "Effects of improvisational music therapy vs enhanced standard care on symptom severity among children with autism spectrum disorder: The TIME-A randomized clinical trial." *JAMA 318*, 6, 525–535. doi: 10.1001/jama.2017.9478.

Blanca Gutiérrez, J., Blanco Alvariño, A., Luque Pérez, M., and Ramírez Pérez, M. (2008) "Experiencias, percepciones y necesidades en la UCI: Revisión sistemática de estudios cualitativos." *Enfermería Global 7*, 1, 1–14. www.redalyc.org/pdf/3658/365834748003.pdf

Bøtker, J.Ø. and Jacobsen, S.L. (2023) "The experience of authenticity across three music disciplines; Music therapy, music teaching, and music performance: Preliminary findings of a phenomenological interview study." *Voices: A World Forum for Music Therapy 23*, 1. https://doi.org/10.15845/voices.v23i1.3464

Bright, R. (1991) *La musicoterapia en el tratamiento geriátrico: Una nueva vision* [*Music in Geriatric Care: A Second Look*]. Buenos Aires: Editorial Bonum.

Broqua, G.I. (2020) "Accesibilidad en musicoterapia. La especificidad terminológica en la interdisciplina." *ECOS – Revista Científica De Musicoterapia Y Disciplinas Afines 5*, 1, 1–16. https://dialnet.unirioja.es/servlet/articulo?codigo=7970254

Broqua, G. (2021) "Music Therapy, Rehabilitation and Ethics in Argentina." 1st International Conference CRE Program on Neuro-Socio-Psycho Rehabilitation. Rayat-Bahra University. www.youtube.com/watch?v=4XbluqEOqxE

Broqua, G.I. (2022) *Música accesible con Tecnología Asistiva.* Buenos Aires: Editorial Autores de Argentina.

Broqua, G.I. (2023a) "Formación de musicoterapeutas a distancia con Tecnología Educativa: el desafío del nivel académico." En V.A. Cannarozzo y V. Díaz Abrahan (comp.) *Desarrollos Disciplinares de la Musicoterapia: Construir Redes Desde y Hacia el Sur* (pgs.139–156). La Plata: Universidad Nacional de La Plata. https://sedici.unlp.edu.ar/bitstream/handle/10915/159540/Documento_completo.pdf?sequence=1

Broqua, G.I. (2023b) "Posgrados de actualización en Musicoterapia en Argentina." En XV Congreso Internacional de Investigación y Práctica Profesional en Psicología y V Encuentro de Musicoterapia. Facultad de Psicología, Universidad de Buenos Aires. www.aacademica.org/graciela.ines.broqua/7.pdf

Broqua, G.I. (2023c) "Posgrados de Musicoterapia a distancia en lengua española." Tesis de Maestría. Universidad Abierta Interamericana. https://repositorio.uai.edu.ar/items/ddacb262-9963-4ee7-bdb1-eb13eca54eab

Broqua, G.I. (2023d) "Tecnología asistiva para la ejecución de aerófono con traqueotomía." *Revista do Núcleo de Estudos e Pesquisas Interdisciplinares em Musicoterapia InCantare 17*, 2, 70–74. https://doi.org/10.33871/2317417X.2022.17.2.8279

Cadena, K., Dehasse, J., and Romero Haaker, J.R. (2023) "Logros, innovaciones y desafíos de Panamá para la erradicación de la pobreza." Banco Mundial Blogs. Octubre 19. https://blogs.worldbank.org/es/latinamerica/logros-innovaciones-desafios-panama-erradicacion-pobreza

CAMTI (Colonialism and Music Therapy Interlocutors) Collective (2022) *Colonialism and Music Therapy*. Dallas, TX: Barcelona Publishers.

Cannarozzo, V.A. (2020a) "El ejercicio profesional desde el enfoque de derechos humanos. Interrogantes y reflexiones a partir del ejercicio profesional de la Musicoterapia en un hospital público especializado en rehabilitación." En V.A. Cannarozzo y D.H. Gonnet (comp.) *Musicoterapia en la Provincia de Buenos Aires: Oportunidades y desafíos para su inclusión en la agenda pública* (pp.17–35). La Plata: Universidad Nacional de La Plata. http://sedici.unlp.edu.ar/bitstream/handle/10915/118048/Documento_completo.pdf?sequence=1&isAllowed=y

Cannarozzo, V.A. (2020b) "La inclusión como paradigma fundamental de la educación universitaria significa construir oportunidades para todos: Entrevista a Fernando Tauber." *ECOS – Revista Científica De Musicoterapia Y Disciplinas Afines 5*, 2, 129–146. https://revistas.unlp.edu.ar/ECOS/article/view/10804

Cannarozzo, V.A. and Díaz Abrahan, V. (2023) "Presentación." En V.A. Cannarozzo y V. Díaz Abrahan (comp.) *Desarrollos Disciplinares de la Musicoterapia: Construir redes desde y hacia el Sur* (pg.6–10). La Plata: Universidad Nacional de La Plata. http://sedici.unlp.edu.ar/bitstream/handle/10915/159540/Documento_completo.pdf?sequence=1

Cannarozzo, V.A. and Díaz Abrahan, V. (comp.) (2023) *Desarrollos Disciplinares de la Musicoterapia: Construir redes desde y hacia el Sur*. La Plata: Universidad Nacional de La Plata. http://sedici.unlp.edu.ar/bitstream/handle/10915/159540/Documento_completo.pdf?sequence=1

Cannarozzo, V.A., Godetti, E., Mancini, F., Moscuzza, C.A., Gonnet, D.H., and Díaz Abrahan, V. (2021) "Consonancias: Una experiencia musicoterapéutica en el ámbito público hospitalario durante la pandemia de COVID-19." *ECOS – Revista Científica De Musicoterapia Y Disciplinas Afines 6*, 1, 4. https://doi.org/10.24215/27186199e004

Caplan, S. (2019) "Intersection of cultural and religious beliefs about mental health: Latinos in the faith-based setting." *Hispanic Health Care International 17*, 1, 4–10. https://doi.org/10.1177/1540415319828265

Cárdenas, R., Horacio, J., Topelberg, A., and Suárez, E. (2008) "Historia de la musicoterapia en la Argentina." En XV Jornadas de Investigación y IV Encuentro de Investigadores en Psicología del Mercosur. Buenos Aires: Facultad de Psicología, Universidad de Buenos Aires. www.aacademica.org/000-032/100.pdf

Carrizo, L.J. (2021) "Musicoterapia en la estrategia de atención primaria de la salud en el marco de la pandemia por Covid-19: Experiencia en un hospital rural." *ECOS – Revista Científica De Musicoterapia Y Disciplinas Afines (Especial) 009.* https://dialnet.unirioja.es/servlet/articulo?codigo=8718246

Case, A. (2021) "Exploring Music, Imagery, and Racial-Ethnic-Cultural Identity with Youth in a Community Music Program: A Community Engagement Project." Expressive Therapies Capstone Theses. 462. https://digitalcommons.lesley.edu/expressive_theses/462

Cavanagh, E. and Veracini, L. (eds) (2016) *The Routledge Handbook of the History of Settler Colonialism.* Abingdon, New York: Routledge.

Cerebello-González, E. (2023) "Musicoterapia en Latinoamerica. Una Reflexion Sobre el Desafio Institucional." Essay. En V.A. Cannarozzo y V. Díaz Abrahan (comp.) *Desarrollos Disciplinares de La Musicoterapia: Construyendos Redes Desde y Hacia El Sur* (Capítulo 3). La Plata, Argentina: Catedra Libre.

Chang, D.C., Oseni, T.O., Strong, B.L., Molina, G., *et al.* (2021) "The other global pandemic: Scientific racism and the normality bias." *Annals of Surgery 274,* 6, e646–e648. https://doi.org/10.1097/SLA.0000000000005168

Chlan, L.H., Weinert, C.R., Heiderscheit, A., Tracy, M.F., *et al.* (2013) "Effects of patient-directed music intervention on anxiety and sedative exposure in critically ill patients receiving mechanical-ventilatory support." *JAMA: Journal of the American Medical Association 309,* 22, 2335–2344. doi: 10.1001/jama.2013.5670.

Chomsky, N. (2015) "Globalization." *Chomsky's Philosophy.* Lecture, July 20. www.youtube.com/watch?v=4RxHzQTHhKk

Chuchuy, I.G. (2023) "Perfil del graduado en la formación en musicoterapia. Un análisis de contenidos curriculares de los planes de estudio de la Universidad de Buenos Aires." En V.A. Cannarozzo y V. Díaz Abrahan (comp.) *Desarrollos Disciplinares de la Musicoterapia: Construir redes desde y hacia el Sur* (pgs.50–68). La Plata: Universidad Nacional de La Plata. https://sedici.unlp.edu.ar/bitstream/handle/10915/159540/Documento_completo.pdf?sequence=1

CLAM (Comité Latinoamericano de Musicoterapia) (2021) *Procesos de formación profesional de musicoterapia en América Latina y el Caribe.* www.musicoterapiaclam.com/_files/ugd/32eca6_b0d94540c1f841a397ded65332609cdo.pdf

CONASAMI (Comisión Nacional de Salarios Mínimos) (2023) *Informes mensuales sobre el comportamiento de la economía: Dirección técnica.* www.gob.mx/conasami/documentos/informes-mensuales-sobre-el-comportamiento-de-la-economia-del-ano-2023

Congreso de la Nación Argentina (1995) *Ley de Educación Superior [N° 24.521].* www.argentina.gob.ar/normativa/nacional/ley-24521-25394/actualizacion

Congreso de la Nación Argentina (2015) *Ley de Ejercicio Profesional de la Musicoterapia [N° 27153].* www.argentina.gob.ar/normativa/nacional/ley-27153-248823

Congreso de la Nación Argentina (2016) *Ley Personas con Discapacidad. Deber de Informar sobre sus Derechos al Momento de Entregar el Certificado de Discapacidad [N° 27269].* www.argentina.gob.ar/normativa/nacional/ley-27269-264950/texto

CONEVAL (Consejo Nacional de Evaluación de la Política de Desarrollo Social) (2022) "Medición de la pobreza." www.coneval.org.mx/Medicion/Paginas/PobrezaInicio.aspx

Conservatório Brasileiro de Música (2011) *Anais do XVII Fórum Estadual de Musicoterapia e IX Jornada Científica de Musicoterapia "Construindo história na musicoterapia: Clínica, formação, pesquisa e política".* Rio de Janeiro, Brasil. https://content.amtrj.com.br/wp-content/uploads/2024/05/anais_2011-XVII_ FORUM_ESTADUAL_DE_MUSICOTERAPIA_IX_JORNADA_CIENTIFICA_ DE_MUSICOTERAPIA.pdf

Costa, C. M. (Org.). (2020). *Musicoterapia no Rio de Janeiro: Novos Rumos* (2ª ed. rev.). Associação de Musicoterapia do Rio de Janeiro.

Cuadrado-García, M., Montoro-Pons, J. D., & Miquel-Romero, M.-J. (2023). Music studies as cultural capital accumulation and its impact on music genre preferences. International Journal of Music Education, 41(1), 38-51. https://doi. org/10.1177/02557614221092417

Cunha, R. (2016) "Musicoterapia social e comunitária: uma organização: crítica de conceitos." ["Social and community music therapy: A critical organization of concepts."] *Revista Brasileira de Musicoterapia [Brazilian Journal of Music Therapy] 18*, 21, 93–116.

da Silva, L.T. (2021) "Sonoridades latino-americanas na música popular do brasil nos anos 1970" ["Latin American sonorities in Brazilian popular music in the 1970s"]. Master's dissertation, Federal University of Uberlândia. https://repositorio.ufu.br/handle/123456789/33958

Dam Lam, R. and Gasparatos, A. (2023) "Unpacking the interface of modernization, development and sustainability in Indigenous Guna communities of Panama." *People and Nature 5*, 2, 774–794. https://doi.org/10.1002/pan3.10452

De Backer, J. and Sutton, J. (eds) (2014) *The Music in Music Therapy: Psychodynamic Music Therapy in Europe: Clinical, Theoretical and Research Approaches.* London: Jessica Kingsley Publishers.

de Carvalho, S.M.G. and Pio, P.M. (2017) "A categoria da práxis em Pedagogia do Oprimido: sentidos e implicações para a educação libertadora" ["The category of praxis in Pedagogy of the Oppressed: Meanings and implications for liberatory education"]. *Revista Brasileira de Estudos Pedagógicos 98*, 249, 428–445. doi: 10.24109/2176-6681.rbep.98i249.2729.

de Castro, A.A.G., Valentin, F., and de Sá, L.C. (2015) "Atuação e perfil do musicoterapeuta organizacional" ["Performance and profile of the organizational music therapist"]. *Revista Brasileira de Musicoterapia [Brazilian Journal of Music Therapy] 19.* https://musicoterapia.revistademusicoterapia.mus.br/index.php/ rbmt/article/view/103

de Souza Oliveira, E. and Lucini, M. (2021) "O pensamento decolonial: Conceitos para pensar uma prática de pesquisa de resistência" ["Decolonial thinking: Concepts for thinking about a research practice of resistance"]. *Historian Bulletin 8*, 1. https://periodicos.ufs.br/historiar/article/view/15456

Denis, N.A. (2015) *War Against All Puerto Ricans: Revolution and Terror in America's Colony.* New York: Nation Books.

Díaz, D.H.S., Garcia, G., Clare, C., Su, J., *et al.* (2020) "Taking care of the Puerto Rican patient: Historical perspectives, health status, and health care access." *MedEdPORTAL 16*, 10984. https://doi.org/10.15766/mep_2374-8265.10984

Díaz, J. (2023) "Musicoterapia feminista y salud mental comunitaria: El canto y la expresión corporal como experiencias de transformación identitaria y colectiva." En V.A. Cannarozzo y V. Díaz Abrahan (comp.) *Desarrollos Disciplinares de la Musicoterapia: Construir redes desde y hacia el Sur* (pgs.85–109). La Plata: Universidad Nacional de La Plata. https://sedici.unlp.edu.ar/bitstream/handle/10915/159540/Documento_completo.pdf?sequence=1 dos Santos, A. (2022) *Empathy Pathways: A View from Music Therapy*. Cham, Switzerland: Palgrave Macmillan.

Duany, J. (2002) *The Puerto Rican Nation on the Move: Identities on the Island and in the United States*. Chapel Hill, NC: The University of North Carolina Press.

Duany, R. (2004) "Solve the colonial dilemma to gain the Puerto Rican vote." *Miami Herald*, April 18, p.2.

Dubbin, L.A., Chang, J.S., and Shim, J.K. (2013) "Cultural health capital and the interactional dynamics of patient-centered care." *Social Science & Medicine 93*, 113–120. https://doi.org/10.1016/j.socscimed.2013.06.014

Elencwajg, J. (2020) "Procesos de formación profesional: Licenciatura en Musicoterapia de la Universidad Juan Agustín Maza, Mendoza." *ECOS – Revista Científica De Musicoterapia Y Disciplinas Afines 5*, 3, 19–38. https://revistas.unlp.edu.ar/ECOS/article/view/10870

Englert, S. (2022) *Settler Colonialism: An Introduction*. London: Pluto Press. https://doi.org/10.2307/j.ctv2x6f052

Escobar, A. (2011) *Encountering Development: The Making and Unmaking of the Third World*. Princeton, NJ: Princeton University Press. https://doi.org/10.1515/9781400839926

Eslava Mejía, J. (2019) "¿Una musicoterapia latinoamericana? Polifonía y polirritmia en el desarrollo disciplinar y profesional de Latinoamérica." *Revista InCantare 10*, 1, 1–166. https://periodicos.unespar.edu.br/index.php/incantare/article/download/3504/2287/8922

Estrella, K. (2017) "Music Therapy with Hispanic/Latino Clients." In A. Whitehead-Pleaux and X. Tan (eds) *Cultural Intersections in Music Therapy: Music, Health, and the Person* (Chapter 4). Dallas, TX: Barcelona Publishers.

Falicov, C.J. (2014) *Latino Families in Therapy* (2nd edn). New York: Guilford Press.

Fajardo, A. (2009) "Accordions can cry: Music for healing among Latinos." Open to Hope, September 10. www.opentohope.com/accordions-can-cry-music-for-healing-among-latinos

Fallek, R., Corey, K., Qamar, A., Vernisie, S.N., *et al.* (2019) "Soothing the heart with music: A feasibility study of a bedside music therapy intervention for critically ill patients in an urban hospital setting." *Palliative Support Care 18*, 1, 47–54. doi: 10.1017/S1478951519000294.

Federico, G. (2016) *El niño con necesidades especiales: Neurología y musicoterapia*. Argentina: Editorial Kier.

Federico, G. and Tosto, V. (comp.) (2018) *Lo que suena en las sesiones: Casos clínicos musicoterapéuticos*. Editorial Kier.

Fernando, G. (2008) "Assessing mental health and psychosocial status in communities exposed to traumatic events: Sri Lanka as an example." *American Journal of Orthopsychiatry 78*, 2, 229–239. https://doi.org/10.1037/a0013940

Ferrari, K.D. (sin fecha) "Musicoterapia en Latinoamérica." *Scribd*. www.scribd.com/document/284785193

Ferrari, K. (2013) *Musicoterapia: Aspectos de la sistematización y la evaluación de la práctica clínica*. Buenos Aires: MTD Ediciones.

Ferreira, M. de M. (2015) "Construção e gestão do conhecimento no Ensino Superior de Musicoterapia no Brasil." *Brazilian Journal of Music Therapy 19*. https://musicoterapia.revistademusicoterapia.mus.br/index.php/rbmt/article/view/101

Fisher, E. (2014) "Constitutional struggle and Indigenous resistance in Latin America: The case of Panama." *Latin American Perspectives 41*, 6, 65–78. https://doi.org/10.1177/0094582X14547505

Flint Rehab. (2021) "Stroke affecting speech: Diagnosis, treatment, and timeline." www.flintrehab.com/stroke-affecting-speech-aphasia [**Now** "When stroke affects speech: How to overcome aphasia, dysarthria, or apraxia of speech".]

Flores, E., Tschann, J.M., Dimas, J.M., Bachen, E.A., Pasch, L.A., and de Groat, C.L. (2008) *Discrimination Stress Scale* [Database record]. APA PsycTests. https://doi.org/10.1037/t03611-000

Flores, G. (2020, October 18). Hispanic Heritage month 2020: 5 times Los Tigres del norte spoke out against social injustice. Billboard. https://www.billboard.com/music/latin/los-tigres-del-norte-social-injustice-9327502

Flores, J. (2000) *From Bomba to Hip-Hop: Puerto Rican Culture and Latino Identity.* New York: Columbia University Press.

Florido, A. (2020) "Puerto Rico, island of racial harmony?" NPR, April 24. www.npr.org/2020/04/23/842832544/puerto-rico-island-of-racial-harmony

Freitas, M.S.P., Lourenço, S.C., and Pitta, S.C. (2014) "Saudade: um estudo etimológico." UniÍtalo in Research.

Fuentes, C. and Valdeavellano, R. (2015) *Chicago Boys* [Film]. La Ventana Producciones.

Freire, P. (1972) *Pedagogy of the Oppressed.* London: Penguin Education.

Gaiada, A. (2020) "Musicoterapia en el ámbito hospitalario. Recorridos y experiencias." En V.A. Cannarozzo y D.H. Gonnet (comp.) *Musicoterapia en la Provincia de Buenos Aires: Oportunidades y desafíos para su inclusión en la agenda pública* (pg.52–62). La Plata: Universidad Nacional de La Plata. http://sedici.unlp.edu.ar/bitstream/handle/10915/118048/Documento_completo.pdf?sequence=1&isAllowed=y

Gallardo, R.D. (1998) *Musicoterapia y salud mental: Prevención, asistencia y rehabilitación.* Ediciones Universo. Buenos Aires, Argentina.

García, D. (2022) "Conoce la fragilidad médica de ser afrodescendiente" ["Learn about the medical fragility of being of African descent"]. *Noticias*, May 30. https://prensa.css.gob.pa/2022/05/30/conoce-la-fragilidad-medica-de-ser-afrodescendiente

Garcia-Preto, N. (2005) "Puerto Rican Families." In M. McGoldrick, J. Giordano, and N. Garcia-Preto (eds) *Ethnicity & Family Therapy* (3rd edition) (pp.242–255). New York: Guilford Press.

Gauna, G., Giacobone, A., Licastro, L., and Perea, X. (2008) *Diagnóstico y abordaje musicoterapéutico en la infancia y la niñez.* Argentina: Editorial Koyatun.

Gattino, G.S. (2021) *Essentials of Music Therapy Assessment.* [*Forma e Conteúdo Comunicação Integrada*]. Florianópolis, Brazil.

Gattino, G.S. (2022) *Music Therapy and the Autism Spectrum: An Integrative Overview.* Dallas, TX: Barcelona Publishers.

Gilman, V. (2022) "Ableism and Colonialism in International Music Therapy Service-Learning Settings: A Critical Discourse Analysis." In S. Gilbertson, S. Hadley, D. Keith and S. Uhlig (eds) *Qualitative Inquiries in Music Therapy 16.* Dallas, TX: Barcelona Publishers.

Gobierno de la Provincia de Buenos Aires (2006) *Ley de Ejercicio Profesional de la Musicoterapia [N° 13635].* https://normas.gba.gob.ar/documentos/VRNEbc5V.html

Godetti, E., López, M., and Díaz Abrahan, V. (2023) "Musicoterapia e investigación. Un análisis preliminar sobre su estado en Argentina." En V.A. Cannarozzo y V. Díaz Abrahan (comp.) *Desarrollos Disciplinares de la Musicoterapia: Construir redes desde y hacia el Sur* (Capítulo 12). La Plata: Universidad Nacional de La Plata. https://sedici.unlp.edu.ar/bitstream/handle/10915/159540/Documento_completo.pdf?sequence=1

Godetti, E., Moscuzza, C. A., Gonnet, D., Cannarozzo, V., and Díaz Abrahan, V. (2020) "Revista ECOS: Logros y nuevos desafíos para la construcción de conocimiento en América Latina." *ECOS – Revista Científica De Musicoterapia Y Disciplinas Afines 5*, 2, 1–4. https://revistas.unlp.edu.ar/ECOS/article/view/10682

Golino, A.J., Leone, R., Gollenberg, A., Christopher, C., *et al.* (2019) "Impact of an active music therapy intervention on intensive care patients." *American Journal of Critical Care 28*, 1, 48–55. doi: 10.4037/ajcc2019792.

Gombert, D.J. (2022) "Who is being silenced? Sociocultural and privilege dynamics within music therapy education." *Music Therapy Perspectives 40*, 2, 164–173. https://doi.org/10.1093/mtp/miac023

Gómez-Carretero, P., Monsalve, V., Soriano, J.F, and de Andrés, J. (2007) "Alteraciones emocionales y necesidades psicológicas de pacientes en una Unidad de Cuidados Intensivos." *Medicina Intensiva 31*, 6, 318–325. https://scielo.isciii.es/scielo.php?script=sci_arttext&pid=S0210-56912007000600006

Gonzales, S.M. (2019) "Cultivating familismo: Belonging and inclusion in one Latina/o learning community." *International Journal of Inclusive Education.* http://dx.doi.org/10.1080/13603116.2019.1602362

Grande, S. (2004) *Red Pedagogy: Native American Social and Political Thought.* Lanham, MD: Rowman & Littlefield.

Green, V.L. and Poppe, S.V. (2021) *Toward a More Perfect Union: Understanding Systemic Racism and Resulting Inequity in Latino Communities.* Position Paper, April. UnidosUS. www.unidosus.org/wp-content/uploads/2021/08/unidosus_systemicracismpaper.pdf

Grimmer, M.S. and Schwantes, M. (2018) "Cross-cultural music therapy: Reflections of American music therapists working internationally." *The Arts in Psychotherapy 61*, 21–32. https://doi.org/10.1016/j.aip.2017.07.001

Grocke, D. and Moe, T. (eds) (2015) *Guided Imagery & Music (GIM) and Music Imagery Methods for Individual and Group Therapy.* London: Jessica Kingsley Publishers.

Gullick, J.G. and Kwan, X.X. (2015) "Patient-directed music therapy reduces anxiety and sedation exposure in mechanically-ventilated patients: a research critique." *Australian Critical Care 28*, 10, 3–5. doi: 10.1016/j.aucc.2015.03.003.

Hadley, S. (2017) "I Don't See You as Black/Gay/Disabled/Muslim/etc.: Microaggressions in Everyday Encounters." In A. Whitehead-Pleaux and X. Tan (eds) *Cultural Intersections in Music Therapy: Music, Health, and the Person* (Chapter 2). Dallas, TX: Barcelona Publishers.

Halbmayer, E. (2021) *Amerindian Socio-Cosmologies between the Andes, Amazonia and Mesoamerica: Toward an Anthropological Understanding of the ISTHMO-Colombian Area.* Abingdon: Routledge.

Harrison, R., Walton, M., Chauhan, A., Manias, E., *et al.* (2019) "What is the role of cultural competence in ethnic minority consumer engagement? An analysis in community healthcare." *International Journal for Equity in Health 18*, 1, 191. https://doi.org/10.1186/s12939-019-1104-1

Heiderscheit, A., Chlan, L., and Donley, K. (2011) "Instituting a music listening intervention for critically ill patients receiving mechanical ventilation: Examples from two patient cases." *Music Med 3*, 4, 239–246. doi: 10.1177/1943862111410981.

Held, M.B.E. (2023) "Decolonizing science: Undoing the colonial and racist hegemony of Western science." *Journal of MultiDisciplinary Evaluation 19*, 44, 88–101. https://doi.org/10.56645/jmde.v19i44.785

Heras La Calle, G., Martín, M.C., and Nin, N. (2017) "Buscando humanizar los cuidados intensivos." *Revista Brasileira de Terapia Intensiva 29*, 1, 9–13. https://doi.org/10.5935/0103-507x. 20170003

Hernández, A.R., Schmidt, S., and Achenbach, J. (2018) "Study: Hurricane Maria and its aftermath caused a spike in Puerto Rico deaths, with nearly 3,000 more than normal." *The Washington Post*, August 28. www.washingtonpost.com/national/study-hurricane-maria-and-its-aftermath-caused-a-spike-in-puerto-rico-deaths-with-nearly-3000-more-than-normal/2018/08/28/57d6d2d6-aa43-11e8-b1da-ff7faa680710_story.html?utm_term=.b34b1244367b

Hernández, A.R., Leaming, W., and Murphy, Z. (2017) "Sin luz: Life without power." *The Washington Post* [presentation]. www.washingtonpost.com/graphics/2017/national/puerto-rico-life-without-power/?utm_term=.6b3cc1e461a7

Hernandez Romero, C.J. (2019) "Proyecto Jardín Community Garden: Traditional Medicine & Health Among Latinx in Boyle Heights." UCLA. https://escholarship.org/uc/item/37t0z838

Hernandez-Ruiz, E. (2005) "Effect of music therapy on anxiety levels and sleep patterns of abused women in shelters." *Journal of Music Therapy 42*, 2, 140–158. https://doi.org/10.1093/jmt/42.2.140

Hernandez-Ruiz, E. (2023) "Virtual parent coaching of music interventions for young autistic children in Mexico." *Music Therapy Perspectives 41*, 1, e21–e29. https://doi.org/10.1093/mtp/miac030

Hernandez-Ruiz, E. and Sullivan, J. (2023) "Who are the music therapists in Mexico and how do they practice? An online survey with professionals and students." *Voices: A World Forum for Music Therapy 23*, 3. https://voices.no/index.php/voices/article/view/3785

Higgins, M., and Kim, E.-J.A. (2019) "Decolonizing methodologies in science education: Rebraiding research theory-practice-ethics with Indigenous theories and theorists." *Cultural Studies of Science Education 14*, 111–127. doi :10.1007/s11422-018-9862-4.

Hunter, B.C., Oliva, R., Sahler, O.J.Z., Gaisser, D'A., Salipante, D.M., and Arezina, C.H. (2010) "Music therapy as an adjunctive treatment in the management of stress for patients being weaned from mechanical ventilation." *Journal of Music Therapy 47*, 3, 198–219. doi: 10.1093/jmt/47.3.198.

INEGI (Instituto Nacional de Estadística y Geografía) (2019) *Los delitos en México*. www.inegi.org.mx/app/biblioteca/ficha.html?upc=702825193096

Isla, C. and Demkura, M. (2023) "Desarrollos, desafíos e implicancias de la musicoterapia orientada en salud comunitaria en la formación de profesionales en Argentina." En V.A. Cannarozzo y V. Díaz Abrahan (comp.) *Desarrollos Disciplinares de la Musicoterapia: Construir redes desde y hacia el Sur* (pgs.157–172). La Plata: Universidad Nacional de La Plata. https://sedici.unlp.edu.ar/bitstream/handle/10915/159540/Documento_completo.pdf?sequence=1

Johnson, K., Fleury, J., and McClain, D. (2018) "Music intervention to prevent delirium among older patients admitted to a trauma intensive care unit and a trauma orthopaedic unit." *Intensive Critical Care Nursing 47*, 7–14. https://doi.org/10.1016/j.iccn.2018.03.007

Jones, N., Marks, R., Ramirez, R. and Ríos-Vargas, M. (2020) "2020 Census illuminates racial and ethnic composition of the country." US Census Bureau. https://bit.ly/3pYfnix

Kim, S.-A. (2021) "Music as an Acculturation Strategy in Culturally Informed Music Therapy." In M. Belgrave and S.-A. Kim (eds) *Music Therapy in a Multicultural Context: A Handbook for Music Therapy Students and Professionals* (pp.9–42). London: Jessica Kingsley Publishers.

Knight, A.J., LaGasse, A.B., and Clair, A.A. (eds) (2018) *Music Therapy: An Introduction to the Profession*. Silver Spring, MD: American Music Therapy Association®.

Krogstad, J.M., Passel, J.S., Moslimani, M., and Noe-Bustamante, L. (2022) "Key facts about US Latinos for National Hispanic Heritage Month." Pew Research Center. www.pewresearch.org/short-reads/2023/09/22/key-facts-about-us-latinos-for-national-hispanic-heritage-month

Kusch, R., Mignolo, W., Lugones, M., and Price, J.M. (2010) *Indigenous and Popular Thinking in América* (translated by María Lugones and Joshua M. Price). Durham, NC: Duke University Press.

Lanzoni, A. and Gómez, M. (2020) "Importancia de la incorporación de la Musicoterapia en el Equipo de Neurorehabilitación Transdisciplinaria con niñas y niños con discapacidad." En V.A. Cannarozzo y D.H. Gonnet (comp.) *Musicoterapia en la Provincia de Buenos Aires: Oportunidades y desafíos para su inclusión en la agenda pública* (pg.36–51). La Plata: Universidad Nacional de La Plata. http://sedici.unlp.edu.ar/bitstream/handle/10915/118048/Documento_completo.pdf?sequence=1&isAllowed=y

Law No. 14,842, of April 11, 2024. Provides for the professional activity of a music therapist. Brasília, DF. www2.camara.leg.br/legin/fed/lei/2024/lei-14842-11-abril-2024-795494-publicacaooriginal-171525-pl.html

Lecourt, E. (2006) *El grito está siempre afinado: Viñetas de la clínica musicoterapéutica*. Barcelona: Editorial Lumen.

Lee, N. (2020) "Navigating the experience of burnout of immigrant music therapists in the United States." *Theses and Dissertations 84*. https://digitalcommons.molloy.edu/etd/84

Madrid Martínez, J.E. (2020) "Políticas sociales y pobreza indígena en Panamá. Análisis cualitativo." *Cátedra 17*, 57–66. https://doi.org/10.48204/j.catedra.n17a4

Maeda, N.O. (2020) "Considerations for Music Therapists Working Across a Language Barrier." Master's thesis, Drexel University. https://doi.org/10.17918/00000010

Malacalza, B. and Fagaburu, D. (2022) "Empathy or calculation? A critical analysis of vaccination geopolitics in Latin America." *Global Governance 28*, 3, 432–546. https://doi.org/10.1163/19426720-02803006

Maldonado-Torres (2008) "La descolonización y el giro des-colonial" ["Decolonization and the decolonial turn"]. *Tabula Rasa 9*, 61–72. www.revistatabularasa.org/numero009/la-descolonizacion-y-el-giro-des-colonial

Maldonado-Torres, N. (2022) "El giro decolonial, el Caribe y la posibilidad de una filosofía poscontinental." *Transmodernity 9*, 8. https://doi.org/10.5070/T49857559

Marquina, M. (2004) *Panorama de las titulaciones en el sistema de educación superior argentino: Aportes para un estudio comparado*. Buenos Aires: Comisión Nacional de Evaluación y Acreditación Universitaria (CONEAU). www.coneau.gob.ar/archivos/1333.pdf

Martinez, M.A. (2022) "Mariachis pay emotional tribute to victims of Uvalde School shooting." *New York Post*. https://nypost.com/2023/05/24/uvalde-anniversary-brings-mariachis-mourners-to-pay-respects

McCaffrey, R. (2006) "The effect of music on pain and acute confusion in older adults undergoing hip and knee surgery." *Holistic Nursing Practice 34*, 9, 234–245.

McCaffrey, R.G. and Good, M. (2000) "The lived experience of listening to music while recovering from surgery." *Journal of Holistic Nursing 18*, 4, 378–390. doi: 10.1177/089801010001800408.

McCaffrey, R. and Locsin, R. (2004) "The effect of music listening on acute confusion and delirium in elders undergoing hip and knee surgery." *Journal of Clinical Nursing 13*, 2, 91–96. doi: 10.1111/j.1365-2702.2004.01048.x.

McFerran, K., Chan, V., Tague, D., Stachyra, K., and Mercadal-Brotons (2023) "A comprehensive review classifying contemporary global practices in music therapy." *Music Therapy Today WFMT 18*, 1, 474–493. www.researchgate.net/publication/374157705_466_A_Comprehensive_Review_Classifying_Contemporary_Global_Practices_In_Music_Therapy_467_COMPREHENSIVE_REVIEW_OF_GLOBAL_MUSIC_THERAPY_PRACTICES_Background_to_the_Project

McLeod, S. (2024, February 14). *Cultural capital theory of Pierre Bourdieu*. Simply Psychology. https://www.simplypsychology.org/cultural-capital-theory-of-pierre-bourdieu.html

Mental Health America (2023) "Latinx/Hispanic Communities and Mental Health." www.mhaopc.org/bipoc-mental-health-awareness-month/latinx-hispanic-communities-and-mental-health

Mignolo, W.D. (2009) "Epistemic disobedience, independent thought and decolonial freedom." *Theory, Culture & Society, 26*, 7–8, 159≠181. https://doi.org/10.1177/0263276409349275

Mignolo, W.D. (2012) *Local Histories/Global Designs: Coloniality, Subaltern Knowledges, and Border Thinking*. Princeton, NJ: Princeton University Press.

Mignolo, W.D. (2018) "Decoloniality and phenomenology: The geopolitics of knowing and epistemic/ontological colonial differences." *Journal of Speculative Philosophy 32*, 3, 360–387. https://doi.org/10.5325/jspecphil.32.3.0360

Mignolo, W.D. (2019) "Reconstitución epistémica/estética: La aesthesis decolonial una década después." *Calle 14: Revista de investigación en el campo del arte 14*, 25, 14–33. https://doi.org/10.14483/21450706.14132

Ministerio de Educación Nacional (2014) "Resolución 1198/2014." República Argentina. https://ar.vlex.com/vid/525369186

Moslimani, M., Lopez, M., & Noe-Bustamante, L. (2023, August 16). *11 facts about Hispanic origin groups in the U.S*. Pew Research Center. https://www.pewresearch.org/short-reads/2023/08/16/11-facts-about-hispanic-origin-groups-in-the-us

Motta, F.C.P., Alcadipani, R., and R.B. Bresler, R.B. (2001) "A valorização do estrangeiro como segregação nas organizações" ["The valorization of foreigners is seen as segregation in organizations"]. *Revista de Administração Contemporânea 5*, special issue, 59–79. https://doi.org/10.1590/S1415-65552001000500004

Mulvaney-Day, N.E., Earl, T.R., Diaz-Linhart, Y., and Alegría, M. (2011) "Preferences for relational style with mental health clinicians: A qualitative comparison of African American, Latino and Non-Latino White patients." *Journal of Clinical Psychology 67*, 1, 31–44. doi :10.1002/jclp.20739.

Muñoz, R. (2024) "El simposio de musicoterapia en Panamá llega a su doceava edición." *Revista Ellas*, 4 enero. www.ellas.pa/estilo-de-vida/cultura/el-simposio-de-musicoterapia-en-panama-llega-a-su-doceava-edicion

Murray, M. and Lamont, A. (2012) "Community Music and Social/Health Psychology: Linking Theoretical and Practical Concerns." In R. MacDonald, G. Kreutz, and L. Mitchell (eds) *Music, Health and Wellbeing* (Chapter 6). Oxford: Oxford University Press.

Murrey, A. (2019) "Between appropriation and assassination: Pedagogical disobedience in an era of unfinished decolonisation." *International Journal of Social Economics 46*, 11, 1319–1134. https://doi.org/10.1108/IJSE-02-2019-0133

Myrie, C., Breen A., and Ashbourne L. (2022) "'Finding my Blackness, finding my rhythm': Music and identity development in African, Caribbean, and Black emerging adults." *Emerging Adulthood 10*, 4, 824–836. doi: 10.1177/21676968211014659.

NAMI (National Alliance on Mental Illness) (2023, September 13). *NAMI State Legislation Report: Trends in State Mental Health Policy (2022)*. https://www.nami.org/nami-news/nami-releases-latest-report-exploring-state-level-mental-health-legislation-in-2022

Nicholls, T. (2011) "Colonialism." In D.K. Chatterjee (ed.) *Encyclopedia of Global Justice* (pp.161–165). New York: Springer. https://doi.org/10.1007/978-1-4020-9160-5_229

NMTSA (Neurologic Music Therapy Services of Arizona) (2011) "What is Neurologic Music Therapy®?" www.nmtsa.org/what-is-nmt

Nunes, R. (2021) "Jornal português denuncia que crianças do país 'só falam brasileiro'" ["Portuguese newspaper denounces that children in the country 'only speak Brazilian.'"]. *Correio Brasiliense*, 11 November. www.correiobraziliense.com.br/mundo/2021/11/4962302-jornal-portugues-denuncia-que-criancas-do-pais-so-falam-brasileiro.html

OMH (Office of Minority Health) (2023) "Hispanic/Latino health." US Department of Health and Human Services. https://minorityhealth.hhs.gov/omh/browse.aspx?lvl=3&lvlid=64

Oselame, M., Barbosa, R., and Chagas, M. (2017) *Musicoterapia e promoção da saúde: Caminhos possíveis*. London: Novas Edicoes Academicas.

Palacios Picos, A. (2004) "El crédito europeo como motor de cambio en la configuración del Espacio Europeo de la educación superior." *Revista Interuniversitaria de Formación del Profesorado 18*, 3, 197–205. www.redalyc.org/pdf/274/27418312.pdf

Papalía, M. (1998) *Musicoterapia: La función terapéutica de la expresión musical*. Buenos Aires: Erre Eme.

Pardavila Belio, M.I. and Vivar, C.G. (2012) "Necesidades de la familia en las unidades de cuidados intensivos. Revisión de la literatura." *Enfermeria intensiva 23*, 2, 51–67.

Pensa, E. and Godetti, E. (2017) "Consultas frecuentes sobre matriculación y monotributo." *ECOS – Revista Científica De Musicoterapia Y Disciplinas Afines 2*, 1, 18–23. https://revistas.unlp.edu.ar/ECOS/article/view/10513

Pérez Rosario, V. (2014) "Affirming an Afro-Latin@ identity: An interview with poet María Teresa (Mariposa) Fernández." *Latino Studies 12*, 3, 468–475. https://doi.org/10.1057/lst.2014.48

Pew Research Center. (2023, September 22). *Key facts about U.S. Latinos for National Hispanic Heritage Month.* https://www.pewresearch.org/short-reads/2023/09/22/key-facts-about-us-latinos-for-national-hispanic-heritage-month

Pfeiffer, C. and Zamani, C. (2017) *Explorando el cerebro musical: Musicoterapia, música y neurociencias.* Madrid: Editorial Kier.

Poder Ejecutivo Nacional (1981a) *Ley N° 22.431: Sistema de protección integral de los discapacitados.* www.argentina.gob.ar/normativa/nacional/ley-22431-20620/texto

Poder Ejecutivo Nacional (1981b) *Ley N° 22.431: Sistema de protección integral de los discapacitados.* [Text updated with subsequent modifications.] www.argentina.gob.ar/normativa/nacional/ley-22431-20620/actualizacion

Poder Legislativo Provincial de Entre Ríos (2012) *Ley N° 10134. Ejercicio Profesional. Creación del Colegio de Musicoterapeutas.* https://e-legis-ar.msal.gov.ar/htdocs/legisalud/migration/html/20471.html

Queen Margaret University (QMU) (2022) "The 12th European Music Therapy Conference." www.qmu.ac.uk/conferences-and-events/emtc-2022

Quijano, A. (2007) "Coloniality and modernity/rationality." *Cultural Studies 21*, 2–3, 168–178. https://doi.org/10.1080/09502380601164353

Quijano, A. (2020) *Cuestiones y horizontes: de la Dependencia histórico-estructural a la colonialidad/descolonialidad del poder.* Buenos Aires: CLACSO.

Quijano, A. and Ennis, M. (2000) "Coloniality of power, Eurocentrism, and Latin America." *Nepantla: Views from the South 1*, 3, 533–580.

Reibel, S. (2022) "Abordaje musicoterapéutico en un hospital general: Las canciones como modo de enlace a lo vital." *ECOS – Revista Científica De Musicoterapia Y Disciplinas Afines 7*, 030. https://doi.org/10.24215/27186199e030

Rejane Mendes Barcellos, L. and Carvalho Santos, M.A. (2021) "A musicoterapia no Brasil." *Brazilian Journal of Music Therapy 32*, 4–35. https://doi.org/10.51914/brjmt.32.2021.378

Reschke-Hernández, A.E. (2011) "History of music therapy treatment interventions for children with autism." *Journal of Music Therapy 48*, 2, 169–207. https://doi.org/10.1093/jmt/48.2.169

Ridder, H.M.O. and Tsiris, G. (2015) "Music therapy in Europe: Paths of professional development." *Approaches. Music Therapy and Special Music Education 7*, 1, 127–130. http://approaches.gr/special-issue-7-1-2015

Robles, F., Davis, K., Fink, S., and Almukhtar, S. (2017) "Official toll in Puerto Rico: 64. Actual deaths may be 1,052." *The New York Times*, August 9. www.nytimes.com/interactive/2017/12/08/us/puerto-rico-hurricane-maria-death-toll.html

Rodríguez, J.S. (2017) "Efectos del abordaje musicoterapéutico con niños atendidos en dupla en el servicio de salud mental del Hospital de Niños Pedro de Elizalde." *ECOS – Revista Científica de Musicoterapia y Disciplinas Afines 2*, 2, 10-46. https://revistas.unlp.edu.ar/ECOS/article/view/10506/9145

Rodríguez Espada, G. (comp.) (2020) *Pensamiento estético en musicoterapia II. Territorializaciones: formación, improvisación, técnica y escucha.* Buenos Aires: Editorial Autores de Argentina.

Rojas, V. (2019) "Humanización de los cuidados intensivos." *Revista Médica Clínica Las Condes 30*, 2, 120-125. doi: 10.1016/j.rmclc.2019.03.005.

Rojas, V., Lallana, P., Zamora, G., Maya, R., et al. (2020) Impacto de la musicoterapia en los integrantes del equipo clínico de una unidad de pacientes críticos: Una
mirada desde el cuidador cuidado [Impact of Music Therapy on the Members of
the Clinical Team of a Critical Patients Unit: A View from the Caregiver Care].
Providencia: Revista Chilena de Medicina Intensiva. www.medicina-intensiva.
cl/congreso2019/pdf_tr/15.pdf

Rolleti, F. (2019) "La investigación no es para algunas personas, es para todos, absolutamente: Entrevista a Nadia Justel." ECOS – Revista Científica De Musicoterapia Y Disciplinas Afines 4, 2, 54–67. https://revistas.unlp.edu.ar/ECOS/article/
view/10493

Ruud, E. (1990) Los caminos de la musicoterapia: La musicoterapia y su relación con
las teorías terapéuticas actuales [Music Therapy and its Relationship to Current
Treatment Theories]. Buenos Aires: Editorial Bonum.

Sabbatella, P. (2004) "Intervención musical en el alumnado con necesidades educativas especiales: Delimitaciones conceptuales desde la pedagogía musical
y la musicoterapia." Tavira. Revista Electrónica de Formación de Profesorado en
Comunicación Lingüística y Literaria 20, 123–139. https://dialnet.unirioja.es/
revista/1920/A/2004

Saltzman, L.Y., Lesen, A.E., Henry, V., Hansel, T.C. and Bordnick, P.S. (2021)
"COVID-19 mental health disparities." Health Security 19, 1, 5–13. https://doi.
org/10.1089/hs.2021.0017

Sardo, S., Almeida, P., and Godinho, S. (2012) "Portugal e Brasil: partilha e despa-
trialização da música" ["Portugal and Brazil: Sharing and dematerialization of
music"]. Camões: Revista de Letras e Culturas Lusófonas 21, 57–67.

Satinosky, S. (2006) Musicoterapia clínica. Buenos Aires: Editorial Galerna.

Schapira, D., Ferrari, K., Sánchez, V., and Hugo, M. (2007) Musicoterapia: Abordaje
plurimodal. Buenos Aires: ADIM Ediciones.

Segato, R. (2018) Contra-pedagogías de la crueldad. Buenos Aires: Prometeo Libros.

Segato, R. (2021) "Pedagogy of cruelty is all that cosifies life." CE Noticias Finan-
cieras. [English version.]

Sokolov, L. and Curcio, M.F. (2021) "Embodied VoiceWork: Moviéndose hacia la
totalidad en el campo musical del juego." ECOS – Revista Científica De Musicoterapia Y Disciplinas Afines 6, 2, 18. https://doi.org/10.24215/27186199e018

Stige, B. (2014) "Community music therapy and the process of learning about and
struggling for openness." International Journal of Community Music 7, 1, 47–55.
https://doi.org/10.1386/ijcm.7.1.47_1

Sue, D.W. and Sue, D. (2013) Counseling the Culturally Diverse: Theory and Practice
(6th edn). New York: Wiley.

Thaut, M.H. (2005) Rhythm, Music, and the Brain. New York and London: Taylor
& Francis Group.

Thaut, M.H. and Hömberg, V. (2014) Handbook of Neurologic Music Therapy.
Oxford: Oxford University Press.

Thurner, M. (ed.) (2019) The First Wave of Decolonization. New York: Routledge.

Torres, L., Driscoll, M.W. and Voell, M. (2012) "Discrimination, acculturation,
acculturative stress, and Latino psychological distress: A moderated medi-
ational model." Cultural Diversity and Ethnic Minority Psychology 18, 1, 17–25.
https://doi.org/10.1037/a0026710

Tosto, V. (2016) "Musicoterapia e investigación: La construcción de conocimientos
disciplinares." ECOS – Revista Científica De Musicoterapia Y Disciplinas Afines
1, 1, 1–12. https://revistas.unlp.edu.ar/ECOS/article/view/10586

Trinh, J. (2022) "Cumbiatón, a safe space for LA's queer and Latinx communities, grows virtually." PBS SoCal, March 16. https://bit.ly/3DmicHh

UBAM (União Brasileira das Associações de Musicoterapia [Brazilian Union of Music Therapy Associations]) (2020) "Análise do 10 censo nacional de estudantes e profissionais de musicoterapia" ["Analysis of the first national census of music therapy students and professionals"]. https://drive.google.com/file/d/1D7iYBfCs27GJ8KmaAX09mC9lDDGpxooK/view

UBAM (2024a) "Breve história da Musicoterapia no Brasil" ["A brief history of music therapy in Brazil"]. https://ubammusicoterapia.com.br/institucional/musicoterapia/historia-no-brasil

UBAM (2024b) "Cursos de Formação" ["Training Courses"]. https://ubammusico terapia.com.br/formacao-em-musicoterapia/cursos-de-formacao

UNAM (Universidad Nacional Autónoma de México) (2022) "Plan de estudios (sistema escolarizado): Licenciatura en educación musical." http://oferta.unam.mx/planestudios/musicaeducamusical-plan-de-estudios13.pdf

United States Census Bureau. (2023, September 28). *Hispanic Heritage Month*: 2023. https://www.census.gov/newsroom/facts-for-features/2023/hispanic-heritage-month.html

UnidosUS (2021) "Key statistics." www.unidosus.org/facts/statistics-about-latinos-in-the-us-unidosus

Uzal, P. (2016) "La construcción del rol del musicoterapeuta en el equipo de Salud Mental del Hospital General de Niños Pedro de Elizalde." *ECOS – Revista Científica De Musicoterapia Y Disciplinas Afines 1*, 2, 34–64. https://revistas.unlp.edu.ar/ECOS/article/view/10594

Vakis, R. and Lindert, K. (2000) *Poverty in Indigenous Populations in Panama: A Study using LSMS Data.* World Bank. https://documents.worldbank.org/en/publication/documents-reports/documentdetail/681861468775528487/poverty-in-indigenous-populations-in-panama-a-study-using-lsms-data

Valdivieso-Mora, E., Peet, C.L., Garnier-Villarreal, M., Salazar-Villanea, M., and Johnson, D.K. (2016) "A systematic review of the relationship between familism and mental health outcomes in Latino population." *Frontiers in Psychology 7*. https://doi.org/10.3389/fpsyg.2016.01632

Västfjäll, D., Juslin, P.N., and Hartig, T. (2012) "Music, Subjective Well Being, and Health: The Role of Everyday Emotions." In R. MacDonald, G. Kreutz, and L. Mitchell (eds) *Music, Health, and Wellbeing* (pp.405–423). Oxford: Oxford University Press. https://doi.org/10.1093/acprof:oso/9780199586974.003.0027

Vega, W.A., Rodriguez, M.A., and Gruskin, E. (2009) "Health disparities in the Latino population." *Epidemiologic Reviews 31*, 1, 99–112. https://doi.org/10.1093/epirev/mxp008

Vesco, C. and Marasco, A.I. (2021) "Relatos de espera: Experiencias musicoterapéuticas en el Hospital de Quemados: Musicoterapia en sala de espera." *ECOS – Revista Científica De Musicoterapia Y Disciplinas Afines 6*, 1, 5. https://doi.org/10.24215/27186199e005

Villa, L. (2019) "How Bad Bunny bridges LGBTQ and Latinx identities with his inclusive 'Caro' video." MTV.

WFMT (World Federation of Music Therapy) (2017) "News from Latin América region: Music therapy in Chile." www.wfmt.info/post/news-from-latin-america-region-music-therapy-in-chile

WFMT (2011) "About WFMT: What is music therapy?" www.wfmt.info/about

Wheeler, B.L. (2006) "Foreword." In F. Baker and J. Tamplin, *Music Therapy Methods in Neurorehabilitation: A Clinician's Manual* (pp.9–10). London: Jessica Kingsley Publishers.

Wood, D.F. (2003) "Problem-based learning." *BMJ 336*, 7384, 328–330. doi: 10.1136/bmj.326.7384.328.

World Bank (2021) "GDP per capita (current US$) – Latin America & Caribbean." https://data.worldbank.org/indicator/NY.GDP.PCAP.CD?locations=ZJ&most_recent_value_desc=true

World Bank (2022) *Panama Pandemic Response and Growth Recovery Development Policy Operation 2*. (P175930). https://projects.worldbank.org/en/projects-operations/project-detail/P174107

World Bank (2024) "The World Bank in Panama: Overview." www.worldbank.org/en/country/panama/overview#:~:text=Over%20the%20last%20thirty%20years,of%20people%20living%20in%20poverty

Yearby, R., Clark, B., and Figueroa, J. (2022) "Structural racism in historical and modern US society." *Health Affairs (Project Hope) 41*, 2, 187–194. doi: 10.1377/hlthaff.2021.01466.

Yosso, T. (2005) "Whose culture has capital? A critical race theory discussion of community cultural wealth." *Race Ethnicity and Education 8*, 1, 69–91. https://doi.org/10.1080/1361332052000341006

Zain, J. (2014) *Escuchar el silencio: Musicoterapia vibroacústica*. Buenos Aires: Editorial Kier.

Zarate de Perez, P. (2020) "Cambio de paradigma en la educación musical." *La Prensa*, August 9.

Zarate de Perez, P. (2023) *Reimagining Panama's Musical and Cultural Narratives of Jazz: Panamanian Suite*. Lanham, MD: Lexington Books.

Zarate de Perez, P. and Wu, W. (2023) "Invisible Silence, Loud Music: The Transmusical Journey of a Jazz Musician." In C.A. Lee (ed.) *The Oxford Handbook of Queer and Trans Music Therapy* (Chapter 29). Oxford: Oxford University Press. https://doi.org/10.1093/oxfordhb/9780192898364.013.33

Žižek, S. (2008) *Violence: Six Sideways Reflections*. London: Picador.

THE CONTRIBUTORS

Patricia Zarate de Perez, MT (US, Panama, Chile)

Patricia graduated with a first class in her Music Therapy major at Berklee College of Music (Boston, US) in 1999. Since then, she has worked as a music therapist with people of all ages and a wide variety of health conditions, and has been an avid advocate of music therapy within the Latinx/e diaspora. She has published papers on music therapy in the *Revista Médica de Chile* (*Journal of Medicine of Chile*) (2001), *Revista Chilena de Pediatría* (*Journal of Pediatrics of Chile*) (2002), *Revista Médica de Panamá* (*Medical Journal of Panama*) (2013), *ReVista: Harvard Review of Latin America* (2016), and the *Oxford Handbook of Queer and Trans Music Therapy* (2022), among others. She co-founded the Latin American Music Therapy Network (LAMTN) in 2012, founded the Latin American Music Therapy Symposium in 2013, the Music Therapy Center of Panama (Centro de Musicoterapia de Panamá, CMP) in 2015, the Global Music Therapy Center (Centro de Musicoterapia Global, CMTG) in 2020, and the Music Therapy Center of Chile (Centro de Musicoterapia de Chile) in 2024. She currently directs the Master's in Global Music Therapy (GbMT) program in Panama, serves as President of the Music Therapy Association of Panama (Asociación Panameña de Musicoterapia, APAMU), as Vice-President of the Latin American Music Therapy Committee (Comité Latinoamericano de Musicoterapia, CLAM), and is part of the faculty of Berklee College of Music's Music Therapy Department and the Berklee Global Jazz Institute in Boston, MA.

Jeniris M. Garay, EdM, MT-BC (Puerto Rico)

Born and raised in Puerto Rico, Jeniris is a board-certified music therapist, clinical educator, and co-founder and past president of the Latin American Music Therapy Network (LAMTN). Fluent in four languages and proficient in over ten musical instruments, Jeniris has taught at the University of Rhode Island, pioneered international service learning trips, and presented at numerous conferences across the United States, Latin America, and the Caribbean. She currently serves as an early intervention music therapist and service coordinator. She also provides bilingual workforce development seminars for early childhood staff across the state of Massachusetts in the US. In her spare time, Jeniris is a professional singer and dueling pianist for weddings and corporate events. She lives in Boston, MA with her husband Rikky and their two children, Logan and Liam. Jeniris holds a Master's in Human Development and Psychology from the Harvard Graduate School of Education, and a Bachelor's in Music Therapy from Berklee College of Music with a minor in psychology.

Talia Girton, MT-BC, RMT, MA

Talia is a music psychotherapist and educator based in London, where she directs a music school and music therapy center. She is a former trustee of the European Piano Teachers Association UK and has served as the editor of *Piano Professional* magazine. Fluent in Spanish, Talia has been invited to lead workshops and seminars throughout Latin America. In 2015, she became the first music therapist in residence at the Music Therapy Center of Panama (Centro de Musicoterapia de Panamá, CMP), where she supervised students and provided therapeutic services to hundreds of clients. She also contributed as a professor in Panama's inaugural music therapy diploma program, and currently teaches in the Master's in Global Music Therapy (GbMT) program, working alongside director Patricia Zarate de Perez. Talia is pursuing advanced studies in integrative arts psychotherapy, with plans to incorporate various creative modalities—such as dance, movement, poetry, and visual arts—into her therapeutic practice.

Cynthia Pimentel Koskela, MT-BC, EdM (US, Mexico)

Cynthia Pimentel Koskela is a passionate advocate, music therapist, educator, and mother. She has extensive clinical experience as a music therapist and entrepreneur in establishing music therapy programs in early intervention, hospital, and school-based settings. She holds a Bachelor's degree in Music Therapy from Berklee College of Music and a Master's in Human Development and Psychology from Harvard Graduate School of Education. As a first generation Mexican American, her passion has always been to advocate for the expansion of culturally responsive music therapy services, particularly for immigrant communities. Her work includes the development of Esperanza Academy's first music therapy program and co-founding the Latin American Music Therapy Network (LAMTN), a community that aims to support and connect Latinx/e-identifying music therapists in the US and abroad. She currently holds a position as the inaugural clinical director for the Center for Music Therapy at Berklee College of Music (Boston, MA).

Ricardo Maya, MT (Chile)

After graduating with his degree in Psychology from the University of Salamanca (Universidad de Salamanca), Ricardo studied music therapy in the postgraduate course at the University of Chile (Universidad de Chile) and specialized in Neurologic Music Therapy® at the University of Toronto Academy of Neurologic Music Therapy®. He has presented his research at the Latin American Music Therapy Symposium and teaches at the Master's in Global Music Therapy (GbMT) program. He has worked as a music therapist in a hospital setting and an intensive care unit, and currently works privately and collaborates with the Music Therapy Center of Chile (Centro de Musicoterapia de Chile) as the music therapist in residence.

Eugenia Hernandez-Ruiz, PhD, MT-BC

Eugenia is a US-trained Mexican music therapist. She is currently associate professor at Arizona State University, having worked as a full-time clinician in Mexico for ten years. Her current research and clinical interests are parent coaching of music interventions for autistic children, music neuroscience, and music therapy education. She has presented in regional, national, and international conferences, and her research has been published in the *Journal of Music Therapy*, *Music Therapy Perspectives*, *Nordic Journal of Music Therapy*, *Psychology of Music*, *The Arts in Psychotherapy*, and *Review Journal of Autism and Developmental Disorders*. She serves on the Certification Board for Music Therapists and is Associate Editor of *Music Therapy Perspectives*. She is also part of the Editorial Board of *Journal of Music Therapy*. She is a frequent reviewer for the premier journals in her field, and has participated in review panels for the National Institutes of Health and National Endowment for the Arts, US.

Graciela Broqua, MT

Argentine music therapist Graciela Broqua graduated from the University of Buenos Aires (Universidad de Buenos Aires, UBA). She holds a Master's in Educational Technology from the Interamerican Open University (Universidad Abierta Interamericana), and is currently a PhD student and postgraduate professor in psychology at UBA and a professor of higher education at the National Technological University (Universidad Tecnológica Nacional). Since 2005 she has worked in the neurorehabilitation of infants and adolescents, and serves as a teacher, juror, and thesis tutor in the Bachelor's degree in Music Therapy at UBA. She has been a member of the Communication Commission of the Latin American Music Therapy Committee (Comité Latinoamericano de Musicoterapia, CLAM) since 2020, and is a member of the Latin American Music Therapy Network (LAMTN). She serves as an evaluator of articles at the magazines *Anuario de Ciencias* (Faculty of Psychology, UBA) and *InCantare* (Faculdade de Artes do Paraná). She is author of the book *Accessible Music with Assistive Technology* (Editorial Autores de Argentina) as well as numerous articles and book chapters.

Gustavo Schulz Gattino, MT

Gustavo Schulz Gattino, PhD, is a music therapist and associate professor in the Department of Communication and Psychology at Aalborg University (Denmark), where he teaches in the Bachelor's, Master's, and doctoral programs in Music Therapy. Gustavo is accredited as a music therapist by the Portuguese Music Therapy Association (Associação Portuguesa de Musicoterapia, APMT). He is the North region coordinator and Denmark's country representative in the European Music Therapy Confederation (EMTC), and a member of the International Music Therapy Assessment Consortium (IMTAC). Gustavo is a guest lecturer for the Master's programs in Music Therapy at Pablo Olavide University (Universidad Pablo de Olavide de Sevilla) (Spain), University of Barcelona (Universitat de Barcelona) (Spain), Music, Art and Process Institute (Instituto Música, Arte y Proceso) (Spain), and Codarts (Netherlands).

INDEX

Page references to Figures or Photographs will be in *italics*